THE MERCHANT REPUBLIC OF LEBANON

The Merchant Republic of Lebanon

Rise of an Open Economy

Carolyn L. Gates

The Centre for Lebanese Studies
in association with
I.B.Tauris Publishers
LONDON • NEW YORK

The Centre for Lebanese Studies would like to thank Mr George Asseily and Mr Tony Asseily for their generous donation which made possible the printing of this book

Published in 1998 by The Centre for Lebanese Studies, Oxford
in association with I.B.Tauris & Co Ltd
Victoria House, Bloomsbury Square, London WC1B 4DZ

In the United States and Canada distributed by St Martin's Press
175 Fifth Avenue, New York NY 10010

ISBN 1 86064 047 8

A full CIP record for this book is available from the British Library
A full CIP record for this book is available from the Library of Congress

Library of Congress Catalog card: available

Typeset in Times New Roman by Oxford Publishing Services
Printed and bound in Great Britain by Biddles Ltd, Guildford and King's Lynn

Contents

List of Tables and Figures

Tables

Figures

Acronyms and Abbreviations

£L	Lebanese pound (in circulation after 1948)
£S	Syrian pound (in circulation after 1948)
£SL	Syro-Lebanese pound (in circulation between 1920 and 1948)
£T	Turkish pound
ARAMCO	Arabian-American Oil Company
AUB	American University of Beirut
BSL	*Banque de Syrie et du Liban*
CERMOC	*Centre d'études et de recherches sur le Moyen-Orient*
CFLN	*Comité français de la libération nationale*
CGI	capital-goods industrialisation
CNF	*Comité national français*
COL	cost-of-living
CSIC	*Conseil supérieur des intérêts communs*
CSR	*Commission supérieure de ravitaillement*
DHP	*Compagnie française du chemin de fer de Damas, Hama et prolongements*
DUP	directly unproductive profit seeking
EER	effective exchange rate
EOI	export-oriented industrialisation
EP	export-promoting
ERI	Economic Research Institute
FAO	Food and Agriculture Organisation (of the United Nations)
FF	French franc
GNP	gross national product
ICI	Imperial Chemical Industries

ICOR	incremental capital-output ratio
IPC	Iraq Petroleum Company
IRFED	Institut de recherche de formation en vue de développement
ISI	import-substituting industrialisation
LDC	less-developed country
MAE	*Ministère des affaires étrangères*, Paris
MESC	Middle East Supply Centre
NCF	net capital formation
NIE	newly industrialising economy
NIL	national income of Lebanon
NNP	net national product
OEG	*Office de l'économie de guerre*
PRO	Public Record Office
SCAIL	*Société libanaise de crédit agricole et industriel du Liban*
SDN	*Société des nations*
SERIAC	*Société d'études et de réalisations industrielles, agricoles et commerciales*
SLEP	*Société libanaise d'économie politique*
TAPLINE	Trans-Arabian Pipeline Company (Saudi Arabia)
UKCC	United Kingdom Commercial Corporation
USNA	United States National Archives

Foreword

This study of Lebanon's open economy, symbolised by the rise of the 1950s' Merchant Republic, has evolved over many years. Parts of this examination are drawn from my doctoral thesis; additional research, analysis and interpretative results are a product of work I have pursued more recently. *The Merchant Republic of Lebanon: Rise of an Open Economy*, which has brought together many of my interests in economic theory and comparative economic systems, has been written with three main objectives in mind. First, the analysis is framed to highlight the important role played by Lebanon's postwar institutions and organisations in shaping its economic path and performance. Second, this work raises many theoretical debates about economic growth, change and development. Using Lebanon's economy as a case study, it seeks to shed light on these more universal issues. Finally, it makes available a large amount of primary and secondary material on the Lebanese economy, which other economists and scholars may find useful for future research.

This book appears as we approach the next millennium. My research on Lebanon's economy, however, began when I was a student living in Beirut in a very different era: the tumultuous, yet oddly hopeful period of the 1970s. My interest in Lebanon's political economy was stoked by the conditions at that time, which were full of conflict, contradictions and anticipation. One heard the much quoted but possibly apocryphal story of the Belgian economist and advisor to the Lebanese government, Paul van Zeeland, who was supposed to have remarked: 'I don't know what makes the economy work, but it's doing very well and I wouldn't advise you to touch it.' By the mid-1970s, it was very apparent that many things in Lebanon were about to be touched, not only in the economy, but throughout the state and society. During the later stages of the civil war, when there seemed to be no end in sight of turmoil, violence and vast destruction, one was reminded over and over again about the very different faces of Lebanon: its long internal conflicts in the first half of the nineteenth century; its 'golden age' as a Merchant Republic and Switzerland of the Middle East in the 1950s and 1960s; and the shifts, adaptive responses, twists and turns between crisis and progress.

Lebanon's economy, society and state have been the subjects of research by serious scholars and commentators. I have benefited enormously from their many thoughtful, persuasive and provocative analyses. But I came to believe that the role of institutions and organisations was under-appreciated in the examination of Lebanon's economic evolution. This study, therefore, shifts the emphasis to a more institutional analysis of its economic activities and experiments that led to the rise of the Merchant Republic. I have sought to place my hypotheses, empirical data and their supportive evidence in a framework that draws from evolutionary and neo-institutional economics to illuminate the many choices, debates and behaviour that gave rise to Lebanon's open economy. Thus, this study has dissected the institutions, policy framework and economic behaviour that prompted the development of characteristic economic structures, dynamics and performance in Lebanon. It is also hoped that as Lebanon's project of reconstruction proceeds, a few lessons may be drawn from this analysis of the manifold complexities of the modern Lebanese economic order.

Many scholars and practitioners have generously assisted me over the years in my research and pursuit of understanding the many aspects of this subject. I gratefully acknowledge an intellectual debt to a number of people and their important works that have influenced this study: Albert Badre, Irene Gendzier, Michael Gilsenan, Albert Hourani, Charles Issawi, Boutros Labaki, Salim Nasr, Douglass North, Roger Owen, Elias Saba, Peter Sluglett, Irina Smilianskaya, Raghid Solh and Jan Tinbergen. My sincere appreciation also goes to the Centre for Lebanese Studies, Oxford, particularly to its director, Nadim Shehadi, and chairman of the Board of Governors George Asseily, for their generous support. In addition, I wish to thank Margaret Owen, who edited this manuscript. My deepest gratitude is reserved for my husband, David Truong, and family who have patiently and ceaselessly encouraged me in all of my pursuits. Without their moral support, the completion of this work would have been impossible. Nevertheless, while I have been the recipient of much generosity and assistance in my work, I, alone, bear responsibility for the contents of this study.

Carolyn L. Gates
Singapore
December 1997

CHAPTER ONE

Outward Orientation and Lebanon: Introductory Comments

Since the nineteenth century, outward-looking economic agents[1] have acted as a powerful force for change in Lebanon, shaping the evolution of an economic order that reached its golden age during the 1950s' Merchant Republic. As elsewhere, the development of Lebanon's economic order was greatly influenced by the material interests of its dominant elite. After the establishment of an independent Lebanese state in 1943, this elite broadly consisted of a socio-economic class of merchants and financiers and the politically and confessionally based *zu'ama*. Building on Lebanon's historically-rooted political economy, it set out to create the institutions ('rules of the game'[2]) and facilitate the development of economic organisations and skills that made possible Lebanon's rise as the centre of international trade, finance and services in the Middle East. Lebanon's Merchant Republic emerged over the decade following the evacuation of Anglo-French occupation forces in 1946: its newly enacted institutions and previously established position permitted Lebanese organisations to seize expanding opportunities that both the international and regional economies were providing at that time. Further, the institutionalisation of an open service economic model was viewed as a critical bulwark of a viable Lebanon, supporting both Lebanese sovereignty and material sustainability.

To examine the institutions and organisations that supported Lebanon's outward-looking economy, the period after the end of the Second World War, notably during its first 15 years of independence, provides ample evidence. Data will be marshalled to analyse Lebanon's rise as a financial and commercial capital, its resulting economic performance, and other effects of this model of development.

The rise of the Lebanese Merchant Republic was not a result of a new governing elite adopting and executing a rationally chosen economic model on a *tabula rasa*. Nor was the economy's outward orientation a theoretical construct of policy-makers or intellectuals. Rather, its post-independent economic system *evolved* from nineteenth- and early twentieth-century economic and political experiences in the Lebanese provinces and surrounding areas. Thus, Lebanon's open economic system is viewed here as the outcome of an evolutionary process, whereby it continuously responded and adapted to movements in the international, regional and local arenas.[3] This work, therefore, proceeds from the nineteenth century. Important transformations during this period include the growth of European foreign trade with, and investment in, Beirut and Mount Lebanon; the rise of a Lebanese bourgeoisie; a developing European–Lebanese economic and political nexus; and expanding Franco-Lebanese relations. The emerging externally-oriented environment determined the path of growth and sectoral, locational and other structural changes in the economy. Hence, by the early twentieth century, primary export production had initiated Lebanon's participation in the international market; Beirut had become a nucleus of economic activities in the eastern Mediterranean; and the 'propulsive activities' of trade, finance and intermediary services had been implanted. These, and other economic and institutional shifts that will be discussed at length in later chapters, laid a base for an outward-looking economic order that culminated in the Lebanese Merchant Republic.

A common thread running through much of Lebanon's modern political economy has been its outward orientation. The concept of outward orientation or openness is specified here, rather than economic liberalism: the interests shaping Lebanon's political economy were primarily concerned with developing an apparatus and institutions to facilitate a competitive position in the international market, offering growing opportunities in *entrepôt* trade, finance and offshore operations. In contrast to the various forms of mercantilism and bureaucratic regulation that had governed the economic framework of Ottoman, French and Allied rule in Lebanon, openness was adopted after Lebanese independence. However, the deepening of competitive market institutions and organisations within the Lebanese economy never became a priority, mainly because *laissez-faire* threatened powerful interests. Consequently, Lebanon's modern economic order has had little to do with the ideals of efficiency and competition in its domestic market, but has concentrated on accumulation and growth based on its external economic role.

Outward and inward orientation revisited

In the vast economic literature on outward and inward orientation, prominent attention has been focused on Japan and a small group of successful Asian newly industrialising economies (NIEs), which consciously adopted a strategy of export-oriented industrialisation (EOI) in the first two decades after the Second World War.[4] In this literature, East Asian EOI has been contrasted with import-substituting industrialisation (ISI), widely established in Latin America, South Asia and elsewhere. Unlike the case of Lebanon, the EOI model of development has emphasised openness primarily in one sector and direction: the export of manufactured goods to advanced industrial economies. Moreover, in contrast with Lebanon's minimalist state, the developmental states of Japan and most Asian NIEs have been activist and interventionist. Due to the strong influence of the ISI and EOI paradigms over the past 40 years, however, the literature seldom looks at the rarer export-oriented service economies such as Lebanon. To define more precisely Lebanon's own model of outward orientation, we must first diverge into a brief discussion about outward, export, inward and import-substituting orientation, concepts that are often conflated and confused in the literature.

Developing countries have employed three main models of industrialisation: ISI, EOI and capital-goods industrialisation (CGI).[5] ISI gained favour in the 1950s and 1960s in Latin America and many regions of decolonising Asia and Africa. This was due to pessimism about primary exports and doubts about the absorptive capacity of the markets of advanced countries if all less-developed countries (LDCs) simultaneously became successful exporters of manufactured commodities. Furthermore, outward orientation, or more specifically EOI, was rejected in favour of ISI because of economic and political limitations: foreign exchange and balance of payments constraints; political hostility towards colonial 'unequal exchange'; and the nationalistic appeal of industrialising through self-reliance and 'learning by doing'. Placed in its proper historical context, however, it is evident that the choice of ISI by many LDCs was as much a consequence of a general political rejection of outward orientation as of the very real constraints of EOI.

After the Second World War, policy-makers and economists in developing countries became pessimistic about outward or export orientation as a result of their experiences with colonial economies. Specifically, their analysis provided a critique of neo-mercantilist relations by which foreign and large domestic owners of primary resources in the colonies produced inputs for the metropolitan economy and, in return, imported manufactured and higher value-added finished goods from the mother country. Pioneering development economists perceived primary commodities, which have made up the largest share of exports of LDCs, as subject to declining terms of trade *vis-à-vis* manufactured imports and subject to price instability. Further, they argued that the benefits of rising labour productivity — a central element in economic development — within the primary export sector of LDCs were transferred to the advanced countries through higher wages and profits.[6] Others contested the wisdom of export production of primary commodities because of low price and income elasticities of demand, and a shift from natural to synthetic inputs in advanced countries' manufactures.[7] For these and other reasons, LDCs have viewed import-substituting industrialisation as a means of increasing the rate of economic growth and quickening the pace of development.

Inward orientation emphasises the often vague notions of self-reliance, closed economic conditions and 'the educational effects of learning to do things for oneself'.[8] In contrast, the execution of an ISI strategy, a subset of inward orientation, is based on specific and well defined policies: trade measures such as high tariffs, quotas and non-tariff barriers to protect infant industries; multiple exchange rates designed to discourage consumer imports and encourage non-traditional (non-agricultural) exports; preferential credit policies for manufacturers. By the 1970s, after several decades of ISI experience, neoclassical critics and even many structuralists concluded that the achievements of ISI had not matched their objectives. In their verdict of ISI failure, they argued that it had produced inefficient resource allocation and X-inefficiency; it had been unable to exploit widened markets, growing choices, and economies of scale; it was vulnerable to rent-seeking and directly unproductive profit-seeking (DUP) activities;[9] and ISI's bureaucratic regulation had increased inefficiencies and inequalities in the macroeconomy. In the meantime, a growing number of countries, especially small and medium-sized countries in East Asia, influenced by their limited natural resources, vast economic challenges and cold war politics, had adopted EOI. Some, accumulating years of experience of export promotion, eventually became the tigers of East Asia; and other countries adopted export-oriented policies because of a failure of, or a need to adjust, the ISI strategy in their own economies.

An EOI strategy, a subset of outward orientation, has been defined in different ways. Some economists have measured EOI and ISI by separating output growth into categories, which they then impute to EOI, ISI and other growth strategies or policies.[10] A more transparent concept of an EOI or export-promoting (EP) strategy focuses on an economy's effective exchange rate (EER). An EP strategy is said to be operative when an economy's EER is approximately neutral between producing for domestic (import) and export markets, $EER_x \approx EER_m$; and a pro-export-bias strategy, or ultra-EP strategy, is defined as $EER_x > EER_m$.[11] With an EP strategy, an EER_m which produces £3 = $1 of imports, for example, will yield £3 = $1 of exports under the EER_x. Thus, a producer will receive the same value (in terms of exchange) from domestic sales as exports; and under an ultra-EP strategy, the producer will receive more than £3 from export sales. To avoid a long discussion of the diverse policies and instruments utilised in various EOI strategies, which does not further our analysis, we will merely state that we are using a modified form of the second definition which, in addition to the exchange mechanism concept, considers the effects of different sectoral emphases of outward orientation, for example export promotion of manufactured goods versus services.

Evidence from country studies and cross-sectional analyses tends to support the argument that the benefits of an EP strategy go far beyond static theories of comparative advantage, such as those of Ricardo or Heckscher–Ohlin–Samuelson.[12] It employs openness to exploit both the static and dynamic comparative advantages of an economy. Its effects can include more efficient allocation of foreign and domestic resources; greater technical efficiency and increased productivity; widened markets and economies of scale; higher savings; and innovation.[13] Bhagwati argues that an EOI or EP strategy is less likely than ISI to lead to DUP and rent-seeking activities that divert energies and resources of an economy and reduce the transparency of any system.[14] Furthermore, Krueger has concluded that this strategy has had positive effects on efficiency and growth; but more importantly, through an emphasis on labour-intensive activities, it has produced high employment and income effects and, therefore, contributed to an alleviation of poverty.[15]

Theoretically, modern EOI and EP theories utilise and support the argument of classical economists that there is a positive relationship between trade and economic growth. In Adam Smith's model, for example, free trade is the central institution, which promotes domestic productivity by widened markets and, hence, economic growth.[16] The often argued claim of EOI advocates that a higher rate of savings and accumulation can be achieved through trade, resulting in higher rates of investment and growth, echoes Smith's argument. A precursor of those claiming that EOI stimulates dynamic innovation and behavioural and institutional changes, J. S. Mill, argued that trade encourages the transfer of knowledge and produces powerful educational, intellectual and 'moral' (cultural) effects that promote progress.[17] The neoclassical school has almost unanimously supported export promotion on the grounds of efficiency and productivity effects. Critics of the strategy have been many, and a number of studies have marshalled evidence showing that liberal trade and financial regimes can reduce growth and produce other negative economic effects.[18] But the weight of current evidence, focused on export-oriented economies that have also achieved macroeconomic stability,[19] supports the basic tenet that trade can be a potent force for economic growth and change. Nevertheless, as the protracted debate on trade and protection suggests, some of the contention over these issues emanates more from national and group self-interest than theoretical discord, just as the eighteenth and nineteenth century classical economists were influenced by England's 'great power' status and dominating head start in manufacturing, trade and transport. Thus, ideology and material interests can never be completely removed from this debate.

Applicability of outward orientation theories to the Lebanese economy

In contrast to Lebanon's outward orientation, the EOI model of development has emphasised openness primarily in one sector and direction: the export of manufactured goods to advanced economies. It has been applied by some of the most successful Asian economies through a powerful, interventionist developmental state, greatly diverging from Lebanon's weak minimalist state. Therefore, evidence provided by case studies on EOI economies showing that expanded trade is correlated with improved efficiency and higher rates of growth, savings, investment and innovation, among other things, may indicate very little about Lebanon's outward-looking service-oriented development.[20]

One problem of using EOI theories to analyse Lebanon's outward-looking economy is that the concept of outward orientation cannot be conflated with EOI; nor can it be translated merely into liberal trade and investment institutions and policies. As the Lebanese case shows, outward orientation can encompass various economic sectors and activities oriented towards foreign demand and investment. Hence, a distinction must be made between outward-looking strategies and policies based on primary (agriculture, raw materials), secondary (manufacturing) and tertiary (service) activities.[21] Typical of the primary outward-looking economy was the colonial economy producing raw materials and agriproducts for the metropolitan economy. The secondary outward-looking economy is exemplified by post-Second World War East Asian economies such as Japan, South Korea and Taiwan, which have focused on export-oriented manufacturing. Lebanon is representative of tertiary outward-looking economies, which in the past were typically city states located on strategic trade routes engaging in *entrepôt* services. However, the Lebanese economy has also displayed features of primary and secondary outward orientation. For instance, after Lebanon lost free access to Syria's hinterland upon the dissolution of the Syro-Lebanese Customs Union in 1950, Lebanese producers were forced to restructure supply, distribution and marketing mechanisms to penetrate export markets; and in response to the altered conditions, the Lebanese government instituted a number of EP measures which targeted regional markets to sell Lebanese agriproducts and manufactured goods. Because Lebanon's tiny internal market was simply too small to utilise its manufacturing and agricultural productive capacity, primary and secondary export production became a matter of survival for many Lebanese industries and firms.

In the nineteenth century, Mount Lebanon's economic outward orientation was based on export production of primary and semi-finished goods, above all cocoons and silk yarn. The development of trade, finance and shipping associated with the silk industry in Beirut, Mount Lebanon and neighbouring areas expanded outward-oriented services in the region. The nature of Lebanese outward orientation shifted during French mandatory rule, due to several factors: the decline of the Lebanese silk industry; the onset of the Great Depression; the establishment of modern industrial enterprises; and the intensification of Franco-Lebanese quasi-colonial arrangements, facilitated by the introduction of French mandatory institutions and privileges extended to French capital.

Lebanon's outward-looking economic structure was interrupted by the Second World War when Allied strategic objectives in the occupied Levant temporarily modified economic conditions and formal institutions. The relatively weak colonial economic system that prevailed in French-ruled Lebanon was abruptly transformed into a highly-regulated, semi-autarkic war economy. Closed economic conditions and wartime necessity brought import-substitution policies, allowing Lebanon's infant industries (most of which had been established in the 1930s when trade was interrupted during the Great Depression) to grow under sheltered markets and bureaucratic regulation. However, closed markets and regulation raised costs and did not promote the development of externally-competitive manufacturing in Lebanon. After the end of the war when the Lebanese economy was reopened, opportunities to engage in highly profitable external trade, finance and services expanded. The new opportunities, and shifting domestic institutions, made Lebanon's inward-oriented and non-competitive postwar industry even less attractive. Both these factors encouraged the new governing elite to reject inward orientation and protectionism. The reversal of Lebanon's outward-looking economic path during the war, thus, was a mere interstice in the evolution of Lebanon's economic order. With the achievement of political independence and a changing economic environment in Lebanon and the Middle East, Lebanon's economy shifted to a higher path of outward orientation.

It was only after independence, when Lebanese agents obtained maximum freedom of action, that outward orientation in Lebanon reached its fruition. In the early postwar period, the governing bloc adopted free trade and capital as key institutions of the new order. This had little to do with economic theories: it is doubtful that Lebanon's leadership ever debated the comparative merits of, for instance, the Keynesian demand-side view of trade as an engine of growth with the demand- and supply-side notion of trade as a 'handmaiden of growth'.[22] On the contrary, the driving force of creating an open environment was little more than an expression of the economic and political interests of the dominant elite. However, if one assumes that the Lebanese governing elite wished to maintain power and reproduce itself, its embrace of outward-looking non-interventionist institutions was a risky strategy. Lebanon was clearly opposing the tide of history in the 1950s when, elsewhere, developed economies were adopting Keynesian demand management and welfare statism; and post-colonial nationalist governments embraced state activism and inward development strategies. On the political level, conventional wisdom would have recommended a strong interventionist state to bolster the idea and legitimacy of the Lebanese nation-state, which was not universally accepted in Lebanon or the Arab world. This strategy also constituted a reversal of policies and institutions initiated during the Second World War that had established a protected market and stimulated domestic production, high profits and employment. Furthermore, the issue was controversial, as important Lebanese interests supported the perpetuation of inwardly-oriented sheltered markets: the most vocal advocates of protectionism were large owner-entrepreneurs, skilled workers and labour organisations, which were associated with more developed sectors of industry. Critics questioned the effectiveness of free trade policies to satisfy a minimum growth of incomes for the majority of the population; and the idea of 'trickle-down' growth was contested.[23] Nevertheless, representing the interests and sentiment of powerful merchants, bankers, as well as Lebanese nationalists, and using skilful manoeuvres in a newly independent Lebanese state apparatus, proponents of liberal trade and financial regimes won the day.

This economic path targeted the development of Lebanon's intermediary role between the West and the Middle East based on the expansion of trade, finance and services centred in the quasi city-state of Beirut.[24] It had little to do with the concepts of superior allocation and coordination functions of the market mechanism or rationality of economic agents, characteristics of the neoclassical paradigm. Lebanese economic liberals never considered the logical implications of Adam Smith's invective against mercantilist regulations and state interventionist policies that supported monopolies and anti-competitive interests of favoured groups in eighteenth-century England. While Lebanon's measure of *laissez-faire* focused on the rights of economic agents to pursue their self interests and the institutionalisation of a non-activist, minimalist state, it did little to reduce obvious market failures or to promote internal competition.

The structures, policies and institutions supporting an open economy that serviced the Middle East, and acted as an intermediary between the advanced and regional economies, shaped Lebanon's economic order until 1958; and in a modified form, they persisted until 1975.[25] Bolstered by the interests of a majority within the power elite, these notions were translated into a model, which, if not always coherent and consistent, is readily identifiable as the Merchant Republic. Through the initiation of certain policies and omission of others, the government established a weakly-regulated market environment conducive to the expansion of an internationalised commercial economy. Among the first policies adopted by Lebanon's independent government were a progressive deregulation of trade and foreign exchange regimes, the stabilisation of the Lebanese currency and the establishment of an environment that logically led to a complete economic break with nationalist Syria. With the implementation of these and other measures, the government made the survival of domestic manufacturing and agriculture dependent upon Lebanon's comparative advantages in regional markets. Moreover, given Lebanon's small size and its adoption of a model of an open economy based on triangular trade and international services, Lebanese policy-makers were constrained in their macroeconomic policy options. They had little choice but to establish or continue policies to maintain a strong currency, surplus budgets and prudent external accounts.

The 'typical' export-promotion model as it developed in East Asia is quite dissimilar to the evolution of Lebanon's model of outward orientation. Beyond their divergence in the role of the state, sectoral emphasis of trade — that is the export of manufactured commodities in the East Asian EOI as opposed to the export of services in the Lebanese model — and ultimate objectives of the strategies, the function of the exchange mechanism is quite different. The typical EOI strategy has focused on maintaining a neutral or pro-export bias of the EER to affect both supply- and demand-side factors of domestic production. On the supply side, a neutral or pro-export EER provides domestic producers with incentives to produce for foreign markets and, on the demand side, they make products price competitive. Consequently, in this paradigm, trade expands; domestic production develops as incomes, savings and investment grow; and the ultimate goals of economic growth and structural change through industrialisation are achieved. By contrast, the function of the exchange rate regime in the Lebanese model, which from 1948 to 1975 comprised a strong gold-backed currency, and after 1952, mainly determined by market forces, was not directed at domestic production or economic growth and change through industrialisation. Although the EER of the Lebanese pound (£L) was approximately neutral (even as multiple exchange rates continued for a relatively small number of transactions), $EER_x \approx EER_m$, the role of the exchange rate mechanism was to encourage international confidence and inward financial flows to support an internationalised service economy, facilitate import and triangular trade movements and manage inflationary pressures. Furthermore, unlike the role of accumulation of industrial capital in the EOI model, a growing share of Lebanon's financial and commercial capital was 'hot', searching for the highest and quickest returns wherever, at an acceptable risk level. With higher profit rates and lower risks in services, a comparatively small share of capital flowed into domestic production. In brief, Lebanon's outward-looking strategy had far smaller growth effects on domestic output, employment and incomes than the East Asian EOI model.

However, there are similarities, at least in application, between the models of outward orientation. Both adopted strong pro-trade policies and institutions and developed open and efficient communications and transport networks linked to the advanced economies to facilitate exchange. The implementation of both models has produced *laissez-faire* tendencies in certain areas of the economies, but neither has aimed to implement an 'ideal' *laissez-faire*: the typical EOI strategy has utilised various forms of interventionism, while Lebanon implemented 'ersatz' *laissez-faire*, intended to permit the mobility of goods and capital, but not to create competitive internal markets. On the whole, both have tended to get important macroeconomic fundamentals right — namely neutral EERs, price stability and sound fiscal accounts — although the aims and modalities to achieve macroeconomic stability were somewhat different in the two.

Methodological issues

Beyond the problem of applying the concept of outward orientation to Lebanon, more prosaic difficulties arise when using Lebanon as a case study of almost any subject. One quandary is the geographical definition of Lebanon. Given the conceptual framework and time span of this work, it focuses on 'central Lebanon', which includes Beirut, Mount Lebanon and neighbouring areas that were economically integrated with the centre. Nevertheless, some socio-economic forces common to Mount Lebanon and Beirut can be found elsewhere; and at the same time, very dissimilar socio-economic movements were occurring in 'peripheral Lebanon' — that is southern and northern Lebanon, the Beka'a — and central Lebanon, which were integrated into the Lebanese state after 1920.

A second problem is data. This work uses data of authoritative primary and secondary sources, some widely available, others collected in archives and publications that are exceedingly difficult to obtain. However, for the entire period of this analysis, the statistical data are very weak due to collection, methodological and collation problems. Time series for even very basic economic indicators, such as national income, investment and foreign trade, can be questioned. Furthermore, some data on enterprise revenues and profits (and household incomes where available) appear to be underestimated because of collection problems and secrecy concerns. To highlight this issue, I have included comparative estimates of some indicators (for example, production, balance of payments and trade). In addition, because Lebanon did not have an autonomous monetary authority until 1964, data on the money supply, credit, gold and foreign reserves and other financial indicators originate from the French-controlled bank of issue, *Banque de Syrie et du Liban* (BSL). As the BSL was a highly politicised organisation, which also had large commercial interests in Lebanon, the data cannot always be trusted. In sum, while a very large amount of data are provided in the text and appendices of this work, they should be viewed with caution. They are meant to indicate magnitudes and suggest basic trends. They cannot be used in anything more than very rudimentary quantitative analysis to obtain meaningful results.

The transliteration of Arabic is always a difficult problem, and it is very confusing to readers used to either standard or popular transliteration of proper names. Because many Lebanese names and places are commonly transliterated in the accepted French manner, they are almost unrecognisable when transliterated by standard English practice. Hence, I have chosen to romanise these names in the most common style found in English-language literature. For example, I have used Kamal Jumblatt, as opposed to Kamal Janbalat.

Organisation

The Merchant Republic of Lebanon: Rise of An Open Economy is organised in seven main chapters and a statistical appendix. Following this introduction, in Chapter 2, 'The International Market Economy and the Establishment of an Outward-looking Environment in Lebanon, 1800–1939', I examine economic agents, institutions, policies and other forces that influenced the early development of Lebanon's outward-looking economic environment. In Chapter 3, 'Looking Inward: Reversal of Economic Policy and Institutional Environment in Lebanon during the Second World War', I analyse the changes and effects of Lebanon's brief war economy. Chapter 4 presents a 'Profile of Selected Sectors of Lebanese Industry, 1929–46'. Chapter 5, 'The Establishment of the Economic Order of the Republic of Lebanon: Open Economy', provides theoretical underpinnings of the Lebanese model of outward orientation adopted in the early postwar era. It also examines the main institutions the newly established Lebanese government adopted to support the vision of an open commercialised service economy. In Chapter 6, 'Outward-oriented Economic Growth and Change, 1946–58', I use empirical data to analyse the implementation of Lebanese outward orientation. In Chapter 7, 'The Lebanese Economic Model: An Evaluation', I summarise the findings of the work and evaluate the Lebanese model during the golden age of the Merchant Republic, according to its own logic and its impact on the growth and development of the economy. A statistical appendix providing data on the Lebanese economy can be found at the end of this work.

CHAPTER TWO

The International Market Economy and the Establishment of an Outward-looking Environment in Lebanon, 1800–1939

European penetration

European demand for silk spurred trade between Europe and Lebanon from the seventeenth century when it began exporting silk to France and Italy.[1] Over the next two centuries, growing European penetration of the region 'in search of food, raw materials, markets and outlets for its energy, capital and population',[2] and its interaction with local agents, organisations and institutions, propelled multifaceted transformations in the Lebanese provinces. Within this complex process, Lebanon increased production for, and exchange with, the international market; capitalist relations developed in Mount Lebanon and the Beirut region; and a class of Lebanese merchants, financiers and intermediaries emerged, as they accumulated capital, skills and influence. As the region was incorporated into a developing international division of labour and specialisation,[3] local supply forces adjusted to meet European demand.

Though this transition occurred over a protracted period, the pace of change quickened during the nineteenth century, as trade between Europe and the Levant expanded,[4] and as shifting economic, political and social forces converged. First, stimulated by a rise in European demand for silk and a few other commodities, supply forces in the Levant responded. Revolutionised sea transport, which made long-distance trade faster and more secure, facilitated this exchange. Second, under the pressures of expanding productive capacity and industrial competition,

European industrial powers began to seek new export markets. Through a variety of political and economic instruments, local markets for European manufactured exports were opened and/or widened. Third, the economic–commercial environment of the region was altered by political changes that favoured European trade, investment and economic influence: for example, the 1831–41 Egyptian occupation of Syria; the conclusion of the Ottoman–European commercial treaties of 1838; the establishment of the *mutasarrifiyya* in Mount Lebanon in 1861. Accompanying these changes was the development of an institutional framework promoting European trade and finance in the region and enforcing European 'rules of the game'. Consequently, political and economic risks for European traders and investors were reduced, transaction costs declined and international markets were widened. Under these conditions, local investment, production and exchange were shifted towards the international market. Lebanon assumed three basic economic roles as it integrated into the international economy: it became a market for European manufactures, an export producer of primary and semi-finished commodities, and an intermediary for international goods and services in the region.

The development of the Lebanese silk industry

Lebanon's position in the nineteenth-century international market economy was shaped by the development of sericulture. While Lebanon had already begun to specialise in raw silk production by the eighteenth century,[5] its economic potential and effects were not realised until the next century when silk exports to France expanded rapidly. Sericulture became the engine of growth in nineteenth-century Mount Lebanon, dominating its economy until the First World War. Although data are difficult to obtain, the nature and pace of growth of silk production and trade can be put into context by several indicators. Rapid growth of output and export of Lebanese silk began in the mid-nineteenth century, as suggested by the elevenfold increase of silk exports from Beirut between 1841 and 1857.[6] This trend peaked between 1873 and 1902 when production of raw silk in Lebanon and Syria increased by over 350 per cent, due entirely to rising foreign (primarily French) demand.[7] Moreover, the weight of silk products in total exports from Beirut's port doubled from about 25 per cent at mid-century to 50 per cent during the 1890s.[8] Silk and cocoon output in Lebanon and Syria grew most rapidly from 1873 to 1915, when export dependence on France became almost complete: 40 per cent of total silk exports were sent to France in 1873, growing to 99 per cent in 1914.[9] Just prior to the war, silk production comprised 73 per cent of total value-added in agriculture and industry (cocoon production accounting for 55 per cent and silk thread for 18 per cent) and 36 per cent of gross product in Mount Lebanon.[10] At the same time, annual operating capital in Mount Lebanon's spinning factories was estimated at FF 9 million of domestic resources and another FF 8–9 million of foreign investment; domestic fixed capital comprised an additional FF 2.3 million and foreign fixed assets amounted to FF 0.2 million,[11] making the industry a recipient of a large share of the total flows and stock of capital in the mountain. Most investment was financed internally: funds retained from net profits in silk reeling, 37 per cent of total factor income being profits,[12] were far higher than what was required for investment and current operations. Two final indicators of the economic importance that silk had attained in Mount Lebanon by the prewar years were that half of Mount Lebanon's population was economically dependent on sericulture and that cocoons, silk thread and waste comprised 62 per cent of total exports from Mount Lebanon.[13]

As incentives and security increased, French and other foreign interests invested in industry to produce silk thread in Lebanon. By 1852, five of the nine silk-reeling factories were owned by French capital, and British firms owned another two.[14] After the establishment of the European-backed *mutasarrifiyya* in Mount Lebanon in 1861, French investment in silk rose further: by 1870, French interests owned ten silk-reeling factories and some modernised their plants.[15] As economic opportunities expanded, Lebanese producers and intermediaries increased their investment in silk reeling, particularly after the 1870s. Coinciding with growing Lebanese participation in silk production, however, was a large reduction in French ownership of silk-reeling factories, declining from 56 per cent of the total in 1852 to less than 5 per cent in 1885.[16] In brief, Lebanese investment in silk increased just as French capital was pulling out of that industry.

The ascendancy of sericulture multiplied Lebanese dependence on French industry, commerce and finance.[17] The demand for, and earnings from, Lebanon's silk exports were highly unstable, not only because of the nature of the international market for primary commodities, but also because Lebanese suppliers were dependent on one market. Foreign demand was highly sensitive to, for example, the *pébrine* epidemic that hit French sericulture in the 1850s, the 1870s depression, and competition from silk producers in the Far East; and, as would be expected, there was high variance of prices for cocoons and raw silk.[18] The subordination of Lebanese sericulture, which was structurally weak and technically inefficient, to French interests ultimately blocked the necessary reorganisation of all phases of production.[19] Technical backwardness, in addition to stagnant international prices for silk, low wages in sericulture (encouraging emigration and an outward flow of labour to other industries) and high land prices, were responsible for the onset of a crisis in sericulture by the late nineteenth century. Among the economic consequences of this pattern of development were capital flight; loss of potential value-added as a result of producing mainly primary (cocoons) rather than processed goods (thread or cloth); deindustrialisation; and emigration.[20]

More important for the future of Lebanon was its participation in the highly profitable silk trade. Trade, finance and services associated with the silk industry (shipping, insurance, brokerage) were concentrated in a few French, Lebanese and joint venture firms. Under this structure of ownership, management and influence, the silk industry was vertically integrated: a small number of French and Lebanese controlled production, finance and exchange of silk commodities.

The rise of Beirut

The seeds of Beirut's role as a leading commercial, financial and communications intermediary between Europe and the Middle East were planted during this period. Just as the silk industry was an important stimulus for industrialisation and then deindustrialisation in Mount Lebanon, it was an impetus to the development of Beirut's export sector and financial, shipping and insurance services. All silk exports to France (90 per cent of total Lebanese silk exports) were shipped through the port of Beirut. The port of Beirut was also favoured by Europe's communications and transport revolution and economic expansion to the detriment of the older ports of Sidon, Tyre, Tripoli and Acre. Furthermore, the predominance of French interests in Beirut promoted its rising influence. For instance, the French *Compagnie ottomane de la route Beyrouth–Damas* was a prime mover in the formation of the Beirut Port Concession.[21] French interests financed a large share of Beirut's infrastructure through direct investment in Lebanese concessionary companies such as the *Compagnie du gaz de Beyrouth* and the *Eaux de Beyrouth*.[22] As links between Europe and Lebanon tightened and Beirut's international role grew, regional commercial–economic bonds loosened.[23] Most notably, Beirut's previously large volume of trade with Egypt and Turkey suffered a relative decline.

In less than a century, Beirut's population grew by an estimated twentyfold: from 8000 in 1825 to between 150,000 and 200,000 in 1913.[24] During that period, Beirut became an important commercial and financial centre, an administrative and political capital as an Ottoman *vilayet*, a seat of European consuls and concessionary offices, and an influential educational and cultural centre in which French, American, British and other foreign institutions were established. Furthermore, the rich and influential bourgeois families migrated to the environs of Beirut to take advantage of the growing opportunities Beirut offered.[25] Beirut thus became the most prosperous city in the region.[26] Simultaneously, the foundations of its future role were laid, and its westernisation first became evident in the customs and habits of its bourgeoisie.[27]

The emergence of a mercantile-financial bourgeoisie

The emergence of a class of merchants and financiers, whose wealth and power grew with that of foreign trade and services, was instrumental in the evolution of Lebanon's outward-looking economic order. This bourgeoisie prospered from its close association with European interests, but its long-term viability depended on expanding its own economic and political influence. Moreover, based in a small, newly-emerging commercialised economy, Lebanon's embryonic bourgeoisie acquired highly diversified interests: they included land, agri- and industrial (particularly silk) production, trade and finance. The bourgeoisie's importance became more manifest after Lebanon's role as silk producer decreased and its intermediary function increased. Local merchants took advantage of new opportunities in re-export and, through expanding commercial networks, they became distributors of European merchandise to the hinterland.

Fortunes were made during the First World War by this class, especially those who dealt in grains and other essential commodities. As effective wartime economic controls were not imposed, speculators and black marketeers were able to make large profits on scarce commodities when the Turkish blockade and local constraints reduced supplies. Prospering Beirut and Tripoli merchants reinvested a substantial share of their war profits in large domains of rural property, especially in the Beka'a and Mount Lebanon.[28]

Foreign trade and investment trends

European efforts to penetrate new export markets and Ottoman 'anti-mercantilist' trade policies favoured the expansion of imports, in contrast to exports, in Greater Syria.[29] In the Syrian region, 65 per cent of imports were covered by exports between 1825 and 1865, and this share dropped to 60 per cent between 1870 and 1900, and to 50 per cent between 1910 and 1920.[30] However, with high European demand for silk goods, Beirut's exports expanded rapidly in several cycles, and its import coverage tended to increase from 1825 to the early 1870s, after which the growth of exports did not keep pace with that of imports. The data in Table 2.1 on Beirut's trade show an import coverage of 67 per cent from 1825 to 1850, rising to 103 per cent from 1851 to 1857, declining to 85 per cent from 1851 to 1872 and to 52 per cent from 1896 to 1910. The large growth in the volume of European exports is underlined by this trend, given the improved net barter terms of trade of Syria and Beirut: Syria experienced a rise in its terms of trade between the 1870s and 1913[31] and Beirut, similarly, from the 1840s to before the First World War.[32] Nevertheless, the region experienced an unfavourable secular balance of trade that was not completely covered by invisibles or capital transfers. Consequently, gold flowed to Europe, domestic price levels rose, the local currency depreciated,[33] and foreign ownership of local assets increased. In the two decades preceding the First World War, however, data suggest that trade deficits were largely offset by an inflow of foreign capital financing large infrastructure projects (see Figure 2.1).

Table 2.1: *Trade of Beirut, 1825–1910 (%)**

Years	Growth rate	Average annual growth rate	UK + French/ total trade	Export–import ratio
1825–1850	333	12.8		67
1825			59	68
1850			60	72
1851–1857	112	16.0		103
1851			50	71
1857				100
1851–1872	21.7	1.0		85
1872			75*	60
1872–1896	35.5	1.4		50
1896			64	46
1896–1910	18.2	1.2		52
1910			62	38

Note: *Import trade only.

Source: Charles Issawi, *The Fertile Crescent 1800–1914: A Documentary History* (New York and Oxford, 1988) pp. 154–5.

While Britain was the largest exporter to the region until the First World War, supplying over 33 per cent of all imports to Syria and over 48 per cent to Beirut on the eve of the war,[34] it was the French who dominated foreign investment in the area. Pre-First World War French investment, estimated at FF 200 million, was the single most important within the Syrian region.[35] Principal French investments in Beirut and Mount Lebanon accounted for about half that amount. The largest share of French capital was invested in the communications and transport system, public utilities, banking, commercial houses and insurance; only a modicum flowed into agriculture and industry, mainly in the silk industry.[36]

The establishment of direct French control over Lebanon

Following the First World War, the League of Nations granted France the mandate over Lebanon and Syria. This award was a confirmation by the military victors of France's sphere of influence in the area,[37] something that had been recognised earlier by Britain and France in the Railways Understanding of 1910, the Sykes–

Picot Agreement of 1916 and the Lloyd George–Clemenceau Agreement of 1919. Soon after, the French high commission in Beirut proclaimed the establishment of the State of Greater Lebanon, expanding the borders of Mount Lebanon to include the Beka'a, Akkar, southern Lebanon and coastal areas of Tripoli, Beirut, Sidon and Tyre.

Figure 2.1: *Principal European investments in infrastructure in the Levant, 1890–1913*

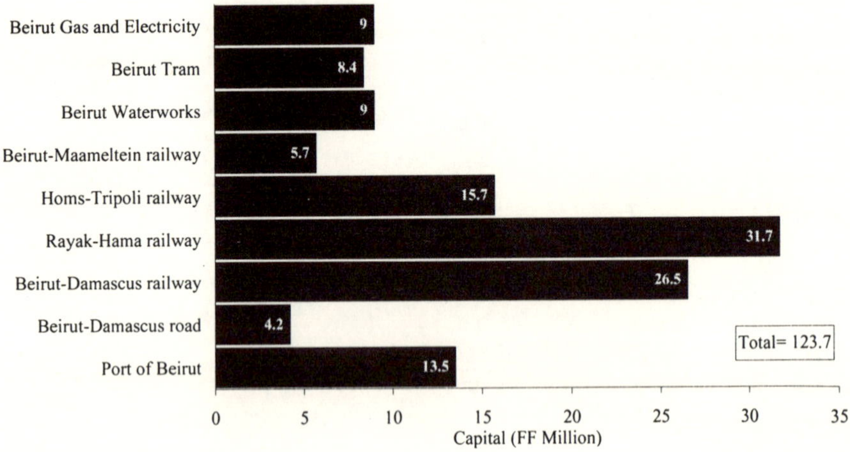

Source: Boutros Labaki, *Introduction à l'histoire économique du Liban* (Beirut, 1984) p. 219; Jacques de Monicault, *Le Port de Beyrouth et l'économie des pays du Levant sous le mandat français* (Paris, 1936) p. 32; Issawi, *The Fertile Crescent,* p. 135.

The imposition of the French mandate over the newly-established states of Lebanon and Syria destroyed economic, commercial and financial unity that had existed in the Greater Syria region under Ottoman rule. However, to coordinate and rationalise economic management of Lebanon and Syria, the mandatory established *de jure* customs and monetary unions and a *de facto* economic union between the two.

Direct control heightened the ability of French capital to compete in the area, temporarily improving its comparatively weak international position.[38] French mandatory economic policy promoted neo-mercantilist exchange (*économie de traité*) by the establishment of relationships with the Levant states similar to those that prevailed in France's colonies. The *économie de traité* encompassed exchange of French manufactures for colonial commodities and semi-finished goods 'in a closed economic circuit designed to exclude foreign traders and shipping'.[39]

Table 2.2: *French investment in Lebanon during the mandate*

Category and Firms	(FFm)	Share (%)
1. Banks	*698.30*	*84.9*
Banque de Syrie et du Liban	300.00	
Crédit foncier de Syrie	6.00	
Crédit foncier d'Algérie et Tunisie	125.00	
Compagnie Algérienne	267.30	
2. Utilities	*77.00*	*9.4*
Electricité de Beyrouth	75.00	
Société d'électricité la Kadicha	2.00	
3. Ports and Entrepôts	*20.50*	*2.5*
Compagnie du port, des quais et entrepôts de Beyrouth	16.00	
Compagnie générale du Levant	4.50	
4. Railroads	*15.00*	*1.8*
Compagnie française du chemin de fer DHP	15.00	
5. Miscellaneous	*11.30*	*1.4*
Radio-Orient	3.30	
Grand hotels du Levant	8.00	
TOTAL	*822.10*	*100*

Source:, Mohamed Amine El-Hafez, *La structure et la politique économique en Syrie et au Liban* (Beirut, 1953) p. 48.

The extension of mandatory privileges to French capital was implemented through two main modalities. First, the establishment of the mandate in Lebanon shifted policy making and execution from Turkish and local bureaucracies to a French high commission, which was greatly influenced by industrial, commercial and financial interests in Lyon and Marseilles.[40] This shift brought about a number of institutional changes that governed the Lebanese economy. Second, French bureaucrats consistently promoted French over competing foreign or local economic interests. While French interests had previously held a dominant foreign position in the most profitable areas of the economy, after the establishment of the mandate, French companies were able to take control of a number of concessions that had formerly belonged to other European interests;[41] and they were able to impede the ability of foreign competitors to enter into new economic activities in Lebanon.

Policy and institutional changes under French rule: financial system

Even before the formal institution of the mandate over the Levant states, the French introduced a rudimentary financial system. Modelled on French colonial financial systems elsewhere, the mandatory authority granted the privilege of note issue to the BSL in 1919. With its relatively large foreign capital base and a dual role as a commercial bank and the bank of issue, the BSL was endowed with extensive power over monetary policy and credit allocation. It also dominated both foreign banks and domestic financial institutions.

The Syro-Lebanese paper currency, which was pegged to the French franc, created dislocations for the local economy, especially in coastal cities where the currency was in greater use. The local currency suffered from extreme fluctuations of the franc until the French currency was placed on the gold standard in 1928, and subsequently from frequent devaluations of the French franc. As a result, in the first years of the mandate, 1919–26, the local economies lost an equivalent of £T 10 million;[42] and, from 1920 to 1939, the Syro-Lebanese pound was devalued by more than 64 per cent against the US dollar[43] (see Table 2.3). Second, the Syro-Lebanese monetary union, which incorporated the two economies into the French financial system, eliminated Ottoman-imposed financial unity, thereby contributing to declining trade and other economic relations with some regional economies like Egypt and Turkey.

Although financial intermediation was not highly developed in Lebanon during this period, a comparatively wide range of credit instruments existed, particularly after 1930. Financial markets in Lebanon were characterised by dualism, whereby an organised sector in Beirut employed relatively modern methods of intermediation and transactions, and unorganised rural markets were dominated by landlords, merchants and moneylenders. Organised financial markets in Beirut were largely controlled by French interests, and to a lesser extent other foreign financial groups.

Beirut's commercial banks were the cornerstone of Lebanon's organised financial system. After the recovery of the Lebanese economy in the 1920s, both foreign (four of the five largest foreign banks being French),[44] and domestic banking expanded. Foreign banks, which secured a large part of their capital from parent banks in Europe, were established in Beirut to finance international trade and related operations. By contrast, the essential function of smaller local banks and discounting houses was to provide loans to domestic borrowers, particularly in rural areas. However, foreign banks expanded the scope of their operations in Lebanon during the Depression. Because interest rates tended to be higher in Beirut than in European markets, and because of the general European financial crisis in the 1930s, capital flowed into Lebanon, pursuing higher returns. With the expansion of their capital base, foreign banking institutions began to penetrate internal markets.[45] The inflow of private foreign capital into Syria and Lebanon from 1922 to 1941 has been estimated at £SL 21 million (US$ 10–15 million).[46]

Table 2.3: *Exchange rates and currency cover of £SL, 1919–39*

Year ending	£SL	French assets/cover	FF = US $1 (average)	FF = Sterling £1 (average)
1919	–	–	7.3	31.8
1920	9.0	100.0	14.3	52.7
1921	10.1	100.0	13.5	51.9
1922	9.1	100.0	12.3	54.6
1923	9.8	100.0	16.6	75.7
1924	7.9	99.7	19.3	85.3
1925	9.8	98.2	21.2	102.6
1926	9.8	96.2	31.4	152.7
1927	7.9	95.1	25.5	123.9
1928	8.6	95.7	25.4	124.1
1929	8.7	95.7	25.4	124.0
1930	11.7	96.7	25.5	123.9
1931	11.4	96.7	25.5	115.6
1932	12.0	95.9	25.5	89.2
1933	12.9	96.2	20.6	84.6
1934	12.9	96.2	15.2	76.7
1935	15.0	95.9	15.2	74.3
1936	21.3	95.8	16.7	83.0
1937	23.7	92.4	25.1	124.4
1938	35.9	92.4	35.0	170.6
1939	46.9	88.6	39.8	176.7

Source: Edmond Asfour, *Syria: Development and Monetary Policy* (Cambridge, MA, 1959) p. 47.

Several other important sources of capital existed in the Lebanese economy at this time. One was the Lebanese and French trading houses, which favoured commerce, financial and international services. In general, Lebanese investors preferred trade, finance and property, where risks were low and rewards high. However, merchant capital operated throughout the Lebanese economy in both the formal and informal markets, its availability determined by commercial criteria. Industrial capital was mobilised from several sources, one of which was Lebanese emigrés returning to their homeland with both savings and experience. Emigrés were instrumental in establishing modern industry in Lebanon in the 1930s; they also invested relatively large capital in the construction and tourism sectors. An unknown share of emigrant remittance transfers, which reached FF 30 million per annum between 1920 and 1926,[47] also helped finance small retail, handicraft and off-farm enterprises. Other sources of capital were war profits, estimated at £T 7 million in 1914, and £T 18 million in 1918, in Syria and Lebanon;[48] and Palestinian-Jewish immigrants who invested in Lebanese industries, banks and tourism. Moneylenders, mainly merchants, landlords and village buyers-up, provided most rural credit, but it was available only at extremely high interest rates on short-term conditions, preventing most peasants from making the long-term investments necessary to improve the technically backward conditions that characterised small agriculture.

While credit was generally available to the domestic economy, some sectors had far greater access than others, an important mechanism shaping the investment environment and structure of the national economy. Public investment in the Lebanese economy was small. The French High Commission, whose budget was always under pressure, did not provide credit for undercapitalised but important sectors of the economy. Instead, French policy aimed to regain local confidence in the economy and the French-backed currency so that Lebanon's private sector would invest in the domestic market.[49] Stagnating economic conditions showed that this policy was unsuccessful, forcing the mandatory power to establish state-backed lending institutions. However, few credit constraints were alleviated because financial intermediaries were undercapitalised and their lending practices were inefficient and ineffective. One common misuse of state-guaranteed agricultural credit was lending to landlords, who then advanced the same capital at far higher rates to the peasantry.[50] As state-backed financial institutions only lent to the peasantry as a last resort,[51] they were almost totally left out of the organised credit markets.

Balanced budgets and *ad hoc* fiscal instruments

The sole objective of mandatory fiscal policy was to collect enough revenue to finance state expenditures. To meet this elementary goal, the High Commission imposed taxes and fees on an *ad hoc* basis to pay for essential expenses. As long as the mandatory authority met its budget requirements, fiscal management was not questioned: issues of efficiency, equity and economic effects were not considered. Further, the mandatory-imposed tax structure never completely integrated the old tax systems (applied to two different regions of Lebanon before 1920), resulting in a generally lower tax burden for Mount Lebanon.[52] The fiscal system was also highly regressive: indirect taxes generated the bulk of revenues (in 1932, 80 per cent of all tax receipts originated from customs duties and excise taxes).

On the expenditure side, the fiscal system was more complex. The French created three basic budgets: the Common Interests budget (joint Syro-Lebanese revenues and expenditures), the states' (Lebanese and Syrian) budgets and the French High Commission budget. Of Common Interest revenues, 95 per cent were generated by customs receipts, and its expenditures were allocated for joint Syro-Lebanese services — namely financial and economic services, customs administration, *sûreté générale*, *troupes spéciales* and railways. The surplus of the Common Interests budget, which was distributed to the states in no fixed proportion until 1943, was the largest source of revenue for the local budgets. The expenditures of the state budgets were allocated for local administration, security, welfare and development. Finally, the bulk of the French High Commission budget went towards the expenses of the Levant army and the High Commission bureaucracy. The triplication of administration resulted in inefficient and expensive budget management. It also obscured the nature and distribution of revenues and expenditures and made any effective system of accountability very difficult.

Tariff policy

The objectives of tariff policy, which was executed through the French-controlled Syro-Lebanese Customs Union, were ambiguous; but clearly it did not protect the territories' industries.[53] Although industrialists pressed for higher tariffs, influential commercial interests effectively opposed protectionism. In any case, the League of Nations' 'Open Door' policy for mandated areas exposed Lebanon to low 'normal' tariffs granted to all League members and the USA. These policies favoured commerce between the industrialised countries and Lebanon; and in the 1930s they facilitated the competitive search of industrialised economies for export markets in Africa and Asia, including the Levant.[54] As a consequence, Japan, the USA, Britain and Italy expanded their volume of exports to Syria and Lebanon in the 1930s. By contrast, regional protectionist policies had been established after the imposition of British and French mandatory rule in the Middle East.[55] Subsequently, some favourable tariff agreements were concluded between Lebanon/Syria and its neighbours, which supported the growth of Syro-Lebanese exports to the region in the 1930s. Finally, the mandatory and Lebanese government approved the creation of a free trade zone in Beirut to promote re-export trade between international and regional markets.

The nominal rate of Syro-Lebanese tariff protection rose from about 11.5 per cent in 1921 to 28 per cent in 1934,[56] with lower effective rates of protection — barriers too weak to protect Lebanon's infant industries. Due primarily to the decline of prices of international imports in the 1930s and to the expansion of Syro-Lebanese exports to the region, Syro-Lebanese import–export ratios improved: import coverage rose from 25 per cent in the years between 1920 and 1933 to between 30 and 60 per cent in the years from 1933 to 1939.[57]

Sectoral trends during French rule

During the interwar years, three important sectoral trends can be discerned:

- a continued decline in agriculture, as indicated by a reduction in sectoral investment, output and income and its weakened position *vis-à-vis* trade and services; at the same time, there was little or no reduction of surplus labour, even in very low marginal product agriculture;[58]
- industrialisation in the 1930s, whereby modern manufacturing was established to produce consumer goods for the local market, accompanied by a continuing decline of traditional industry;
- stabilisation of the economic base for foreign trade and services, facilitated by the development of physical infrastructure, but impeded by the Depression of the 1930s.

Agriculture

At the time of the establishment of Greater Lebanon in 1920, almost two-thirds of the population were dependent upon the agrarian sector, which was in a state of crisis as a result of the First World War and the decline of sericulture. With large surplus labour in agriculture, value-added was too low to provide even a subsistence income for the population dependent upon this sector. While in the previous century, some of Mount Lebanon's surplus workers had been transferred abroad through emigration or to the more productive silk industry, these avenues were almost closed after the war, due to the decline of the silk industry and to depressed employment in the Americas and elsewhere in the 1930s. Hence, employment pressures on agriculture were high, but profits and incentives were too low to attract the large investment necessary to modernise and restructure the sector. On the other hand, Lebanon's agricultural potential was increased with the addition of fertile lands surrounding Mount Lebanon: to the 80,000 hectares of land that was cultivable (but not high-yielding) in the mountain was added another 140,000 hectares of fertile land in the Beka'a, Akkar, Koura, areas around Tripoli, and the plain between Beirut and Tyre, representing 64 per cent of cultivable lands in the new state.[59]

French and Lebanese authorities introduced policies to promote the revival of sericulture,[60] but output of cocoons in the Levant never reached more than two-thirds of prewar levels.[61] With the failure of the silk industry to restructure, it was virtually destroyed during the Depression by falling world prices and wider distribution of artificial silk. Attempts to introduce a substitute were unsuccessful. Purely technical constraints involving agricultural production on mountain terraces (where mulberry trees had been grown) hampered the development of alternative agro-exports. Nor did the growth of fruit farming and industrial plantation production compensate for the loss of income from sericulture. Finally, falling international prices for primary commodities reduced incentives for the redevelopment of Lebanon's agriculture sector. Nevertheless, cultivation was extended and intensified in the 1920s and stabilised in the 1930s in Lebanon, primarily due to an increase in local demand.[62]

Public and private investment in agriculture was comparatively low; and technical reorganisation and technological advances in the sector were insufficient to overcome structural problems. Mandatory and Lebanese government policy promoted the establishment of irrigation and drainage projects,[63] but on the whole, public investment was not sufficient to complete the projects. Inadequate water resources remained a major constraint to expanding production. Probably the most important public investment that benefited agriculture was in transport infrastructure, which before 1930 had been very poor and a major impediment to expanding agricultural markets.[64] During this period, private interests began to invest in farm mechanisation, which was introduced slowly and unevenly to the coastal areas of Sidon and Tyre and in the grain-growing areas of the Beka'a and Akkar.[65] Furthermore, modern methods of cultivation, organisation and marketing were initiated. However, capital flowing into agriculture was comparatively small because investment was riskier and the rate of return was lower and slower than that available to investors in commercial and financial ventures. Thus, long-term investment in agriculture was simply too small to reverse the process of decay, making it the weakest sector in the Lebanese economy.

Industry

Before the First World War, Lebanese industry, which had employed from 10 to 25 per cent of the labour force[66] and paid higher wages than either commerce or agriculture,[67] had developed around a small number of export and consumer goods such as silk, tobacco, leather goods and foodstuffs. Except for a limited modernisation of the silk industry, organisation of these industries remained traditional.

Under the conditions of the first decade of the mandate, Lebanese industry was not restructured and modernised; and silk manufacturing became a sunset industry. Development of modern industry in Lebanon faced numerous problems: notably, a small internal market dominated by western imports; influential Franco-Lebanese interests, which favoured import and re-export trade; and the imposition of the French mandate, which did not promote industrialisation.[68] Nevertheless, during the next decade, capital began to flow into industry. Investment in modern manufacturing was stimulated by depressed trading conditions, the return of Lebanese emigrés with capital and industrial experience, and favourable supply factors including a low-wage surplus labour force and improved physical infrastructure. The timing of industrial investment suggests that the impact of the Depression, which reduced import competition and allowed industrialists to exploit local advantages, played a key role in laying a base for industrialisation in Lebanon. Emigré capital, which was seeking economic opportunities during the slump, was instrumental in establishing import-substituting industries, such as textiles, construction materials and food-processing.[69] The best known example of the émigré industrialist is George Arida, who invested capital made in Mexico into a cotton-spinning mill in Tripoli, which in the early 1930s produced the equivalent of 12 per cent of Syro-Lebanese imports.[70] In addition, domestic, regional and foreign capital flowed into Lebanese industry during this period. Maronite Monseigneur Antoun Arida, influenced by Zionist industrial policies in Palestine, established the Kadicha electricity company in 1922 and the Chekka cement company in 1929. Kadicha was financed by funds of the Arida family and Palestinian Jews,[71] while Chekka's capital originated from the Arida family and Maronite religious orders in association with French interests.[72]

Figure 2.2: *Establishment of industrial enterprises in Lebanon, 1913–40*

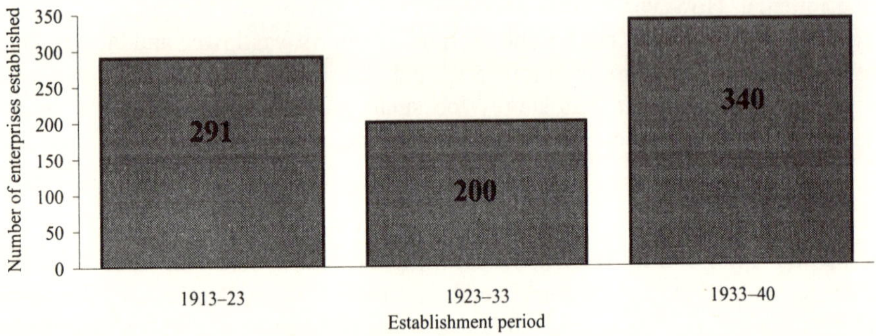

Source: Ministère du plan et mission IRFED, *Besoins et possibilités de développement du Liban*, étude preliminaire, vol. 1 (Beirut, n.d.) p. 198.

The number of modern industrial enterprises in Syria and Lebanon, which more than doubled between 1932 and 1933,[73] increased from 400 in 1930 to 900 in 1939.[74] Evidence of a large industrial expansion and modernisation during the early 1930s is supported by the growth of capital imports and industrial construction licences. Annual imports of capital goods expanded by thirtyfold from 1925 to 1934: they grew from 1420 tons in 1925, to 3159 tons in 1930, to 19,863 tons in 1932, peaking at 44,107 tons in 1934. Thereafter, they dropped to an average of 4300 tons per annum between 1934 and 1939.[75] The number of industrial licences grew from 110 in 1930 to 139 in 1932, dropping to 30 in 1934.[76]

Table 2.4: *Largest Lebanese-owned industrial enterprises during French mandate*

Enterprise (core products)	Year established	Place established	Capital (£SL)
Société des ciments libanaise (cement)	1929	Chekka/Tripoli	240 000
Arida Brothers (cotton-spinning and weaving)	1935	Bashas/Tripoli	490 000
Achkar & Cie (silk-spinning)	1935	Dubayé/Beirut	400 000
Connatry Jabre & Cie (vegetable oils)	1937	Beirut	494 680
Clouterie libanaise-syrienne (nails and wire netting)	1938	Beirut	1 200 000

Source: Compiled from *Le Commerce du Levant* as cited by Kurt Grunwald, 'The industrialization of the Lebanon and Syria', *Weltwirtschaftliches Archiv*, vol. 76, no. 1 (1956) Table 8, p. 155.

Grunwald assessed 1937 employment in modern industries in Beirut at 3957 workers, and in Tripoli at 894 workers;[77] another source, however, shows in the same year a total employment of 16,753 workers in the modern industries in Beirut and only 354 workers in those in Tripoli[78] (see Tables 2.4 and 2.5). According to French data, employment in modern manufacturing in 1937 made up 42 per cent of total industrial employment in Lebanese centres (Beirut, Tripoli and Sidon), in contrast with 15 per cent in Syrian industrial centres (Damascus, Aleppo, Homs and Hamah).[79]

In 1932, Lebanese industry comprised 272 factories, which employed more than 4000 workers; and 12 of these factories employed more than 100 workers each. Between 1932 and 1934, newly established Lebanese industrial enterprises were found in the sectors of cement, cigarettes, beer and alcohol, cotton-spinning, food-processing and electricity.[80] A number of these were established to meet changing tastes in Lebanon, for example, ice, beer and repair of motor vehicles. Others satisfied traditional consumer demand. By the end of 1938, modern manufacturing firms located in Beirut and its environs produced knitwear and hosiery; silk, cotton and wool textiles; leather and shoes; processed foods and beverages; beer and alcohol products; soap; matches; furniture; tiles, pipes and cement; nails, iron and metal works.[81] Tripoli was the home of the important cotton-spinning and weaving factories, the Chekka cement factory, tile and pipe works, and soap producers. Modern tanneries were established in Zahlé, replacing some of its older cottage workshops, and in Chtaura.

Accompanying the movement of the rise of modern industry was an acceleration in the decline of traditional industries in Lebanon. Based on inefficient manual labour and simple cottage organisation, many traditional industries were faced with restructuring or collapse, thereby displacing large numbers of artisans and workers. In Lebanon, this trend proceeded faster than in Syria: older industries, which were relatively more important and numerous in Syria, were better able to resist the new competitive forces. Decline in Lebanon was concentrated in the traditional Tripoli soap industry and Zahlé tanneries.

Table 2.5: *Employment in Lebanese modern and traditional industries, 1937*

Industry	Beirut employment	Tripoli employment	Total
Modern	800	–	800
Hosiery and knitwear	350	–	350
Cement and manufactures	500	844	1 344
Shoes (mechanised)	1 050	50	1 100
Petroleum	1 257	–	1 257
TOTAL	3 957	894	4 851
Traditional			
Cocoon breeding	65 800	–	65 800
Boot-making	5 000	1 200	6 200
Tailoring	700	–	700
Cabinet-making and inlaid wood	2 000	–	2 000
Tobacco monopoly	1 900	–	1 900
TOTAL	75 400	1 200	76 600

Source: Grunwald, 'The industrialisation of the Lebanon and Syria', Table 5, p. 149.

Despite the revival of foreign imports in the mid-1930s, Lebanese industry was consolidated until 1937 when it began to overproduce for its limited internal and regional markets, which were again being inundated with foreign imports. In response, merchants stockpiled relatively inexpensive goods, helping perpetuate low prices for manufactured wares until 1940. Consequently, industries such as textiles were threatened with closure when the war broke out in 1939.[82]

The decline of foreign competition and increase of domestic competition during the 1930s in Lebanon catalysed a dual evolutionary process of industrialisation and deindustrialisation whereby the fittest enterprises survived. Nevertheless, industrialisation was founded on a weak base, even though Lebanese industry did not compare unfavourably with regional industries. Industry remained organised on a small scale, preventing the emergence of scale economies. Moreover, it was capable of producing only a fraction of local demand for some goods and overproducing for others. It was also unable to compete with (frequently higher quality and lower priced) foreign production. The revised 1932 tariffs that helped protect industries against, for example, cheaper Japanese and British manufactures, were clearly inadequate measures to shelter Lebanon's infant industries. Beyond the threat of competitive foreign manufactures, Lebanon's industrial sector was dependent on imported capital goods and technology. While typically a constraint on industrialising economies, this factor became a major obstacle to the modernisation, reorganisation and expansion of industry in the next decade, when the Second World War interrupted not only imports of foreign consumer products, but also essential producers' goods.

Foreign trade

French mandatory authorities and commercial interests promoted Franco-Levantine trade, which was also underpinned by the predominant role of French investment in Lebanon and Syria.[83] When France assumed control of Lebanon, international and regional trade was already a well-established part of the Lebanese economy.[84] During the mandatory years, Lebanon's foreign trade structure experienced a number of changes. First, its direction of trade shifted after the intensification of bilateral Franco-Lebanese links and the introduction of a Syro-Lebanese common market. Even with the introduction of colonial economic and financial barriers, Levantine exports to the region expanded. Second, the commodity composition of trade was modified by the demise of silk exports and the increase in capital imports. These changes temporarily benefited French exporters, but harmed Lebanese merchants who had a long association with the silk trade. The trend of import growth outstripping export expansion continued in the first decade of the mandate, but slowed during the 1930s.

Direction of trade

After the establishment of the French mandate in Syria and Lebanon, the direction of regional and international trade shifted. Despite the disruption of regional unity by the introduction of French and British mandatory regimes, the volume and share of Syro-Lebanese regional exports expanded. In the interwar years, about half of all Syro-Lebanese exports flowed to the region, a much higher share than from 1890 to 1914. This was partly due to the decline of silk exports to Europe; but Syria and Lebanon also increased their primary and manufactured commodity exports to regional markets. By 1938, Palestine was Lebanon's most important export market: Syro-Lebanese exports (agriproducts, foodstuffs, textiles, cement, shoes and leather) to Palestine of more than £SL 8 million exceeded those to France by over £SL 2 million.[85] About a quarter of Lebanon's imports originated from the Middle East in both the prewar and mandatory periods. The most important change in European import trade during the mandate was the replacement of Britain by France as Lebanon's largest supplier in 1925. France remained in that position until the Second World War, but never regained that status after the end of the war.

Commodity composition of trade

In 1931, three-quarters of exports were primary commodities, while half of imports were manufactured goods.[86] The structure of Syro-Lebanese trade in the 1930s, when domestic manufacturing expanded, is shown in the following table.[87]

Table 2.6: *Commodity composition of Syro-Lebanese trade in the 1930s*

Category of goods	Share (%)
Imports	
Foodstuffs + textiles + garments + leather footwear	50
Fuels + capital and producer goods	20
Other	30
TOTAL	100
Exports	
Foodstuffs	60
Textiles	20
Leather footwear + garments	5–10
Other	10–15
TOTAL	100

Source: Levant States, CSIC, Service d'études économiques et de statistiques, *Recueil de statistiques de la Syrie et du Liban*, 1945–7 (Beirut, 1948).

Import and triangular trade

Despite the 'balkanisation' of the region and the competition of ports such as Haifa, import and triangular trade in Beirut grew in the interwar years. Mandatory policy encouraged this development by reserving the Syrian market for Beirut merchants in exchange for higher tariff protection for agriculture and industry, which was more important to the Syrian economy.[88] This was further facilitated by the *de facto* Syro-Lebanese economic union. Between 1925 and 1939, about 60 to 80 per cent of the value of aggregate Syro-Lebanese imports entered via Beirut. Transit trade was about four times the value in 1939 as that in 1931, and much of Beirut's transit and re-export trade was destined for Iraq and Jordan and, to a lesser extent, for Palestine, Turkey, Iran and Saudi Arabia. Most of Beirut's re-export and transit-exit trade was to the Middle East, and about a third of its transit-entry trade was from the Middle East.[89]

In the years preceding the First World War, about half of Syro-Lebanese imports were covered by its exports, and this deficit continued to grow in the first decade of the mandatory. In 1930, a reversal of this pattern began as a consequence of the impact of the international Depression. The value of trade dropped during the Depression by about 50 per cent, due mainly to the fall in world prices. The volume of imports only decreased by about 4 per cent, while the volume of exports, principally destined for the region, actually rose by about 85 per cent. The net effect was a decline in the merchandise trade deficit from 1931 to 1937, but it increased to pre-Depression levels in 1938 when the worst effects of the crisis were over. Deficits were generally compensated by foreign capital transfers and service and invisible exports (for example, emigrant remittances, oil transit revenues, tourism and other international services).

Beirut as growth pole of trade, finance and services

The linked set of market relationships of trade, finance and services continued to play an important role in Lebanon's economy under mandatory rule. It, however, became more concentrated in the Beirut region after the demise of sericulture, which had elevated the economic importance of Mount Lebanon before the First World War. Furthermore, French interests promoted Beirut economically and strategically; and large Franco-Lebanese private and public investments flowed into Beirut's physical infrastructure.

French policy played an important role in the expansion of Beirut's regional economic position during the interwar years. A long-term objective was to make Beirut one of two principal French economic and strategic axes of the Middle East, which would service Syria, Palestine, Iraq, southern Persia and Arabia.[90] Second, French policy sought to counter Britain's development of Haifa, and more generally, Palestine. The French mandatory authorities viewed Beirut's regional role to be threatened by the development of industry in Palestine and of Haifa as a port, terminus of the IPC oil pipeline, and communications link to Iraq. Hence, French policy became more activist, particularly after 1933/4 when the new high commissioner Count Damien de Martel established a six-year plan that promoted the development of roads, railways, ports and irrigation.[91] Furthermore, Beirut's commercial and economic position was strengthened and its primacy ensured by the ratification in 1936 of the Franco-Lebanese Treaty of Alliance, which prompted the French to drop their proposal to develop Tripoli as a naval port and centre of military operations.[92]

Table 2.7: *Syro-Lebanese balance of trade, 1913, 1921–39**

Year	General imports[1] (000 tons)	£SL** (00 000)	General exports[2] (000 tons)	£SL** (00 000)	Balance (000 tons)	£SL** (00 000)
1913	–	325	–	150	–	–175
1921	–	300	–	35	–	–265
1922	–	263	–	57	–	–206
1923	–	280	–	123	–	–157
1924	338	398	71	169	–267	–229
1925	449	487	77	229	–371	–258
1926	417	633	77	272	–340	–361
1927	439	641	114	273	–325	–368
1928	544	660	78	267	–466	–393
1929	603	729	122	255	–481	–474
1930	576	635	188	226	–388	–409
1931	588	579	181	208	–407	–371
1932	660	485	129	171	–531	–314
1933	721	452	136	174	–586	–278
1934	593	368	169	156	–423	–212
1935	590	346	208	200	–382	–176
1936	564	339	357	219	–207	–120
1937	671	646	363	375	–307	–271
1938	640	854	460	446	–179	–408
1939	587	922	376	540	–211	–382

Notes: *Numbers are rounded to the nearest thousand; **in current prices; [1] imports include transit-entry goods; [2] exports include re-exports and transit-exit goods.

Source: France, Ministère des affaires étrangères, *Rapports à la Société des Nations sur la situation de la Syrie et du Liban* (Paris, 1934, 1938); France, Haut-commissariat de la République française en Syrie et au Liban, *Bulletin économique trimestriel* (Beirut, 1929); Sa'id Himadeh, *Monetary and Banking System of Syria and Lebanon* (Beirut, 1935) Table III, p. 12.

At the same time, public and private investment flowed into the development of Beirut's infrastructure. The most important area of investment was the communications and transport system, which was centralised in Beirut. Between 1920 and 1943, public investment financed the extension of the road network from 500 to over 2500 kilometres: organised along a grid pattern, the roads ran north to south (linking major strategic, economic and political centres) and east and west (facilitating trade along traditional routes) and was centred around Beirut.[93] Improvement in the road system stimulated the use of the motorcar: the number of

Table 2.8: *Traffic at Beirut Port, 1920–39 (000,000 tons)*

Year	Disembarkation	Embarkation	Total	Transit
1920	132.0	27.6	159.6	n.a.
1922	214.6	26.6	241.2	n.a.
1925	361.8	58.4	420.2	n.a.
1927	350.8	72.1	422.9	n.a.
1928	434.1	34.4	468.5	n.a.
1929	493.5	73.8	567.3	n.a.
1930	441.5	65.8	507.3	n.a.
1931	484.5	53.6	538.1	n.a.
1932	509.7	36.9	546.6	n.a.
1933	514.8	40.3	555.1	n.a.
1934	423.6	40.3	463.9	n.a.
1935	429.1	39.3	468.4	13.4
1936	421.1	58.0	479.1	11.2
1937	448.4	97.5	545.9	22.2
1938	402.6	115.4	518.0	21.5
1939	522.8	110.4	633.2	25.0

Note: n.a. = not available.

Source: Compagnie du Port de Beyrouth as cited by Jean Ducruet, *Les capitaux européens au Proche-Orient* (Paris, 1964) p. 243.

motor vehicles increased from a few hundred after the war to more than 5000 passenger cars and more than 1000 commercial vehicles in 1932;[94] and by 1938, Beirut had almost 100 agencies that imported automobiles.[95] Plans to modernise and expand Beirut's port at an estimated cost of FF 49 million were initiated by the foreign-owned Port of Beirut Company in the mid-1930s.[96] Although modernisation of the port was not completed before the war, improvements were made; a second basin was opened and a commercial free zone was established.[97] The expansion of the port's capacity enabled traffic almost to quadruple between 1920 and 1939 (see Table 2.8).

Capital was also invested in smaller infrastructure projects. An airport at Beirut was inaugurated in 1936 and officially opened in 1939. Beirut urban transport was expanded: bus and taxi companies were established and electric tramway systems maintained. In communications, Radio Orient was founded as a modern and powerful communications link with Paris and New York.[98] Post, telegraph and telephone communication networks were also improved.

Public and private finance promoted the development of tourism services in Lebanon. Beyond investment in public works, the Lebanese budget allocated funds to support tourism infrastructure and to establish a private tourist promotion commission; and the state-backed *Société libanaise de crédit agricole et industriel du Liban* (SCAIL) was authorised to extend credits to build hotels and *estivage* villas.[99] Further, private investment flowed into the development of tourism, which was centred in Beirut and Mount Lebanon. The tourist industry grew during the interwar years: the number of tourists visiting Lebanon and Syria increased from 100 in 1919 to more than 16,000 in 1938; and the number of *estiveurs* grew from 500 to 20,000, respectively.[100] However, more importantly, it established a foundation for greater development after the end of the Second World War.

The shaping of Lebanese economic growth and change in the nineteenth and early twentieth centuries occurred in an evolving, outward-looking economic environment as regards institutions and structures of investment, production and exchange. Beirut became the centre of dynamic economic activities in the country; and the 'propulsive role' of international trade and services was established, laying a base for future growth.

While this outward-looking environment was not translated into a model of development, the seeds of an internationally-oriented service economy, essential to Lebanon's future as the Merchant Republic, were firmly planted during this period. However, the Second World War interrupted the pursuit of this ideal, and the Anglo-French occupation temporarily reoriented the Lebanese economy towards self-reliance.

CHAPTER THREE

Looking Inward: Reversal of Economic Policy and Institutional Environment in Lebanon during the Second World War

The outbreak of the Second World War began to disrupt Lebanon's economy as Europe moved towards war production; international transport became more difficult; and the French mandatory authorities introduced new controls. Economic dislocations mounted in the Levant after France signed an armistice with Germany in 1940. Responses to the installation of a pro-Vichy regime in Beirut were far reaching. Britain blockaded Levantine seaports. Iraq shut the flow of oil to Lebanon through the IPC pipeline. Sterling block neighbours closed their markets to Lebanon and Syria. The Allied occupation of the Levant in 1941 ended its isolation from British-controlled neighbouring economies and the blockade of its seaports. Although Lebanon and Syria did not become permanent members of the sterling block, their status as temporary members gave them full trading and currency rights within the block. Along with these benefits came a new form of interventionism: the broad and multifaceted authority of Allied bureaucracies was extended to the Levant states, allowing the establishment and enforcement of trade, supply, currency and price controls so as to adapt the states' economies to the war. Three different authorities, British, French and Lebanese, regulated (often overlapping) components of Lebanon's economy, which was fashioned according to Allied war requirements and strategic objectives.

Europe's wartime intervention in Lebanon required two broad modifications of the economy to fulfil military objectives. First was the expansion of supply through more efficient and effective utilisation of domestic productive factors and, second, the reorientation of the economy towards inward-oriented productive organisation to satisfy (suppressed) domestic consumption. To shift the economy in this way, it was essential to modify policies and institutions that had facilitated a weakly-regulated quasi-colonial economy to those that would promote a highly-controlled semi-autarkic economic system. Consequently, the occupation authorities initiated four main changes in Lebanon and Syria. First, the war bureaucracies regulated the flow of goods, capital and people to conserve supplies, foreign exchange and transport. The introduction of managed trade modified traditional modes of production, distribution and consumption in the Lebanese economy. Second, the authorities promoted agricultural self-sufficiency by expanding output and reducing export of essential foodstuffs and primary commodities. Without significant investment in capital and land, agricultural output was augmented by utilising surplus labour and improving techniques and processes. Moreover, self-sufficiency required reorientation of agriculture from producing industrial crops for European and US markets to satisfying domestic demand. Because market forces had begun this process earlier and international demand for these goods had been declining or stagnating in the 1930s, output of food and agriproducts (comprising 40 per cent of total Syro-Lebanese exports between 1935 and 1938) could be adjusted in the short run to meet increased domestic demand. Third, occupation policy encouraged rapid import-substitution to reduce dependence on European manufactures, but it did not comprise a long-run and consistent strategy to promote the development of an industrial base. Beyond the fact that it countered British and French long-term interests, the implementation of a typical import-substitution strategy was impossible, given the constraints on time, capital and international supply imposed by the war. Finally, the military occupation interfered with the economy's supply and demand forces by instituting price controls and rationing supply of scarce commodities. The introduction of price and supply controls changed relative prices, thereby disrupting many economic fundamentals; and they were not effective in halting spiralling inflation.

An examination follows of the two basic changes in Lebanon's wartime economy, which shifted it from typical outward orientation to a more inward-directed environment, devised not to stimulate economic growth and development, but to fulfil short- to medium-term foreign military objectives.

Expansion of domestic supply

The Vichy French mandatory authorities initiated policies to utilise domestic resources more effectively and efficiently after the onset of the war: hoarding, speculation and smuggling were countered; essential commodities such as fuels, rice and sugar were rationed; transport and distribution of grains were managed;[1]

the IPC installations were requisitioned. Other emergency measures were established to encourage domestic production. The French military, in conjunction with a group of French and Lebanese companies, constructed a domestic oil refinery at Tripoli, which began to operate in late November 1940.[2] They promoted import-substitution by establishing factories and workshops needed to satisfy civilian and military consumption. Workshops, complementing the principal activities of Tripoli's oil refinery, were created, and they produced items such as pottery and earthenware. A sugar refinery was built at al-Abdé, near Tripoli, and began operating in 1940 when it was given a monopoly over locally-produced sugar cane. In Beirut and its environs, factories and workshops were established to process lignite and manufacture cutlery, scissors and glass products. However, the impact on consumption by the precipitous drop of imports, about 43 per cent by volume in 1939/40, could not be offset by domestic output because of increased demand by the French military and insufficient domestic productive capacity and factors. Between June 1940 and August 1941, economic hardship increased with a growing shortage of goods and foreign exchange.[3] Hoarding, speculation and spiralling prices contributed to a cycle of reduced output and rising inflation and unemployment; and the expanding economic crisis produced fear of political and social unrest.[4]

With the Allied occupation of the Levant, public investment in physical infrastructure in Lebanon was revived. State expenditures on infrastructure had been slashed between 1939 and 1941,[5] and deteriorating roads and declining fuel supplies became major constraints on supply and distribution. The Allied bureaucracy initiated a public works programme to repair war damage and to meet new needs. Thus, the road and rail networks were repaired, improved or extended; a new pier was built in Tripoli; and the IPC pipeline was reopened. British military forces also initiated water and irrigation projects, including the Beirut–Tyre coastal water projects, which were completed in 1944, and a project to irrigate the Beka'a plain, which became operational in 1945. After 1943, however, inflationary pressures in the Levant forced the Allies to restrict infrastructure investment to projects essential to the military.

The Allied occupation also established a stronger bureaucratic structure to expand supply and control distribution of essential consumer and capital goods. The two most important bureaucracies with tasks of improving the supply side of Lebanon's economy were the British Spears Mission economic section,[6] which represented the Middle East Supply Centre (MESC) and the French *Office de l'économie de guerre* (OEG).

A principal assignment of the Spears Mission economic section was to research and analyse the local economies in order to provide appropriate technical and management assistance to increase output, efficiency and capacity of agriculture and industry.[7] Its economic officers were dispatched to factories, mines, fisheries, farms and other enterprises to assess their conditions and productive capacity and utilisation; and they also estimated factor proportions and input requirements to determine supply requirements. To increase economic self-reliance, the Spears Mission established rubber retreading and recycling workshops, pharmaceuticals, paper and glassware factories.[8] It also assisted vital consumer industries (for example textiles, foods and beverages, tobacco, matches and leather goods) to maintain or expand output by authorising them to import producer inputs. Similarly, it helped supply farmers with fertilisers, insecticides, seeds and American lend/lease agricultural machinery. The impact of its control over producer goods cannot be overstated: local enterprises, to which the Spears Mission/MESC did not supply inputs, were generally forced to slash output or cease production altogether. Furthermore, the Mission's supply controls affected industrial expansion, encouraging horizontal rather than vertical integration.

The OEG, administered by the French counsellor for economic affairs, was created in January 1942 to adapt the local economy to war production and to exert greater control over industry. The main tasks of the OEG, which frequently duplicated the functions of the Spears Mission,[9] included providing management advice to private enterprises, establishing workshops and factories and assuming direct control of strategic industries.[10] The OEG, aided by Lebanese universities, managed research and experimental facilities, which in turn provided technical assistance to agricultural and industrial producers. The agricultural section of the OEG sought to increase farming productivity by advising on methods that improved techniques and processes and by supplying seeds and intermediate goods. Its industrial section encouraged import-substitution of essential manufactures. The purchasing section held an import monopoly over scarce commodities. In addition to facilitating the needs of local producers, the OEG produced cloth, shoes, leather and recycled tyres in its factories.[11]

Restructuring to promote autarky

Managed trade

Establishment of trade barriers

After the Anglo-Free French occupation of the Levant in 1941, policies and instruments to regulate trade were expanded and tightened compared with Vichy French emergency measures. At the same time, trade and economic management bureaucracies were fragmented into British, French and Lebanese 'spheres of influence'. These bureaucracies were given the tasks of (1) reducing imports to vital necessities, thereby curtailing demand for Allied supplies, transport and foreign exchange, and (2) supplying essential imports from intra-regional and sterling block sources. To reduce imports efficiently, regulatory measures were applied according to quantity, category and supply origin. However, compared with the rest of the Middle East, Allied bureaucracies were less effective in enforcing trade controls in the Levant: Beirut's well-connected merchants were able to evade import quotas and other trade barriers throughout the war.[12]

The principal agency controlling foreign trade in Lebanon was the Anglo-American MESC,[13] which determined minimum local needs and managed imports to conform with those requirements through licensing and allocation of shipping space for goods that could not be locally produced.[14] The efforts of the MESC and sterling block administration to reduce domestic demand for imports, transport and foreign exchange ended years of neo-mercantilist trade and circulation and promoted a 'regionally-integrated supply pattern'.[15] Through the MESC and British trade monopolies,[16] such as the United Kingdom Commercial Corporation (UKCC),[17] which guaranteed sterling payment for all approved Syro-Lebanese imports, and Imperial Chemical Industries (ICI), which monopolised the supply of chemicals to local industries, Britain expanded its commercial influence in Lebanon and Syria.

Second, the French-controlled *Commission supérieure de ravitaillement* (CSR), acting under the MESC and as intermediary between the MESC and the domestic supply services, assisted in determining import and export quantities. Until 1944 when it was abolished, the CSR organised and regulated internal trade and the distribution of essentials.[18]

The Lebanese Ministry of Supply was created in 1942 to deal with trade, supply and price issues, and it assumed control over import licensing after 1944. Due to widespread rent-seeking and corruption, it was the weakest link in the supply chain. The ministry regularly obstructed the enforcement of trade controls to permit influential Beirut merchants to increase their share of commodity imports in great demand, such as textiles and coffee.[19] One such trading house that imported mainly American goods, F. A. Kettaneh, was reported to have made 'a fortune from illegal US imports'.[20]

Shifts in the structure of trade: concentration, composition and direction

Allied trade policy, which reduced import volume on average by 24 per cent between 1939 and 1945 over 1935–8, and export volume by 71 per cent from 1942 to 1945 over 1935–8, sought to allocate a similar share of the total import market to large domestic trading houses as what they had previously enjoyed. This practice, reinforced by rent-seeking activities and bureaucratic bargaining over access to import licences and foreign exchange, increased commercial concentration of import markets.

France permanently lost its position as primary supplier of the Levant states to Britain and the USA as a consequence of the altered balance of economic and military power of the three in the region and the demands of the war economy. French commercial decline can be illustrated by supply changes in three very important Levantine markets. First, luxury imports (previously dominated by French suppliers) were virtually eliminated. Second, Britain's ICI in Palestine and Egypt gained a monopoly over industrial chemicals, a market that had been dominated by French and German firms before the war. Similarly, French pharmaceutical exporters lost their markets to British and US firms. While British firms regained a prime supply position in the Levant, US exporters gained significant market penetration for the first time. American firms increased chemical, pharmaceutical and transport exports to the Levant while, through lend/lease, agricultural machinery became a US monopoly.[21]

The composition of Syro-Lebanese trade shifted during the war, as shown by the data in Table 3.1.

Table 3.1: *Changes in commodity structure of Syro-Lebanese trade, 1935–45*

Import category	Volume change (%) average, 1939–45/1935–8
Consumer agriproducts	+13
Consumer manufactures*	–45
Capital goods	–26
Luxury goods	–57
Export category	**Average, 1942–5/1935–8**
Consumer agriproducts	–85
Consumer manufactures	–67
Capital goods	–36
Luxury goods	Eliminated

Note: *Textiles comprised the greatest share of manufactured imports.

Source: Levant States, CSIC, *Recueil de statistiques*, 1945–7.

A significant shift in the direction of trade was caused by the tightening of links between the Levant states and the Middle Eastern sterling block countries.[22] The MESC policy of encouraging intra-regional trade expanded Lebanon's commercial links with Middle Eastern sterling block countries: in 1938, only 7 per cent (by value) of total Middle Eastern commerce was among these countries, but this grew to 33 per cent in 1943.[23] By 1943, Middle Eastern countries furnished almost 90 per cent of total Syro-Lebanese imports, compared with 23 per cent in 1938; nearly

97 per cent of Syro-Lebanese exports were sold within the Middle East in 1943, compared with 37 per cent in 1938.[24] Syro-Lebanese imports from six major sterling block countries, the UK, Egypt, Iraq, Palestine, Transjordan and Cyprus, rose from 26 per cent of the total in 1938 to about 47 per cent of the total in 1945, while Syro-Lebanese exports to these countries comprised 75 per cent of the total in 1938 and declined to 64 per cent of the total in 1945.[25] This pattern of regional and sterling block trade was dominant throughout the war, then ceased when Lebanon resumed its large import trade with the USA and Europe after hostilities ended. By 1946, the USA, closely followed by Britain, was the states' major supplier.

Although Lebanon lost agro-export markets in France and other industrialised countries, greater disruption and losses were incurred as a consequence of the reduction of Syro-Lebanese exports to regional markets: the latter dropped to under 25 per cent of the prewar value (adjusted for inflation) and half of the volume. The decline was due to Allied policy. It sought to maintain large supplies in the Levant as a contingency measure — namely to be able to supply the local population and Allied forces if increased troops were required in the region; and Britain discouraged the Levant's best regional customers from purchasing Syro-Lebanese goods, so that they would establish links with other (sterling block) exporters.[26] Thus, in absolute terms, Syro-Lebanese regional exports declined, even though the region absorbed a relatively larger share of their exports. In a few isolated cases, Lebanese wartime exports to regional markets rose absolutely and relatively, for example its export of cement to Iraq. Exports to its most important market, Palestine, plummeted, and wartime volume never reached more than half of its 1937 level.

By contrast, Syro-Lebanese imports from the Middle East increased both relatively and absolutely. After supplies from the industrialised countries were cut off during the war, a growing volume and share of manufactured imports were obtained from Palestine, whose industry was modernising, reorganising and consolidating. In May 1943, an agreement between Syria, Lebanon and Palestine was concluded to exchange Palestinian manufactures for Syro-Lebanese primary goods in order to use the surplus industrial productive capacity of Palestine.[27] Palestine's share of the Syro-Lebanese market grew from about 6 per cent in 1938 to about 14 per cent in 1944.

In sum, the war reduced Syro-Lebanese import and export volume, and it significantly altered the direction of trade. Goods of European and American origin had comprised 67 per cent of the total value of Syro-Lebanese imports in 1938, but only 2.4 per cent in 1943; and Syro-Lebanese exports to Europe and the USA dropped from 55 per cent of the total in 1938 to 3.5 per cent in 1943. India replaced Britain and Japan as Lebanon's major supplier of textiles in the war years.

In fact, the demand for Indian textiles was so great that Britain had to make an independent agreement with the Indian government to restrict textile exports to the Levant, which continued to exceed MESC import quotas.[28]

Figure 3.1: *Direction of Syro-Lebanese trade, 1938–43*

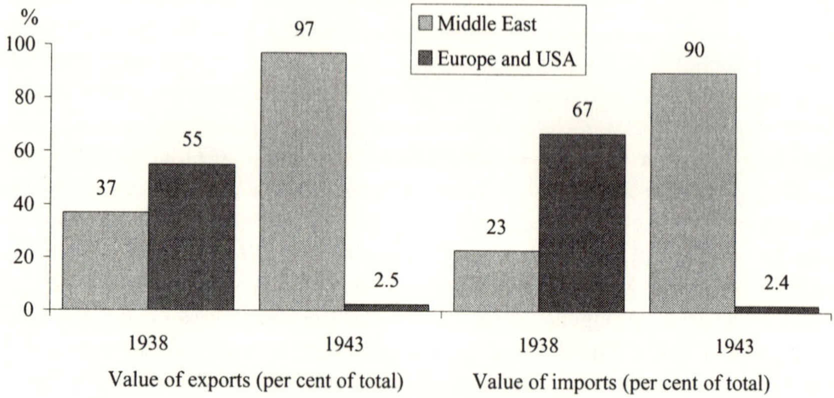

Source: Levant States, CSIC, *Recueil de statistiques*, 1945–7.

Exchange controls

The establishment of the *Office des changes* in December 1939 marked the beginning of strictly-controlled foreign exchange transactions in Lebanon, although previously the French mandate had determined financial policy and regulated capital movements. The *Office des changes*, attached to the French-owned BSL, allocated foreign currency for licensed imports, controlled the flow of foreign capital and currency, and regulated other foreign financial transactions. These regulations were designed to improve France's foreign exchange position in order to fight what was expected to be a long war. Supplying hard currency to the local economy was a much lower priority. The web of exchange regulations allowed the French to borrow £SL 50 million from the Levant states in 1939 to purchase military and civilian supplies needed to prepare the Levant for war.[29]

By 1940, when the Vichy regime was installed in the Levant states, foreign exchange in high demand had largely been exhausted. As dollars were almost unobtainable and sterling accounts were blocked, demand for gold grew: in 1940, an estimated £SL 79 million of gold was hoarded by individuals in Syria and Lebanon.[30] Official gold reserves, a large share of which had been appropriated by the mandatory authority,[31] were completely wiped out by a transfer of £SL 6 million in gold to France in June 1941 by High Commissioner General Dentz.[32]

With stringent restrictions on the official exchange market and growing demand for hard currency, a parallel exchange market developed. Vichy French authorities had tolerated a growing black market in sterling-backed Palestinian pounds.[33] After the entry of the Levant states into the sterling block, speculation in neighbouring currencies continued until the Allies sold sterling on the open market in 1943.

In 1944, the *Office des changes* became an autonomous public service, administered by the French-owned *Banque de Syrie et du Liban* and responsible to the newly created Syro-Lebanese *Contrôle des changes*.[34] At the same time, the Levant states were forced to return to the franc bloc, freeing Britain from its sterling obligations to the economies. The 1944 Catroux Accord, by which the Levant states agreed to re-enter the franc bloc, returned the *status quo ante*: the local economies were again financially dependent on France; and they no longer had secure access to the highly-demanded sterling currency. Thus, black market operations and instability in the local currency markets resumed. These conditions had far reaching ramifications in the early postwar period. Most important, the Lebanese government accepted the Franco-Lebanese Monetary Accord in 1948 to secure release of French franc balances accumulated during the war.

Agricultural self-sufficiency: response to market forces and bureaucratic intervention

Occupation requirements increased demand for domestic agriproducts, bringing about policies that promoted production and discouraged exports: the average volume of agro-exports declined by 85 per cent between 1939 and 1945, as compared with 1935–8, while agro-imports increased by 13 per cent in the same period. During the course of the war, agricultural output increased sufficiently to satisfy domestic demand for grains, vegetables and fruit. Over and above producing for an enlarged domestic market, Lebanon's agrarian sector exported surplus vegetables, fruit and several other agriproducts to Palestine, which were exchanged for Palestinian manufactures. The smuggling of scarce foods to nearby countries, which was common, also expanded demand for Lebanese primary goods.

With a large increase in demand for these goods, and various constraints on supply and distribution forces, prices rose rapidly. Furthermore, profit rates on primary production increased significantly for large landowners/producers. They were particularly high on British contracts to provide food staples for the troops.[35] They were also substantial on products for the civilian market, even under controlled prices. Rising prices, however, generally did not raise profits for small farmers because they depended on middlemen and commission agents to market their output; and credit to finance the higher costs of inputs, such as seeds and fertilisers, was expensive. The large producers not only had better access to investment funds, technical assistance and Allied contracts, but they were also involved in the powerful distribution networks that were the basis of rising profits. In contrast, the goods of small producers were purchased by middlemen, who could frequently sell them in Beirut for three times what they paid to the farmers.[36]

To reduce the power of the middlemen, the British authorities supported the expansion of the Agricultural Cooperative Movement.[37] This comprised a network to market members' produce and supply technical assistance; and it was centred around villages near Beirut, including the largest and most successful, Ubaydiyah (see Appendix Table A16). However, even with official support and an appreciable growth of the cooperative movement, it never became strong enough to challenge the market power of the landowners, merchants and middlemen.

To address the constraint of agricultural credit, the Lebanese government had begun to promote greater state–private cooperation even before the war. It had signed a convention with the BSL in 1937, by which the latter established SCAIL in 1938 with capital of £SL 100,000 to make loans to agricultural and industrial enterprises. Between 1942 and 1944, SCAIL increased its capital to £SL 1 million and augmented its mandate to grant agricultural credit to farmers, landowners and agricultural cooperatives. State–private credit took the form of government-guaranteed loans that were managed through the public *Office du crédit agricole libanais* and executed through the private SCAIL. SCAIL loaned money at 4.8 per cent per annum for government-guaranteed loans.[38] Short-term loans could not exceed one year, and long-term loans were restricted to a maximum of ten years; and both were subject to other regulations.[39] Expanded state–private cooperation in agricultural credit formally gave small farm owners better access to organised credit markets, but due to inadequate capitalisation, corruption and nepotism, they continued to depend heavily on local usurers. The total government-guaranteed loans amounted to almost £SL 4.7 million between 1943 and 1945 (see Table 3.2). Under these constraints — controlled distribution networks and badly-functioning credit markets — and rising production costs, many small farmers could not survive. They were forced to sell their land and to migrate to the cities to obtain war-related employment.

Market forces and bureaucratic intervention stimulated agriproduction, as farmers produced at maximum capacity; but they did not prompt producers to make large investments to restructure agriculture technically and organisationally. The short-term response of the primary sector was due to three main factors. First, obtaining farm machinery and equipment to increase capacity and productivity was exceedingly difficult during the war. Second, a long period, which was likely to extend beyond the war, was required to realise returns on agricultural investment.[40] Finally, uncertain expectations about postwar domestic and export markets, costs and prices did not provide enough information to assess risks and rewards.

Consequently, the growth of fixed investment, as indicated by the import of tractors and other agricultural machinery, was relatively small. The utilisation of tractors was concentrated in the fertile areas of the Beka'a valley and the Akkar plain, so as to maximise agricultural yields in the shortest time possible. However, on the whole, a general movement towards mechanisation and reorganisation of productive forces of agriculture did not emerge during the war years. Agricultural productivity in Lebanon and Syria, while higher than in Iraq or Egypt, was low.

Table 3.2: *Activity of the* Office du crédit agricole libanais, *1943–5*

		Short-term loans		Long-term loans		Total loans	
Muhafazats	*Year*	*Number*	*£SL*	*Number*	*£SL*	*Number*	*£SL*
Beka'a	1943	8	15 900	61	292 680	69	308 580
	1944	11	19 400	120	471 055	131	490 455
	1945	17	33 500	175	658 050	192	691 550
North Lebanon	1943	4	7 000	10	43 200	14	50 200
	1944	5	9 400	36	151 570	41	160 970
	1945	24	46 000	109	622 600	133	668 600
South Lebanon	1943	5	10 000	21	139 500	26	149 500
	1944	3	5 500	48	230 230	51	235 730
	1945	32	63 000	59	462 300	91	525 300
Mount Lebanon	1943	26	41 400	27	99 250	53	140 650
	1944	55	94 500	55	207 780	110	320 280
	1945	148	277 900	123	678 700	271	956 600
TOTAL	1943	43	74 300	119	574 630	162	648 930
	1944	74	128 800	259	1 060 635	333	1 189 435
	1945	221	420 400	466	2 421 650	687	2 842 050

Source: Levant States, CSIC, *Recueil de statistiques*, 1945–7, Table 14.

By 1946, 22 per cent of land in Lebanon was under cultivation, compared with about 17 per cent in 1942, both far less than its potential.[41] With new irrigation projects undertaken during the war, the amount of irrigated land had increased by 1946, but 186,000 hectares (over 80 per cent of total cultivated land) was still not irrigated.[42] At the end of the war, Lebanon was self-sufficient in fruit and vegetables with an exportable surplus. Though Syria and Lebanon together were self-sufficient in grains, Lebanon had to buy annually more than 100,000 tons of wheat and barley from Syria (equivalent to 70 per cent of its requirements), costing more than the combined value of Lebanese production of olive oil, citrus fruit and silk.[43]

Figure 3.2: *Agricultural productivity in Syria–Lebanon and selected countries, 1945 (international units)*

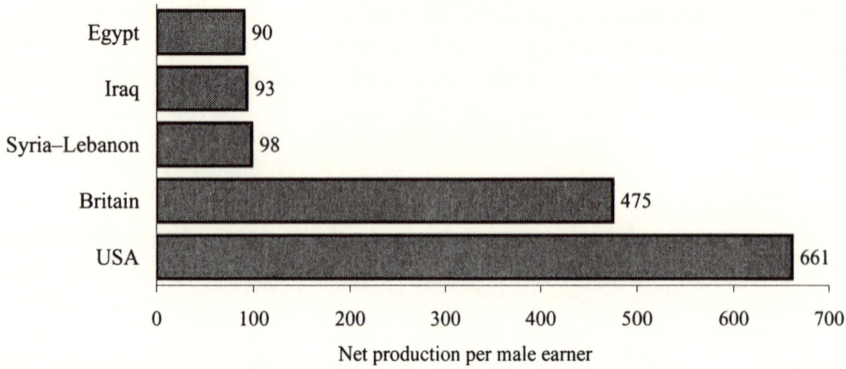

Source: PRO, FO921, file 79, Middle East Economic Conference: the Common Wealth of the Middle East, conference paper no.EC/2, agenda item no. 1(B), 21 March 1945.

Establishment of import-substitution

The logic of Allied objectives in the Levant required a substitution of domestic output for imported commodities. However, with the constraints of military priorities, war conditions affecting the domestic economy, and long-term interests of the powers, a consistent import-substitution strategy to develop Lebanon's industrial base was never considered. Wartime import-substitution in Lebanon deviated from the objectives and rationale of a stylised ISI strategy. The differences between ISI and wartime import-substitution in Lebanon and outcomes of the latter will be discussed in the remainder of this section.

An initial component of an ISI strategy is to secure stable domestic consumer markets by establishing trade and tariff barriers, which are selectively applied to stimulate the growth of consumer industries. However, in wartime Lebanon, import-substitution aimed at replacing all essential consumer imports as rapidly as possible to prevent supply disruption and domestic discontent. Short-term policies supporting this objective contradicted the desired long-term effect of building competitive industries. War conditions also precluded attracting direct foreign investment in Lebanese or joint venture firms, which some ISI strategies incorporate to accelerate technical progress through the transfer of technology, management skills, processes and products. To permit technical reorganisation at the firm level, ISI typically requires large capital imports, which ran counter to the Allied policy of reducing imports and to international supply forces. Similarly, Allied measures to expand primary production in the Levant contradicted in the long run another general goal of ISI: to reduce dependence on primary exports.

Although a number of infant industries had been established or expanded in Lebanon, they were not operating under conditions that would allow them to 'grow up'. As the economic environment shifted towards inward orientation, conditions did not encourage technical and organisational progress that would lower costs, improve quality and permit long-run productivity gains. In other words, the environment was not conducive to making Lebanon's consumer industries competitive with foreign manufactures. Beyond these constraints, Lebanon's wartime industry did not consider the issue of export market development. Given Lebanon's very small size, which typically suggests export-oriented industrialisation in contrast to import-substitution, this would be a crucial determinant of sustainability of Lebanese industry after the end of the war.

The logic of ISI begins with satisfying domestic demand: the internal market is monopolised and domestic supply forces respond to progressively rising demand. Following this scheme, changing demand conditions in wartime Lebanon and the supply responses of its traditional and modern industries will be examined.

An enlarged domestic market for manufactures from 1941 to 1945 was a result of additional Allied military demand and a shift by local consumers to domestic products. Allied demand for 'national security' goods created a new domestic market for goods such as khaki cloth and army boots and a growth market for daily necessities and luxuries such as beer and cigarettes. With the reduction of imported manufactures, the internal market was also enlarged by substitution effects. These two components increased the market for domestic manufactures by at least 50 per cent. Domestic industries benefiting from the rise in demand were textiles, cement, tobacco, foodstuffs, beverages, matches, soap, leather goods, glassware, pottery and metal goods.

The elimination of foreign competition temporarily revived traditional Lebanese industries, which had been slowly strangled by industrial restructuring in the 1930s and foreign competition. Among the cottage industries that escaped collapse because of increased demand during the war were glassware, pottery, soap and silk thread. For a variety of reasons, however, they were unable to reorganise technically to increase their competitiveness. The case of the traditional glass-making industry illustrates this process. The wartime industry, consisting of three relatively large enterprises in Beirut and myriad 'bazaar establishments', produced largely low quality glassware and related products. The most advanced and largest producer of glassware in the Levant was Medawar Glassworks in Jdeidé (near Beirut) which employed about 120 workers.[44] Although Medawar was able to increase wartime output for domestic and export markets, its machinery, processes and organisation were technically inefficient, and it was unable to improve the quality and reduce the costs of its products to make them competitive with imported goods after trade resumed. Thus, a lack of technical progress, combined with a productive capacity that exceeded domestic demand, almost destroyed the entire glassware sector after the end of the war. Because of its uncompetitiveness with US and French imports, early postwar output of this branch plummeted to about half that of 1945.

Increased domestic demand and protected markets prompted maximum utilisation of labour and capital in industry. For those sectors that had been established or restructured and modernised in the 1930s (cement, textiles, tobacco, food and beverages), all of which had been operating at low capacity before the outbreak of war, output could be expanded in the short run by increasing labour and the number of shifts worked. The basic limiting factor to expanding utilisation of capacity in both the modern and traditional industries was the availability of raw materials, many of which had been imported before the war. Thus, the ability or willingness of the Allies to supply enterprises with intermediate goods was a determining factor in the output of industry. Output rose and fell sharply with the fluctuating supply of inputs. Output in the soap industry varied greatly because it was unable to obtain caustic acid after 1942 and was forced to switch to *kali*, a regionally produced material. Production of pasta and related products contracted (in 1943, production was down to about a third of 1940 output) because producers could not secure sufficient supplies of particular grades of flour. Product quality and efficiency of the alcoholic beverage industry declined from the substitution of locally grown (and scarce) grains, seeds and fruits for molasses imported from Czechoslovakia before the war. The newly built al-Abdé sugar factory almost ceased production in 1942 because local sugar growers switched to producing more profitable grain crops.[45] The shortages of intermediate goods, however, encouraged the expansion of other secondary industries: for example, the Beirut-centred paper and cardboard industry expanded with a ready-made market for packaging for Lebanese industries such as cement, cigarettes, salt and sugar.[46]

One temporary solution to this constraint might have been the tightening of supply linkages among domestic industries. However, this movement proceeded very slowly. The strongest intra- and inter-industry linkages existed in the food and beverage sectors, which utilised the low-cost and abundant seasonal produce of local agriculture. For example, Cortas Brothers, the largest canning and preserving factory, established in Beirut just prior to the war, used locally grown goods to produce jams, jellies, sauces, vinegar, canned peas, potatoes, fruits and dehydrated vegetables.[47] However, more generally, Lebanon's primary sector could not supply the quality and quantity of inputs, whether hides, cotton, wool, grains or wood, required by industry, further constraining the growth of backward and forward linkages among Lebanese enterprises, sectors and industries.

A second important constraint on expanding the consumer goods industry during the war was the limited availability of capital goods: machinery, tools and spare parts. Neither Allied forces nor local manufacturers aimed to create industries producing heavy industrial goods and technically advanced intermediate goods. Moreover, the stage of technical development of local industry and restrictions on imports limited their rise. Despite the problems of replacement and repair of machinery, many industrialists employed their machines to produce at as high capacity as possible to take advantage of market conditions. For example, the Arida Cotton Spinning Mill, which employed American machinery from Saco-Lowell shops in Boston, worked one and a half shifts per day in 1942 and Asseily worked two shifts per day in 1942.[48] Some enterprising industrialists resorted to commissioning the construction of machinery and equipment in the Middle East itself, but this was very expensive and technically inferior. With the assistance of military authorities, Kettaneh Brothers, for example, commissioned the construction of an entire match plant in Palestine for its newly-established factory, *La Société allumettière du Levant* in Dubayé, near Beirut.[49]Applications for capital imports flooded the MESC when Allied supply conditions improved, and an increased volume of imported capital goods was allowed in late 1944.[50]

While ISI is often encouraged by a policy objective of employment absorption, this was not a concern in wartime Lebanon. Its economy achieved full employment soon after the Allied occupation, directly providing jobs for more than 30,000 persons in the Levant.[51] However, Lebanon's industrial labour force grew during the war through the transfer of surplus labour from agriculture, a typical objective of ISI. On the whole, this labour force was unskilled, although skilled artisans and workers, many of whom had been employed previously in traditional industries that had collapsed, also occupied its ranks.

Labour-related factors that constrained the development of Lebanon's wartime industries included low productivity and wages rising faster than productivity gains. As techniques of production in the Lebanese manufacturing sector were typically labour-intensive, an improvement in productivity was constrained by the low-skilled workforce. At the same time, skilled labour became comparatively high wage. Competition for skilled labour was intensified as the domestic economy vied with the Allies for a limited number of workers: employment in domestic industry reached 91,000, while modern services employed 24,000.[52] Wage demands, which exceeded productivity gains, grew as consumer prices spiralled upwards and organised labour was tolerated.[53] Consequently, nominal wage increases were typically large: some factories reported nominal wage rises of as much as 800 per cent during the war years. [54] Nevertheless, though nominal wages rose across the board, and workers with Allied services and large industrial firms frequently were able to increase substantially their net earnings by working overtime,[55] real wages tended to fall because the cost of living increased faster than wages[56] (see Table 3.3).

Table 3.3: *Weekly wage rates of IPC workers in Lebanon, 1939–44*

Period of wage rates and indexation	Wage rate (£SL)	Wage index	Cost-of-living index: period
30 November 1939–30 November 1941	12.5	100	100: August 1939
1 December 1941–28 February 1942	21.0	168	340: December 1941
1 March 1942–31 August 1942	21.0	168	340: June 1942
1 September 1942–31 December 1942	28.0	244	368: December 1942
1 January 1943–30 September 1943	31.0	247	457: June 1943
1 October 1943–31 March 1944	37.5	300	522: December 1943
April 1944	40.0	322	559: June 1944

Source: A. R. Prest, *War Economics of Primary Producing Countries* (Cambridge, UK, 1948) p. 231.

As long as profits were easily made, Lebanese manufacturers generally did not fight rising labour costs. Moreover, compared with profits, the wage bill was still very small: for example, it made up about 10 per cent of total factor income of the Arida and Asseily mills in 1942. Conditions that provided large profits for goods of mediocre quality did little to force management to minimise costs, increase efficiency or improve production techniques.

Economic effects of the Second World War

Growth of profits and savings and shift in investment behaviour

As opportunities expanded to profit from high market demand, as well as speculation and market manipulation, the Second World War became a period of large accumulation for Lebanese merchants, financiers, industrialists and landowners. Only one year after the Allied occupation of the Levant, seven Lebanese merchants and industrialists had made £SL 42 million in war-related profits,[57] about half of total demand deposits in Lebanon during the same year, 1942. Not only did Beirut's merchants benefit from their rent-seeking activities and increased market power, but they also largely evaded the newly-established war profits tax. In 1944, Alfred Naccache, the president of the Merchants' Association, estimated that its members owed the government at least £SL 21 million in war profit taxes.[58] £SL 6 million was paid one year later.

Fortunes were made in the war through speculation in commodities, land, buildings, gold and other financial assets. Parallel market operations in commodities, whereby already high-cost goods were priced at three to five times the factory price, were widespread. Wholesale merchants, middlemen and commission agents profited from the manipulation of the markets and from usurious consumer loans.[59]

Meanwhile, politicians and functionaries profited by trafficking in import licences and manipulating bureaucratic regulations.

High-income Lebanese typically diversified their assets through behaviour that is captured by Tobin's portfolio model of asset choice.[60] To reduce the overall long-term risk to their investments, they acquired a number of different assets, such as property, gold, foreign and domestic currencies, stocks and bonds, which were not positively and perfectly correlated. According to this model, individuals will choose to hold money to reduce risk, varying with their expectations about, and returns on, other assets. Holding money in times of high inflation is very risky. In a period of rising prices or expected inflation, asset holders will choose to hold real assets that maintain their price and income, in contrast to money which loses purchasing power. In brief, in a period of (expected) inflation, the demand for real assets should rise, which captures behaviour in wartime Lebanon. Nevertheless, the Lebanese also held growing levels of money denominated in the Syro-Lebanese pound: in real terms, demand deposits doubled from 1939 to 1945. This partially reflects a substitution of banking for cash transactions, but it also suggests an increased demand for money for transactions.

To hedge against inflation, and to reduce risk, profits made by merchants, industrialists and landowners during the war were reinvested in a highly diversified manner in property, gold, foreign currencies, bonds, equities and commodities. Land and buildings, which were not bureaucratically controlled, were particularly favoured investments because of the low risks and very high rates of appreciation in this period. Rural land was attractive because it could often be purchased at a discount: small owners were selling under distressed conditions. Consequently, wealthy urban Lebanese increased their share of rural land-holdings during the war. Despite the fivefold increase in the price of buildings from 1939 to 1943, they were viewed as the best instrument to preserve or increase the value of their holdings.[61] In 1943, registered transactions in buildings and offices amounted to £SL 50 million as opposed to £SL 10 million in 1939,[62] a 200 per cent increase after inflation. The preferred investment in buildings was commercial property in Beirut: private housing rents were controlled, reflected by an insignificant 30 per cent rise in prices for housing during the entire period of the war; and commercial property was expected to appreciate much more rapidly. In addition, investment flowed into villas and property with touristic potential in Mount Lebanon. Although equities and bonds represented a narrow field of investment in Lebanon, they were particularly sought as an outlet for idle cash holdings in the early war years, before the ban on the export of capital was lifted on 30 May 1943. Reflecting speculative capital in the market, the Beirut stock exchange index reached its wartime high in December 1943, after which it declined when investment opportunities expanded (see Table 3.4). The more than 500 per cent

Table 3.4: *Equity prices on the Beirut bourse, 1939–46 (£SL)*

Company	Dec. 1939	Dec. 1940	Dec. 1941	Dec. 1942	Dec. 1943	Dec. 1944	Dec. 1945	Dec. 1946
CGL	11.75	17.50	21.00	65	51	70	135	135.0
Chekka	50.00	62.50	125.00	375	350	275	435	390.0
DHP	32.65	37.50	40.00	100	110	115	115	115.0
PB	62.40	190.00	195.00	450	410	450	350	350.0
Régie	75.00	115.00	200.00	375	280	336	410	280.0
SIB	–	25.00	37.50	55	90	100	105	107.5
SNI	17.50	25.00	100.00	300	185	155	136	100.0
EB	27.10	42.50	70.00	225	169	145	139	112.0
Exchange Index*	105.00	122.00	220.00	426	620	444	458	486.0

Notes: *Base: August 1938–July 1939 = 100; CGL = *Compagnie générale du Levant*; Chekka = *Société des ciments libanaise*; DHP = *Compagnie française du chemin de fer de Damas, Hama et prolongements*; PB = *Compagnie du port, des quais et entrepôts de Beyrouth*; Régie = *Régie des Tabac*; SIB = *Société immobilière Beyrouth*; SNI = *Société nationale industrielle*; EB = *Electricité de Beyrouth.*

Source: Levant States, CSIC; *Recueil des statistiques*, 1945–7; Ministère de l'économie national, *Bulletin statistique trimestriel*, 1950.

rise in equity prices between 1939 and 1944 was large, considering the uncertainty about many companies whose headquarters were located in occupied France.[63] Gold, a traditional form of savings, was in greatest demand during periods of severe crises and very high commodity speculation. Speculation in gold and sterling continued, but the British authorities conducted open market operations for both to dampen inflation. Between August 1943 and May 1944, Lebanese and Syrians purchased £4,886,800 sterling worth of gold (£SL 43,150,444) through the BSL, a little over 15 per cent of Syro-Lebanese notes in circulation in May 1944, £SL 281 million.[64] Between 1941 and 1945, the Lebanese bought more than £SL 600 million in foreign currency (mainly sterling).[65]

Growth of foreign reserves

The Levantine states greatly increased their foreign reserves during the war. Allied expenditures in the Levant from 1941 to 1945 produced a large rise in sterling and French franc balances, amounting to some £SL 500 million.[66] At the same time, Lebanese and Syrians purchased over £SL 800 million in sterling and gold in the open market. This reversed an underlying trend in the Levant whereby current account deficits had resulted in an outflow of gold or were offset periodically by foreign capital inflows.

A surplus position facilitated Lebanon's postwar mercantile economy. Beirut merchants established a leading commercial position after the end of the war, as they were able to satisfy very large pent-up domestic and regional demand with US and European imports. The large accumulation of hard currencies and gold permitted the merchants to use the external surplus as a competitive advantage, giving Beirut an initial edge over other well placed cities and ports in the region. Despite the early postwar increase in all categories of imports, which was not matched by export growth, problematic effects of a trade gap did not develop because of the external surplus.

Inflation and high-cost production structure

Wartime inflation in the Levant was a product of both exogenous and endogenous variables: (1) vast Allied military expenditures were financed by increasing M–2 money by more than 600 per cent between 1939 and 1945, which was backed by sterling and French franc deposits in blocked accounts in London;[67] and (2) private and public sector forces determined upward price movements, which rose by over 500 per cent between 1939 and 1945. Dislocationary effects of the war on the economies in the Levant were great: very large Allied expenditures in small closed economies created severe disequilibrium in supply and demand. From 1941 to 1945, Allied aggregate expenditures amounted to more than £90 million sterling (about £SL 800 million).[68] Between May 1942 and May 1943, military expenditures comprised £28 million sterling, or more than three times the total of the three Syrian and Lebanese budgets and about a third of the total Syro-Lebanese national income.[69] Because the growth in the quantity of money, controlled largely by Britain and France to facilitate strategic objectives, exceeded the amount that individuals wished to hold, excess money balances were spent on goods, services and assets. The increased demand for productive factors and consumer commodities, which greatly surpassed supply, resulted in spiralling prices. With large constraints on expanding productive capacity, supply forces could not restore equilibrium prices. Although there are no reliable data on the growth of investment and output during the war years, it is clear that they did not keep pace with monetary expansion: estimates show that the Levant's wartime money supply expanded annually by about 10 per cent more than national income;[70] and data on imports display a very large drop in capital imports, thus limiting their effects on domestic production and consumption. However, the growth of M–2 money and price rises during the war years in the Levant are weakly correlated. Currency substitution played a role in the monetary aggregates-inflation equation: the private sector controlled large amounts of gold and foreign currency, which were frequently used (and were the unit of accounting) for major transactions. Not only influencing many aspects of financial intermediation in the economy, currency substitution contributed to reducing the velocity of money, and thereby inflationary pressures, during this period.

Table 3.5: *Growth of the money supply and cost of living, 1939–45*

	Annual growth of M–2[1] (%)	Annual rise of general COL[2] index (Beirut) (%)
1939	n.a.	n.a.
1940	65	n.a.
1941	–2	133[3]
1942	102	57
1943	52	21
1944	16	27
1945	22	8

Notes: [1] M–2 = currency + demand and time deposits; [2] COL = Cost-of-Living; [3] December 1941 rise over December 1939; n.a. = not available.

Source: Levant States, CSIC, *Eléments statistiques des états de Syrie et du Liban*, 1947.

Both demand-pull and cost-push pressures contributed to Lebanon's wartime inflation. While the simple models discussed below abstract greatly from reality, they provide an understanding of the fundamental forces working in the economy at that time.

In a very simple demand-pull model, the economy begins at:

$$C + I + G = MV \quad (1)$$

where: C = consumption; I = investment; G = government; M = money supply; V = velocity of circulation. It is easy to see that with wartime full employment and high utilisation of productive capacity, the introduction of Allied spending in an essentially closed economy added more money (M circulated at a given velocity V) on the demand markets for goods and services than what could be supplied at previous equilibrium prices. With restricted potential to increase domestic productive capacity or import consumer goods sufficient to absorb the newly-injected money, an inflationary gap emerged, whereby prices of goods and services rose, which then established new equilibrium prices:

$$C' + I' + G' = M'V' \qquad (2)$$

At the higher prices, nominal wages also increased by that amount, though real wages remained at previous levels.

Cost-push pressures operated in conjunction with demand-pull forces, thereby strengthening upward price movements in this economy. First, wage-push pressures will be examined. In high-profit and high-demand/priority sectors in wartime Lebanon, rises in wage rates were not flexibly determined by productivity gains; in other sectors, supply and demand forces appear to have functioned more efficiently in the labour markets, resulting in greater flexibility of wage rates. Though wages were not indexed, in the high-profit sectors, they typically followed inflation; but they never led to a wage–wage spiral throughout the economy. The rises were not challenged by industrialists because the latter could raise their own product prices so as to maintain (and often raise) their share of factor income. At this point, profits-push inflationary pressures began: producers with large market power to set prices in the short run pushed up prices, attempting to increase their share of income. Countervailing forces did not curtail wage and profit increases, which were then transmitted into price rises in the economy. On balance, it is clear that the winners in Lebanon's inflationary economy were the owners–entrepreneurs in high-demand sectors: while profit rates and shares in manufacturing and import trade soared, wage increases trailed the rises in the cost of living.[71] Elsewhere in the economy, underemployment of unskilled labour seems to have moderated wage demands, thereby limiting wage-push inflation.

Beirut's general price index rose from 100 in its baseline date of December 1939 to 607 in December 1945. Price rises, however, hit certain sectors of the economy harder than others. For example, prices of textiles and garments rose by over 900 per cent, between 1939 and 1945, while food grew by 600 per cent, and housing and water by a mere 30 per cent. Indeed, the rise in prices of textiles and garments outstripped that of every other commodity after the Allies were able to fix the price of grains in June 1942 at seven times the 1939 price and moderated demand for gold and sterling in 1943. At the same time that prices for grain and gold rose moderately and in tandem, from 1943 and 1945, the rise of textile prices increased more rapidly. Typically, in that period, textiles that had been purchased from the manufacturer for £SL 15 per unit were sold retail for between £SL 80 and £SL 100 per unit.[72] By 1944, the price of 'cat and hat' quality cotton was 23 times greater than before the war.[73] Thus, a dissociation of the market developed between the price of gold and wheat, on the one hand, and textiles, on the other.[74] Moreover, the rise of wholesale prices greatly exceeded that of retail prices. This was due to the power of a few large importers and producers in contrast to the atomistic small-scale retailers, who were operating under more competitive market conditions and, at the same time, were subject to greater enforcement of price controls. Wholesale price increases were passed on to the shopkeepers, creating very high profits for large Beirut merchants.[75]

Figure 3.3: *Beirut's wholesale/retail price index, 1938–46*

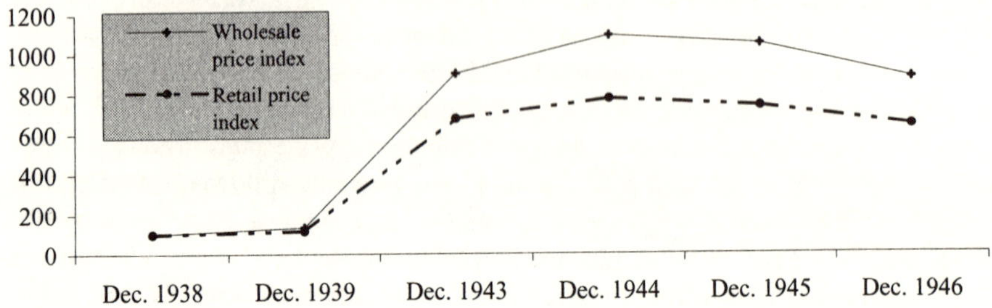

Source: Levant States, CSIC, *Eléments statistiques des états de Syrie et du Liban*, 1947.

British, French and Lebanese bureaucracies attempted to manage rapidly accelerating inflation in the Levant by applying price controls and stabilisation measures, both of which were largely unsuccessful.[76] The urgent need to control inflation became apparent in 1943 when it far exceeded, by up to two or three times, that in the rest of the Middle East. Additional money injected into the economy was not absorbed by taxes or open market operations in government debt. The Allied administration was not prepared to increase its control over prices, supply and distribution. Nor was the Lebanese government ready to increase direct taxation substantially or sell government bonds. Therefore, the Allies were forced to fight inflation by reducing military expenditures, particularly on public works programmes, and by selling sterling and gold in the local markets to reduce liquidity. Meanwhile, the French sought to implement contractionary measures by instructing the BSL to restrict credit, but this was not very effective due to large domestic savings and countervailing French actions elsewhere.[77] The new measures followed the ill-fated war profits tax, initiated by the Lebanese government in November 1942, which levied a tax of between 15 and 33.33 per cent on extraordinary war profits.[78] However, because few complied with the law, it played no role in reducing inflationary pressures. By 1945, when little of the tax had been collected and the government was in desperate need of revenues, Minister of Finance Hamid Frangiyyeh settled on a lump sum payment of £SL 6 million from the most powerful of the Lebanese trade associations, the Association of Beirut Merchants; this was probably less than 25 per cent of what the merchants owed.[79] The government then attempted to obtain another £SL 6 million from domestic manufacturers and foreign companies. In total, the war profits tax rendered revenues of under £SL 10 million, less than 20 per cent of the estimated assessment of £SL 50 million.[80]

While Allied authorities feared that inflationary pressures might lead to the collapse of the Syro-Lebanese pound currency,[81] this did not occur because of optimistic expectations of domestic firms and households. Several factors promoted this positive view. First, the Syro-Lebanese pound was covered by sterling until 1944 and the French franc thereafter. Second, inflation within the Lebanese economy reflected a very large increase in demand for local goods and services by the Allied occupation forces, accompanied by an expansion of the domestic money supply without an enlargement of the real economy. Third, after the Syro-Lebanese sterling and French franc balances were unblocked, the local economies would have very large purchasing power abroad (especially as prices were moderating in the USA and sterling block in the latter stages of the war). According to this logic, even though the domestic purchasing power of the Syro-Lebanese pound had deteriorated in Lebanon's closed economy during the war, inflation was temporary: it would disappear when the British and French repaid their debts by releasing the Levant's foreign currency accounts and import trade returned to normal. Consequently, the Syro-Lebanese pound remained strong throughout the war. The importance of the role of expectations in maintaining the strength of the currency is supported by the growing confidence in the Syro-Lebanese pound as a store of value (savings), alongside the more traditional means of gold and land. As a result, demand for foreign currency and gold was reduced, thereby supporting the value of the Syro-Lebanese pound.

Protectionism: short-run stimulation and long-run constraints on industry

The emergence of sellers' markets stimulated industrial production in wartime Lebanon, but these conditions did not prompt significant restructuring. Responding to rising demand, domestic manufacturers generated additional output from existing resources by utilising previously idle capacity, wherever possible. This meant that firms that had been established or restructured during the 1930s had large advantages over traditional industries in satisfying higher demand. Moreover, with demand exceeding supply, revenues and profits in manufacturing tended to rise greatly, especially for larger firms that operated in highly-concentrated markets. These conditions might have stimulated reorganisation of industry had it not been for other factors occurring simultaneously. With large constraints on capital imports and uncertain expectations about postwar industry, the short-run interests of industrial entrepreneurs prevailed: they chose to maximise current revenues and profits at the expense of future growth. Thus, the wartime impetus to industry did not result in reorganisation, technical progress and long-run competitiveness.

Structural weaknesses of Lebanese manufacturing dominated both modern and traditional branches. One of the most comprehensive reports on Syro-Lebanese industry during the war was prepared by the MESC and Spears Economic Mission.[82] It sketches a picture of Lebanon's wartime industry, centred in Beirut and Tripoli, as an agglomeration of many small and inefficient enterprises which, because of their backward organisation and technology, would have little chance of surviving competition in the postwar era.

Outdated Lebanese cottage industries, which had already begun to be strangled by domestic competition in the 1930s, were temporarily revived during the war. The reprieve was built on wartime chronic shortage markets whereby most enterprises were able to produce at full capacity and sell goods of almost any quality, frequently not meeting demand. Beyond these unusual conditions, other aspects of Lebanon's wartime industry were also problematic for long-term market development: the sectors of industry that tended to expand output most were those satisfying military demand; and enterprises with large cash surpluses could rarely replace capital equipment, much less improve their technologies during the war.[83] Furthermore, Lebanese manufacturing was not diversified sufficiently to meet the needs of its enlarged market. As compared to Palestinian industry, which produced some 500 manufactured goods in 1945, Lebanon manufactured about 50 different commodities.[84]

While this picture is essentially negative, there were a few bright spots. Full utilisation of capacity and high profits for manufactures provided Lebanese industrialists with both the capital and incentives to increase investment in plant, technology and management after the end of the war. Arida and Asseily spinning mills, for example, each made a net profit of over £SL 3 million in 1944/5.[85] Under these conditions, such industrialists amortised their capital, the largest share of which was invested in the 1930s, in the early stages of the war. Moreover, they intensified their collective voice in Lebanon's political economy, which became evident in the early postwar years, as they mobilised support for protectionist industrial policies against traditional mercantile interests.

Conclusion

Allied strategic objectives in the Levant in the Second World War, requiring a large occupation force and local support networks, temporarily changed the rules of the game and market conditions in the Lebanese economy. From an outward-looking, weakly-regulated, quasi-colonial economic system, Lebanon was abruptly transformed into a highly-controlled, semi-autarkic war economy. With increased market demand, production was stimulated; and large internal savings and external surpluses were accumulated. At the same time, high-cost production and spiralling price rises emerged. On a sectoral level, the impact of the war was more complex. The effects on agriculture, industry and trade will be summarised below.

Although agricultural output increased in some branches and production shifted to satisfying domestic consumption, its essentially backward productive structure and technical organisation did not improve with the wartime closed economy. Consequently, agriculture was relegated to being the least productive and lowest value-adding sector in the economy. In 1948, agriculture, from which at least 50 per cent of the population derived its main source of income, contributed £SL 169 million to net national product (NNP).[86] Its per-capita income was about 25 per cent of that in the industrial sector, which contributed £SL 134 million to the NNP and supported not more than 10 per cent of the population.[87]

Lebanon's wartime industrial experience suggests that structuralist policies promoting ISI to secure domestic demand and generate an internal impetus to growth are simply not enough to induce investment for a continuing process of technological innovation and progress. Protectionism is unlikely to sustain technically progressive supply-side dynamics, although it can secure widened markets to exploit economies of scale. Lebanese protectionism and the war conditions themselves led to the development of technical or X-inefficiency, primarily an outcome of market power, which weakened competitive pressures. Thus, Lebanese firms operating in sheltered wartime markets did not have to minimise total costs or promote efficiency. Further, output was less than optimum, not only because of monopolistic pricing policies, but also because managers overworked machines, utilised raw materials that were not technically optimal, and replaced parts and equipment with inferior substitutes. Moreover, Lebanese industry was encouraged by an enlarged market that could only be maintained after the war by continuing to protect the markets of the Syro-Lebanese Customs Union, which industrialists, organised labour and the Syrian government advocated, or by expanding trade, which the majority of Lebanon's elite supported. Wartime price rises also increased the uncompetitiveness of Lebanese industry, as it became a high-cost producer. The development of Lebanon's regional advantage in manufacturing was impeded by its postwar high-cost structure: the general price level in Lebanon was several times that of other Middle Eastern economies; and higher prices were not matched by higher productivity. Primarily for other reasons, Lebanon's postwar leadership chose *not* to pursue a strategy promoting industrialisation, thereby attenuating the issue of high-cost production. Instead, core policy-makers emphasised this constraint to bolster their support for restructuring and enhancing Lebanon's economy as a regional intermediary through international trade, finance and services.

Trade volume during wartime Lebanon was reduced, but its value, decreased in real terms, remained comparatively high. Import volume declined on average by

24 per cent from 1939 to 1945 over the 1935–8 period, and value in current prices increased by 92 per cent in the same period. Export volume was reduced on average by 71 per cent from 1942 to 1945 over the 1935–8 period, and value in current prices increased by 75 per cent in the same period. Although volume shrunk, profit margins on this highly-regulated activity rose. A few merchants who were able to obtain a large share of import licences, cultivate relations with Allied suppliers, and evade bureaucratic controls increased their market power and profit rates. Nevertheless, wartime conditions constrained Lebanon's traditional role in commerce. The return to peace offered Lebanese traders new opportunities that would permit the emergence of the Merchant Republic.

While Lebanon's wartime economy temporarily reversed its outward-looking economic path, this was just a small hiatus in modern Lebanese economic history. With the achievement of political independence, the forging of a 'liberal' politico-economic elite to govern the new state, and the growth of highly profitable external opportunities, Lebanon's postwar economic order took on a shape that resonated of its past and was refined by the possibilities of its future.

CHAPTER FOUR

Profile of Selected Sectors of Lebanese Industry, 1929–46

•

Textiles and garments

Two large modern textile firms existed in Lebanon as it entered the Second World War. The first was Arida Brothers, incorporated in 1935 at Bahsas, near Tripoli. With a capitalisation of £SL 0.5 million, it comprised a spinning mill, established in 1930 and a weaving factory, established in 1936. Second, was *Filature nationale de coton*, a cotton-spinning mill established by the Asseily and Doumit families in Jdeidé al-Metn near Beirut. Although the Arida spinning mill had almost twice the productive capacity of the Asseily plant in the prewar years, wartime utilisation rates were similar: each produced annually about 600 tons of cotton yarn. Because of increased demand, higher prices and profit rates, both enterprises operated their machines at full capacity on one-and-a-half- and two-shift days, limited only by cotton supplies. In 1942/3, profits comprised about 60 per cent of total factor incomes in the two firms.

Lebanon's output of cotton yarn increased in relation to that of Syria during the Second World War. In 1938, each economy produced about half of total Syro-Lebanese cotton yarn output. But, by 1945, Lebanese yarn output amounted to 62 per cent of combined output. The major blockage to expanding output further was an inadequate supply of cotton.

With the entry of Japan into the Second World War, the Allies promoted silk production in Syria and Lebanon by subsidising prices through a British Ministry of Supply monopoly; they also controlled distribution, as the Axis powers were offering very high prices for Levantine silk smuggled through Turkey.[1] During the war years, the number of silk-reeling enterprises in Lebanon increased from 35, existing in the early 1930s, to 65 filatures in 1943, 34 of which were relatively large and modern in 1943.[2] One of the largest was the Dubayé silk factory, owned by Yusuf Ashqar and Tawfiq Doumit, which was established in 1935 with a capital of £SL 0.4 million. By 1943, approximately 4000 to 5000 workers were employed in the silk industry and they produced about 165 tons of reeled silk from 800 tons of cocoons.[3] With the exception of 1940, however, wartime output of cocoons did not reach the levels of prewar production (see Table 4.1).

Table 4.1: *Silk production in Lebanon, 1936–46 (kilograms)*

Year	Cocoon output	Silk filament output
1936	640 000	55 000
1937	766 000	55 000
1938	851 000	60 000
1939	814 000	–
1940	1 200 000	–
1941	700 000	–
1942	600 000	–
1943	612 000	–
1944	535 000	45 000
1945	500 000	40 000
1946	500 000	40 000

Source: Sir Alexander Gibb and Partners, *The Economic Development of Lebanon* (London, 1948) Table 37; Levant States, CSIC, *Recueil de statistiques*, 1942–5.

Lebanon's silk weaving industry, which was far smaller and less important economically than that in Syria, was composed of about half a dozen small workshops in the villages of Zoué and Beit Chehab, which were known for their traditional 'Arab' silk cloth. During the war, silk weaving for civilian use ceased almost totally, and weavers switched to cotton and rayon. Synthetic fibres were increasingly used to produce garments traditionally made of silk. Of the estimated 55 to 57 tons of silk reeled in Lebanon in 1945, only about 20 per cent of the thread was utilised by the local weaving industry.[4] After the end of the war, the silk industry began to decline, as a result of the termination of the British silk monopoly, shifts in the local market, the re-emergence of foreign competition, and the lack of technical progress within the industry.[5] Domestic production of silk thread clashed with cheaper yarn imports: domestic manufacturing could not compete with low-cost foreign producers, notably Japan, especially because cocoon production was more costly in Lebanon. Thus, foreign competition and the existence of cheaper artificial silk reduced the industry's already small share of the world market.

Syria dominated the weaving industry in the Levant. However, Lebanon had a larger mechanical–hand loom ratio, and mechanisation was probably occurring faster in Lebanon than in Syria.[6] The Syro-Lebanese cotton weaving industry had a productive capacity far exceeding that of the spinning industry, and it was, therefore, heavily dependent on yarn imports.[7] Before the war, this industry supplied about a third of local demand, with imports supplying the rest. Dependence on yarn imports was reversed during the war; but, as total output was not increased over prewar levels, domestic consumption of textiles was reduced. In 1944, the industry produced 3600 tons of textiles, while a mere 80 tons were imported, giving an estimated consumption of 3680 tons, as compared with an estimated 13,800 tons in 1939. Due to the almost insatiable demand for textiles, the Allies allowed an increase of textile machinery imports in 1944 to expand local production.[8] As silk and wool yarn were in very short supply, and as looms could be adjusted to weave different types of yarn, many factories switched to the more available cotton and, to a lesser extent, rayon. This change increased the cotton industry's overall productive capacity, adding an estimated 20 per cent to the output of the largest cotton weaving enterprise, Arida Brothers.[9]

La Lainière nationale, at Hazmiyé, owned by the Khattar family, had a declared capital of £SL 300,000 in 1942, and was the largest and most modern wool factory in Lebanon. In fact, it was the only domestic factory technically capable of producing high-quality wool; and during the war, it was frequently requisitioned by the OEG to provide military supplies. The factory, equipped with modern weaving, dyeing, processing and finishing machinery, was capable of producing 250 tons of wool annually, comprising almost half of the total productive capacity of Syria and Lebanon, 500–600 tons of wool per annum.[10] However, due to shortages of raw materials, only 20 out of 140 looms were operating at Hazmiyé in 1943, and these had been adapted to cotton.[11] Operating at full capacity, the factory employed between 450 and 500 workers, but in 1942 only between 120 and 150 workers were employed, which was reduced to 50 in 1944/5.[12] By 1946, this factory, which was equipped to produce 500,000 metres of wool per annum (on a one shift basis), was only manufacturing 100,000 metres because of foreign competition.[13]

Production of knitwear in Lebanon expanded by almost twentyfold between 1939 and 1942, even though its centre was located in Syria.[14] Again, because of the unavailability of silk and wool, most knitwear producers converted to cotton. Though it utilised relatively modern equipment, little factory organisation existed in this industry: production was organised mainly as an 'agglomeration of machines'. In an average establishment, both power- and hand-operated equipment were employed.[15]

Weak integration of the textile sector — partially an outcome of the inability of local reelers to supply sufficient quantities and qualities of yarn to domestic weavers[16] — was a major obstacle to the development of the industry. In addition, the majority of Lebanese dyeing, printing and finishing houses remained small, primitive and inappropriate for the more modern weaving establishments; these village industries remained better suited to the old loom systems.[17] Only a small number of manufacturers had adequate facilities to process their own materials. In fact, after the war, many sent their materials to Palestine for machine printing. Another constraint on the expansion of domestic textiles was the small, traditional ready-to-wear garment industry. The individual and household sectors produced the largest share of garments for the domestic market: individual seamstresses working at home; small cottage workshops employing between one and six sewing machines; and a few European-style tailors.[18] Further, no large inter-firm demand for local textiles emerged.

During the war, technical conditions in the textile industry deteriorated, characterised by a structure of high-cost goods of declining quality. By 1945, the spinning industry operated at under 50 per cent of maximum capacity due to overworked machinery and accelerated depreciation of capital.[19] Because of their large contribution to rising price levels, the Lebanese government attempted to apply price and supply controls to textiles, a plan that was bitterly fought by the textile producers.[20] Matters were only settled after the government had temporarily requisitioned the Asseily and Arida mills.

The textile sector is frequently cited as the major industrial success of the war. However, its expansion was based on technical inefficiency. An MESC/Spears Mission survey of industry[21] reports that while all Syro-Lebanese cotton-spinning mills were equipped with modern machinery, only one factory, Moudarres, located in Aleppo, was operating at high efficiency. It claims that: 'Neglect, ignorance, and greed have all played their part in reducing what should be modern mills to the present bad conditions. The proprietors are simply producing as much yarn as possible with the least possible trouble and expense, happy in the knowledge that whatever the quality they can more or less demand their own price.'[22]

Cement and building materials

The Lebanese cement industry consisted of one factory, the *Société des ciments libanaise* at Chekka (near Tripoli), which was established in 1929 with a capital of £SL 240,000 and which had a capacity to produce 220,000 tons of cement per annum.[23] Chekka was controlled and managed by Swiss nationals, although the family of Patriarch Antoun Arida owned about 20 per cent of its equity.[24] Combined with the output of a smaller cement factory at Damascus, Chekka was able to supply the two states with most of their cement needs by 1936, while it exported 65,000 tons in 1937. The Chekka plant was a modern facility with complete auxiliary services, including its own power supply, laboratories, workshops, loading facilities, water supply and drainage, and sea and rail transport.[25]

Table 4.2: *Syro-Lebanese demand-supply, cotton textiles, 1938–45 (tons)*

	1938	1939	1940	1941	1942	1943	1944	1945
Output Lebanon	–	–	–	–	1100	500	400	400
Output Syria and Lebanon	4 000	3 800	2 800	2 400	4 000	4 000	3 600	3 200
Imports	8 000	10 000	6 800	1 600	3 000	1 300	80	1 200
Estimated consumption	12 000	13 800	9 600	4 000	7 000	5 300	3 680	4 400

Source: Gibb, *The Economic Development of Lebanon*, Table 36, p. 134; Levant States, CSIC, *Recueil de statistiques*, 1942–5.

Table 4.3: *Syro-Lebanese production and imports of cotton yarn, 1938–45*

Year	Lebanese production (tons)	Lebanon (% of total)	Syro-Lebanese production (tons)	Syria + Lebanon (% of total)	Syro-Lebanese imports (tons)	Imports (% of total)	Total production and imports (tons)
1938	820	20	1800	44	2300	56	4100
1939	910	24	1800	47	2000	53	3800
1940	1350	47	2000	70	850	30	2850
1941	1200	49	2100	82	350	18	2450
1942	1150	27	2000	48	2200	52	4200
1943	1500	29	2300	45	2800	55	5100
1944	1700	64	2500	94	150	6	2650
1945	1600	50	2600	81	600	19	3200

Note: *Includes exceptionally large imports of raw cotton.

Source: Gibb, *The Economic Development of Lebanon*, Table 32, p. 131; Levant States, CSIC, *Recueil de statistiques*, 1942–5, 1945–7.

Figure 4.1: *Syro-Lebanese textile import structure, 1938–46 (%)*

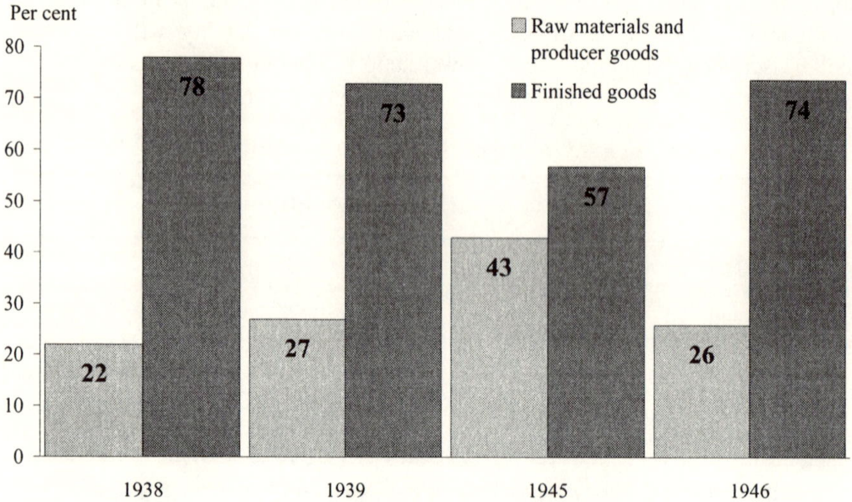

Source: Gibb, *The Economic Development of Lebanon*, Table 56, p. 164.

Table 4.4: *Lebanese cotton-spinning industry: input–output, 1939 and 1946*

City	Enterprise	Spindles (number)		Capacity output of yarn (tons)	
		1939	1946	1939	1946
Beirut	Asseily	5 600	28 000	448	2 240
Tripoli	Arida	10 000	8 000	800	640

Source: Grunwald, 'The industrialisation of the Lebanon and Syria', Table 6, p. 151; FO 921/175, Syria and the Lebanon, Part 4, Industry; FO 922 IP 04500/Syria, 1944–5, Textiles; Gibb, *The Economic Development of Lebanon*, Table 33, p. 132.

During the war, the military assumed control over Chekka, which then employed a large European staff. At that time, Chekka's plant and quarry employed about 750 workers and consumed about 25,000–35,000 tons of fuel oil per annum to drive the diesel engines and fire the furnaces.[26] In 1939, Chekka produced 156,000 tons of cement. Its maximum wartime output was in 1942, when 172,000 tons were produced mainly for use by the military to build public infrastructure in Lebanon. In that year, the military requisitioned 100 per cent of Chekka's output, and even in later years, only a small share of its output was reserved for civilian use.[27] The production of cement for military use required an adjustment of the quality of output: a stronger quality was demanded than that produced for civilian use. Chekka's capacity to produce cement (and its milling capacity of about 456,000 tons per annum) could have been expanded significantly by installing additional rotary kilns. However, British authorities, which had access to such a kiln in Ethiopia, decided against moving it to Chekka, despite the large regional demand for cement and acute shortages in Palestine, Iraq and Cyprus.[28]

Table 4.5: *Profile of Lebanese cotton-spinning enterprises, 1942–3*

A. Input-output

City	Enterprise	Workers (number)	Shifts (number)	Spindles (number)	Yarn output/day (lbs)	Yarn output/year (tons)
Beirut	Asseily	450	2	6000	2000	600
Tripoli	Arida	600	1½	8360	2207	662

B. Total factor income

City	Enterprise	Fixed capital (%)	Labour (%)	Raw materials* (%)	Profit** (%)	Profit/ cost (%)	Total income (%)
Beirut	Asseily	10.4	7.7	20.5	61.4	159	100
Tripoli	Arida	10.3	9.3	18.6	61.8	162	100

Notes: *Ginned cotton; **Asseily profits/day = £1200 sterling; Arida profits/day = £1350 sterling.

Source: FO921/175 Syria and the Lebanon, Part 4, Industry; FO922 IP 04500/Syria, 1944–5, Textiles.

Chekka was relatively modernised and well equipped, but its ex-factory price of £SL 68 per ton of cement compared unfavourably with Britain's superior quality and lower priced cement at £SL 32 per ton in 1946. This was partially due to Chekka's high-cost structure: relatively expensive fuel oil, high-wage labour and unreliable and expensive power sources.[29] More importantly, however, as a monopoly, which was also protected from foreign competition by high transport costs, Chekka enjoyed large economic rents; and it also engaged in black marketeering activities.[30] Given Chekka's monopoly in Lebanon and its duopolistic position in the Levant states, government action against Chekka's pricing and production practices was required to rectify apparent market failure. However, because Chekka was owned by powerful interests, the government was generally unwilling to take on a strong regulatory role; and when it did try to lower cement prices in 1946, Chekka was able to avoid controls by selling cement on the domestic parallel market or by exporting illegally to neighbouring countries.[31]

Table 4.6: *Technical organisation of Syro-Lebanese weaving industry, 1943 and 1946*

Location	Year	Mechanical looms (number)	Hand looms (number)
Beirut	1943*	245	40
Tripoli		250	217
Total Lebanon		495	257
Syria		1302	13659
Tripoli and North Lebanon	1946	237	–
Beirut and South Lebanon		457	300
Total Lebanon		694	300

Note: *These figures are estimates of known enterprises; actual numbers may be 10–20 per cent higher.

Source: Gibb, *The Economic Development of Lebanon*, Tables 34 and 35.

Table 4.7: *Input-output of average Syro-Lebanese weaving enterprise, 1943*

Input-output (number)	Mechanised techniques	Manual techniques
Looms	26.1	60.0*
Workers	77.8	138.0
Hours/day	9.6	9.3
Days/year	300.0	300.0
Output/year (tons)	38.4	34.0

Note: *Looms per contractor.

Source: FO921/175 Industry, p. 23.

The building materials branch — for example, bricks, tiles and cement pipes — was developed primarily as auxiliary operations of glassworks and ceramics factories. The centres of these crafts were Tripoli and Beirut, each of which had at least six small enterprises. Due to their low productive capacity and utilisation, however, they were never able to increase output sufficiently to meet wartime civilian and military demand. The firm with the largest capacity to produce bricks and tiles was Medawar Glassworks, which in 1943/4 produced about five tons a day, or an eighth of its capacity of 40 tons per day.

Table 4.8: *Syro-Lebanese knitting industry: input–output, 1943 and 1945*

Location	Enterprises* (number)		Machines** (number)		Workers (number)		Estimated capacity output (tons p.a.)	
	1943	*1945*	*1943*	*1945*	*1943*	*1945*	*1943*	*1945*
Beirut	7	–	190	–	600	–	600	–
Aleppo	8	–	105	–	170	–	320	–
Damascus	15	–	219	–	360	–	650	–
Tripoli and North Lebanon	–	–	–	22	–	–	–	105
Beirut and South Lebanon	–	–	–	89	–	–	–	285

Notes: *Comprising at least 90 per cent of total enterprises; **about half of all machines were powered; the others were manually operated.

Source: Gibb, *The Economic Development of Lebanon*, Tables 34 and 35; FO 921/175, Industry, part 4, pp. 23 and 24.

Table 4.9: *Input-output of average Syro-Lebanese knitting enterprise, 1943*

Machines	22.3
Workers	29.0
Hours worked per day	8.3
Days worked per year	300.0
Output (tons per annum)	12.2
Capacity output (tons per annum)	61.0

Source: FO 921/175, Industry, part 4, pp. 23 and 24.

Figure 4.2: *Lebanon's knitting industry: output of socks and stockings, 1935–45*

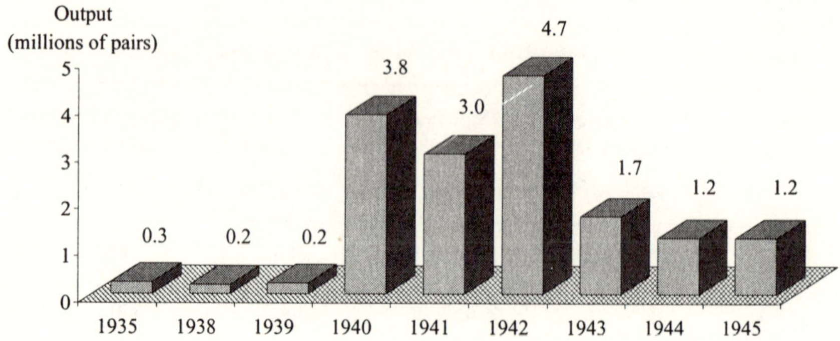

Source: Jewish Agency for Palestine, Economic Research Institute, *Statistical Handbook of Middle Eastern Countries* (Jerusalem, 1945); Levant States, CSIC, *Recueil de statistiques*, 1942–5 and 1945–7.

Figure 4.3: *Lebanon's cement production, 1937–46*

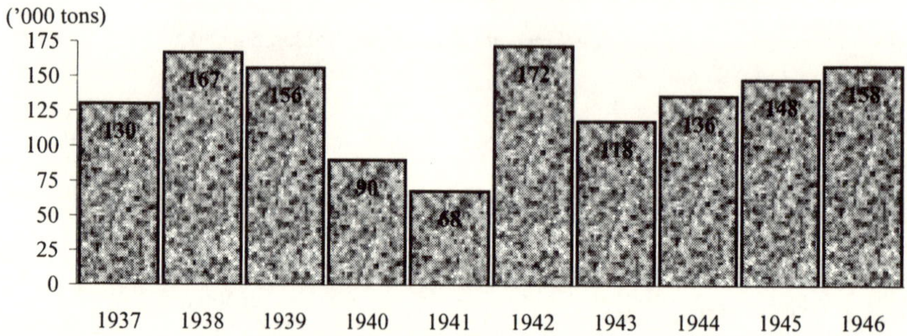

Source: Ministère de l'économie national, *Bulletin statistique trimestriel*, 1951, vol. 2, no. 1.

Tanning and leather goods

Tanning was among the oldest and, traditionally, one of the most important industries in Lebanon. The industry was reorganised and grew between the wars, particularly between 1928 and 1939. By 1939, a modernised tanning industry had begun to develop and production expanded.[32] The establishment of modern leather factories equipped with power-driven machinery made it more dependent on imported hides and tanning extracts to the detriment of locally-produced inputs.[33] By the outbreak of the war, the Levantine tanning industry was producing about 85 to 90 per cent of local needs, exporting some leather products to neighbours, and importing 10 to 15 per cent of its tanned hides from Europe.

During the Second World War, the tanning industry increased its productive capacity by between 30 and 40 per cent by establishing new factories and renovating old facilities.[34] At the end of the war, Beirut was producing 15,000 hides per annum, equivalent to about 90 tons of leather;[35] further expansion of output was limited by scarce raw materials. In 1944, when the Allied Middle East Hides Pool and Control greatly restricted the availability of hides, leather output plummeted to its pre-1939 level, and the industry was working at about 20 per cent capacity.[36]

Figure 4.4: *Tanning production in Lebanon, 1939–46*

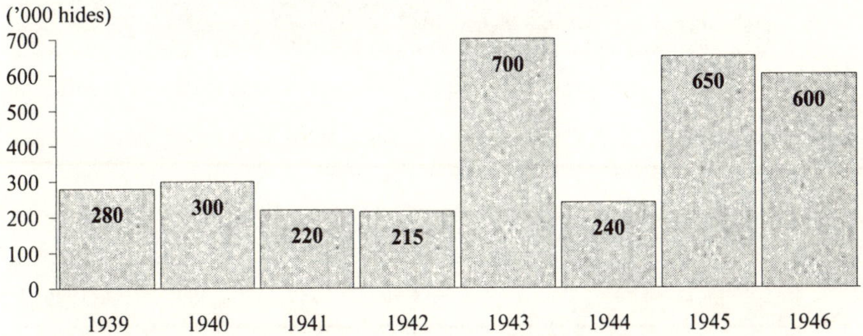

Source: Levant States, CSIC, *Recueil de statistiques*, 1942–5 and 1945–7; Jewish Agency for Palestine, *Statistical Handbook of Middle Eastern Countries*, p. 105.

This industry was centred in Beirut and the village of Mechghara. Of Beirut's six main tanning factories, five (Zabbat, Kevork, Blanga, Ghantous and Borqi) were newly built or equipped in the war.[37] Of Mechghara's 40 tanneries, four (Salamoun, Nassif, Debs and Habouch) utilised modern equipment; they were also among Lebanon's larger producers, each employing between 15 and 50 workers.[38] The industry was divided into three categories of tanneries:

- *the largest tanneries* — located near Beirut or Mechghara, which employed between 15 and 50 workers each, and which were relatively modernised and produced high quality and varied types of leather;
- *small tanneries* — about a quarter the size of the largest tanneries, which were mechanised to a very limited extent and produced a wide range of leather; many of these were located around Sidon;

- *hundreds of small individual or household enterprises* — which utilised vegetable tans to process sheep and goat hides for low quality footwear and leather work; they were not modernised, and after the war, many collapsed due to local competition.[39]

Figure 4.5: *Output of box calf in Lebanon, 1941–6*

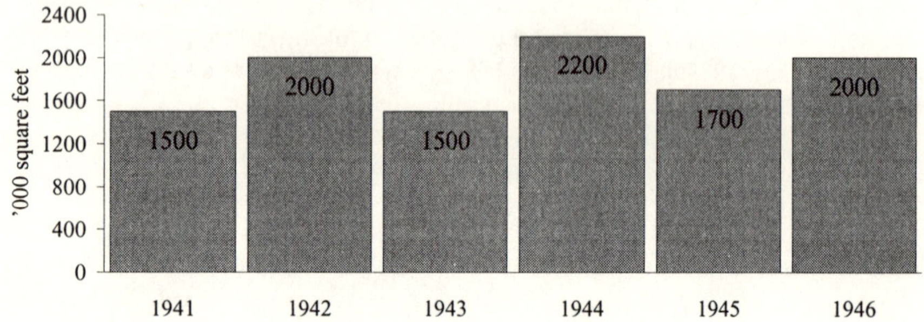

Source: Levant States, CSIC, *Recueil de statistiques*, 1942–5 and 1946–7; Jewish Agency for Palestine, *Statistical Handbook of Middle Eastern Countries*, p. 105.

Table 4.10: *Syro-Lebanese trade in leather goods, 1937–46 (tons)*

	1937	1938	1939	1945	1946
Imports of raw hides	4775	4935	4487	1273	2688
Exports of raw hides	1580	1072	750	–	596
Export of leather	1050	851	465	26	628
Exports of shoes	230	400	415	25	7

Source: Gibb, *The Economic Development of Lebanon*, Table 40, p. 138.

The increase in tanning promoted shoe manufacturing in Lebanon. Of Lebanon's domestically-produced leather footwear, 90 per cent was produced in small workshops employing between two and ten workers.[40] In 1939, the modern Bata Shoe Company, equipped with 83 boot and shoe machines and auxiliary machinery, operated at full capacity, employed 350 workers and produced 2000 pairs of army boots a week.[41] By 1945, output had declined to 250 pairs of shoes a day.[42] The efficiency and quality of Lebanese shoe production declined or stagnated during the war: locally-produced shoes were relatively expensive (two to three times the price of neighbouring countries) and much of the output was of inferior quality.

Shoes that cost £SL 6 before the war cost £SL 65 in 1942, a year in which two million pairs were manufactured locally, or only half the output in normal times.[43]

During the war, Lebanon lost most of its leather export markets, although Jordan and Iraq imported a small quantity of Lebanese shoes and shoe leather in 1944. Syria, whose leather shoe production was only about 5 per cent of that of Lebanon, remained a good customer.[44] After the war, the export market for leather moderately recovered, despite foreign competition and import restrictions in Palestine. However, 1946 shoe exports were only a third of those in 1945. Growing foreign competition in the early postwar period reduced productive utilisation and caused other economic dislocations in this sector.[45]

Alcoholic beverages

Two modern distilleries, which were established in Beirut in 1930, augmented productive capacity and output until 1936, but then barely managed to survive for

Figure 4.6: *Alcohol production in Lebanon, 1939–46*

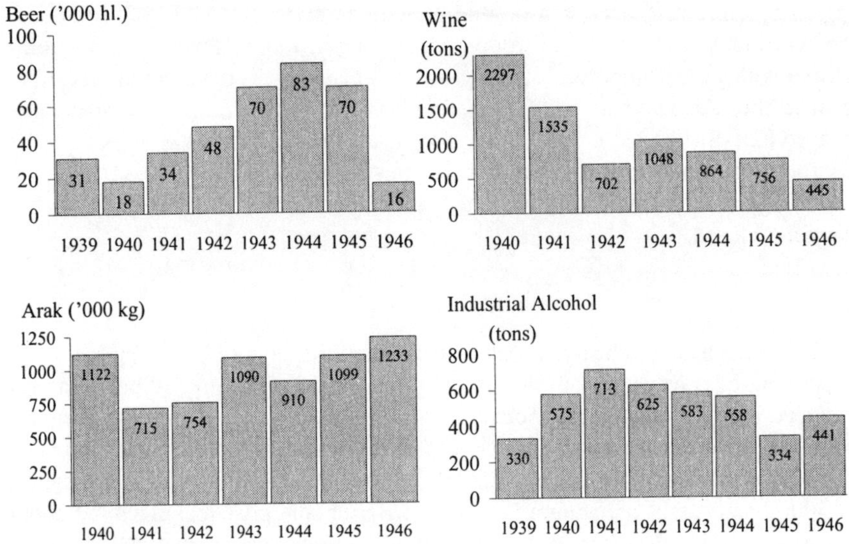

Source: Levant States, CSIC, *Recueil de statistiques*, 1942–5, 1945–7; Jewish Agency for Palestine, *Statistical Handbook of Middle Eastern Countries*; Ministère de l'économie national, *Bulletin statistique trimestriel*, 1951, vol. 2, no. 1.

the next three years because of import competition. With the Allied occupation, the industry was revived, and expansion was constrained mainly by the scarcity of raw materials. Manufacturers were forced to substitute local grains, seeds and fruits for prewar imports from the Axis countries. The industry was centralised in Beirut where the three largest distilleries were located: Beirut accounted for two-thirds of all alcohol production in the Levant states in 1943.[46] Although the growth of output of Beirut's large distilleries was significant, alcohol production was expanded during the war mainly through the establishment of small cottage industries. In 1943, small enterprises produced more alcohol than did the largest Beirut distillery, the *Société nationale industrielle*, then producing 250 tons per annum.[47] By that year, major distilleries and a large number of small household enterprises produced enough alcohol to meet increased demand.

The beer industry in the Levant states was also centralised in Beirut. The two largest breweries were the *Brasserie du Levant* and the *Brasserie franco-libanaise*. After the onset of the war, beer prices rose as the cost of scarce raw materials increased. While local demand for beer fell, military demand more than compensated for the loss. In fact, the breweries worked 24 hours a day, but still could not meet demand; and prices rose by about 300 per cent. Demand continued to rise faster than did supply, even though resources were shifted from producing *'arak* and wine to brewing beer, and despite periodic American and Egyptian imports. The beer industry also suffered from input shortages, and its quality was not competitive with that of imports.[48] Its long-run competitiveness remained in question: because the industry had been over-stimulated by Allied military demand and because Palestine had also built a brewery, its expanded output was unlikely to be absorbed by domestic or regional export markets after the war. Indeed, after the end of the war production plummeted and most of the technically backward breweries closed.

Match industry

The Lebanese match industry, which was well established by 1934, supplied about 70 per cent of consumption in the Levant states.[49] The remaining 30 per cent was produced in Syria. In 1943, the *Société suédoise des allumettes*, located at Damour, employed 250 persons, about 50 per cent of total Syro-Lebanese employment in the industry, and produced about half of all output, some 6000 cases of matches (of 5000 boxes each) per annum.[50] A second Beirut enterprise manufactured about 20 per cent of the domestically produced matches in that year.[51] In 1944, Kettaneh Brothers established the *Société allumettière du Levant* in Dubayé, the most modern match factory in Lebanon.[52] The factors limiting an expansion of output during the war were shortages of poplar wood (which was imported before the war from Poland and Romania) and of chemicals (imported from Britain). Due to these shortages, output dropped by almost 45 per cent in 1942/3 and quality declined. During 1942 and 1943, about half of Syro-Lebanese production was consumed locally, and the remainder was exported to the rest of the Middle East.[53] Total output in 1945 was no greater than the industry's 1935 production. In 1946, the match industry, which was beginning to obtain normal imports of inputs, increased output, only to be almost destroyed by ruinous competition from US imports.

Figure 4.7: *Match production in Lebanon, 1935–46*

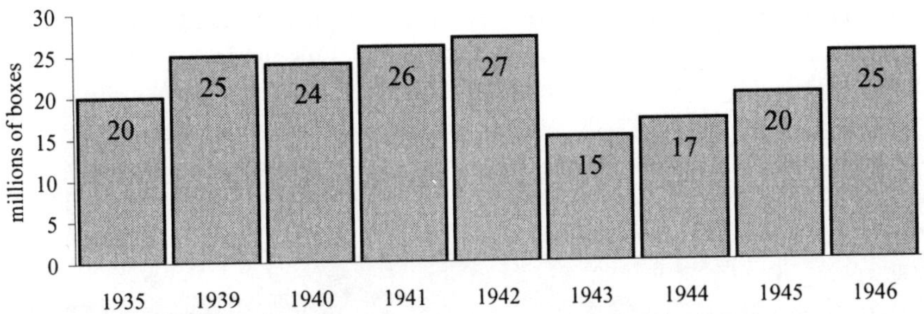

Source: Jewish Agency for Palestine, *Statistical Handbook of Middle Eastern Countries*; Ministère de l'économie national, *Bulletin statistique trimestriel*, 1951, vol. 2, no. 1.

Soap

The soap industry was organised around hundreds of small cottage enterprises centred in Tripoli and Beirut. It was characterised by a great diversity in its units, composed of non-mechanised workshops and a few modern factories. Because of the industry's overall lack of modernisation and growing foreign competition, production had continued to decline from 1913 to 1939. The first modern soap factory was established in 1933. In Syria and Lebanon, about forty new cottage workshops were established between 1939 and 1943. Though the combined Syro-Lebanese output did not increase during those years, remaining at about 10,000 tons per annum, Lebanese production increased by 37 per cent.[54]

Soap had traditionally been made of olive oil and caustic acid, but during the early stages of the war, local producers were forced to substitute *kali* for the previously imported caustic acid. Beirut's smaller, but more modern sector, which had specialised in producing a Marseilles-type laundry soap, switched to producing Tripoli soap during the war. After the UKCC again supplied caustic acid in 1943, production doubled over the previous year. Although olive oil producers preferred producing soap to selling the oil at Allied-controlled prices, continuing shortages of caustic acid constrained production. Thus, existing enterprises were unable to operate to capacity and the sector could not expand further.

Due to the nature of the soap industry, there was no major movement towards modernisation and factory reorganisation. Lebanon's three largest soap factories were the *Savonnerie de Sen et fils*, located in Beirut, which in 1943 was producing at 20 per cent capacity at best and employing 20 workers, a third of full employment; the *Huilerie raffinerie et savonnerie Jabre et Comaty*, also located in Beirut, operating at about 10 per cent capacity in 1943; and Omar & Adra Brothers, located in Tripoli, which was producing at about 40–50 per cent capacity in 1943.[55] After the end of the war, Lebanon's inefficient soap industry was at a great competitive disadvantage when domestic consumers began to substitute the European and Palestinian imports that began to flood the market for locally-made soap.

Figure 4.8: *Soap production in Lebanon, 1939–46*

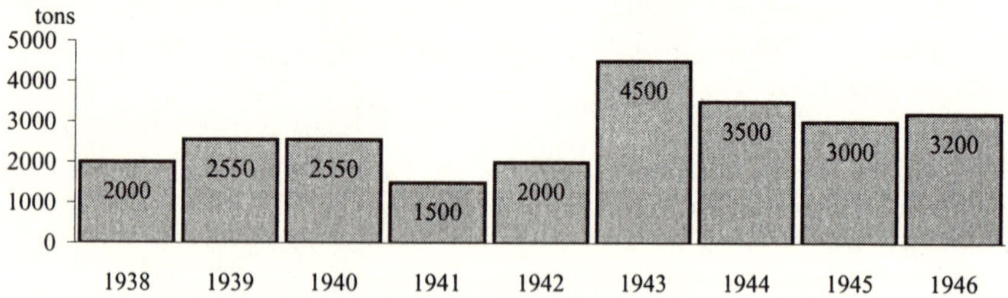

Source: Jewish Agency for Palestine, *Statistical Handbook of Middle Eastern Countries*; Levant States, CSIC, *Recueil de statistiques*, 1942–5, 1945–7.

Figure 4.9: *Syro-Lebanese soap imports/exports, 1936–46*

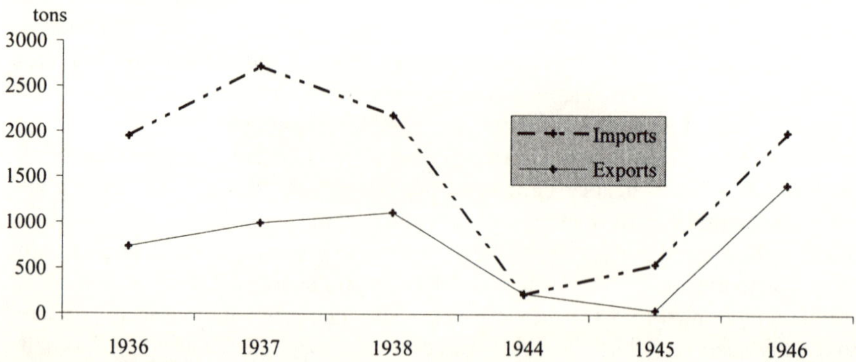

Source: Gibb, *The Economic Development of Lebanon*, p. 40.

Electricity

As the utilisation of electricity is a good indicator of productive organisation, industrialisation and technical change, Lebanon's electricity sector is included in this profile. Lebanon's electrical energy supplies were insufficient to meet industrial and consumer demand, resulting in high costs, power shortages and a large regional variation in energy output. Electric power production in Lebanon almost doubled between 1939 and 1946, but the continued underdevelopment of this industry impeded industrial and economic expansion. Insufficient capacity in electricity production was a result of small investment by the large foreign-owned Beirut Electric Company and the other 14 smaller electrical power facilities located throughout Lebanon.

Utility companies in Lebanon were highly profitable, reflecting small fixed capital, relatively low labour costs and high usage charges. High rates and inadequate supplies made electric energy expensive and insecure for both consumers and producers. Despite Lebanon's large hydroelectric potential, exploitation of this resource was minimal until the development of the Litani River began after the war. Nevertheless, in 1943, eight hydroelectric centres were in existence, along with ten geothermic centres. Electrical power production grew at a much faster rate in Lebanon than in Syria, increasing almost 150 per cent, between 1939 and 1946. Even in 1942, per-capita consumption was almost five times greater in Lebanon than in Syria.[56]

Figure 4.10: *Major consumers of electricity in Beirut, 1942*

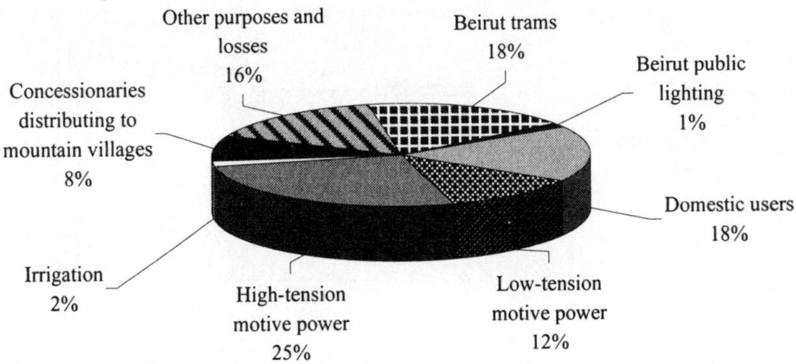

Source: PRO, FO921/175, Industry, p. 28.

Lebanon's largest utility company, the Beirut Electric Company, was a French concessionary company (with French, Belgian and Swiss capital), which generated 57 per cent of total electricity and employed 700 workers in 1942.[57] In 1942, it supplied almost 25 million kilowatt-hours of the total 44 million kilowatt-hours' production to its major users as shown in the following table.

Table 4.11: *Power distribution in Syria and Lebanon, 1942*

Category	Lebanon	Syria
Area (km^2)	10 710.0	171 104.0
Population (estimate)	1 022 114.0	2 883 638.0
Installed power alternating (kVa)	25 034.0	9 021.0.0
Installed power continuous (kW)	72.0	87.0
Consumption of gas oil by geothermic centres (tons)	650.0	3 250.0
Percentage of hydraulic power	94.5	58.5
Power consumed per capita (kWh)	41.3	8.8
Power sold to consumers:		
motive power (kWh)	33 000 000.0	17 000 000.0
lighting (kWh)	9 250 000.0	8 250 000.0

Source: PRO, FO921/175, Industry, p. 28.

Figure 4.11: *Electrical power production in Lebanon, 1939–46*

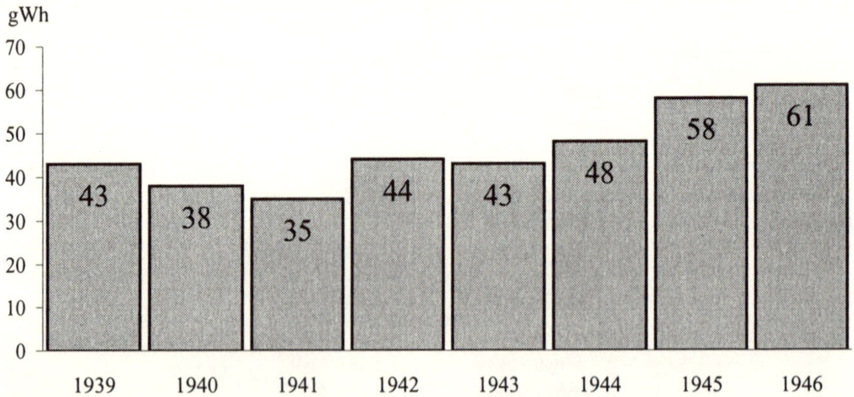

Source: Jewish Agency for Palestine, *Statistical Handbook of Middle Eastern Countries*; Levant States, CSIC, *Recueil de statistiques*, 1942–5, 1945–7.

The second most important electrical utility, Kadicha, which supplied electricity to the Tripoli area, was much smaller, producing 37 per cent of total electricity and employing 70 workers in 1942.[58] The two largest companies serviced Beirut,

Tripoli, Chekka, the Nahr Abu-Ali valley and surrounding areas. The remainder of Lebanon was serviced by smaller electrical power centres located throughout the country, the largest of which was at Zahlé. As 94 per cent of all electricity was generated in the Beirut and Tripoli areas, other regions were at a competitive disadvantage regarding industrialisation. This factor greatly favoured a concentration of industry in Beirut and Tripoli.

CHAPTER FIVE

The Rise of the Merchant Republic: Institutional Change and the Open Economy

> We trust with perfect security that the freedom of trade, without any attention of government, will always supply us with the wine which we have occasion for; and we may trust with equal security that it will always supply us with all the gold and silver which we can afford to employ, either in circulating our commodities, or in other uses.
>
> Adam Smith,
> *An Inquiry into the Nature and Causes of the Wealth of Nations*[1]

Few emerging power elites have accepted so wholeheartedly Adam Smith's entreaty for free trade as did the Lebanese during the first decade of the country's independence.[2] Its embrace of outward-looking non-interventionist ideas during the heated times of nationalism and decolonisation in much of Asia and Africa is remarkable. During the late 1940s and 1950s, these notions were translated into a model, which if not always coherent, is readily identifiable as the Merchant Republic. The model was built on openness, not because it tends to promote a competitive economic environment (which it does), but because openness — consisting of free mobility of goods, capital and 'desirable' people — was essential to dominant mercantile–financial interests. With the adoption of an outward-oriented service model, *laissez-faire* prevailed in the weaker manufacturing and primary sectors; and ultimately their survival depended on developing compara tive and competitive advantages in regional markets. The ideas of an open economy and (at least ersatz) *laissez-faire* shaped Lebanon's political economy until 1958 and, in a modified form, they influenced the structure of economic growth and the evolution of Lebanon's economic order until 1975.[3]

Lebanese policy-makers, however, were not free to adopt any measures they chose. On the contrary, they frequently operated under great political, socio-confessional and economic constraints which threatened the sustainability of enacted policies and institutions and sometimes even the viability of the political economy. For instance, during the early postwar period of rapid deregulation, internal economic conditions greatly worsened for industry, resulting in a conflict between Lebanese manufacturers and merchants and a threat to labour–management coexistence. Consequently, the government vacillated between 'pro-trade' and 'pro-industrial' policies to mediate interests and defuse potential socio-economic conflict. However, as Minister of National Economy Philippe Taqla told the US commercial attaché, regulations introduced in 1949 to protect Lebanon's domestic industry were nothing more than stopgap measures, 'taken to placate local industrialists, chiefly in the textile field, who threatened to dismiss thousands of workers'.[4] Moreover, the choice of policies was limited by the fragile balance of forces within Lebanon and the disparate interests of the power bloc composed of the mercantile–financial bourgeoisie, the urban 'bosses', industrialists and landowning *zu'ama*.

However, conflicting interests were often finessed by back-room deal making. This is readily illustrated by the issue of the Franco-Lebanese Monetary Accord of 1948, which split the powerful into two camps. One centred around the position of President Bishara al-Khoury, who supported the accord because it would lead to the release of blocked foreign balances and support a strong domestic currency, essential for international trade and finance. The second was focused around Prime Minister Riad al-Solh, who was against the accord because of its potential to trigger a rift with Syria and internal political and sectarian discontent. Though it was impossible to reconcile these differences, the two sides bargained an outcome, by which Khoury was allowed freedom to carry out negotiations on the monetary accord in return for Solh's being given authority to deal with the equally contentious issue of Palestine.[5] Finally, Lebanese policy-makers did not have sufficient policy instruments to meet their targets, which often led to policy inconsistency, as stipulated by the 'Tinbergen rule'.[6] With little control over monetary instruments and little willingness to use fiscal policy, Lebanon's policy-makers sought to achieve a number of macroeconomic targets with comparatively few policy instruments. Given their strategic objective of building a deregulated and sustainable economy through a leading external services sector, they viewed as essential those policies which would attract foreign capital; maintain a strong currency, surplus budgets and balanced external accounts; promote international trade and service exports; and mobilise private financial resources to develop the economy. Some of their targets were met, but often with great inconsistency and unintended outcomes.

Three decisive factors supported the adoption of this model: the interests of the dominant commercial and financial elite; optimistic expectations about the viability of the model; and the political and ideological predisposition of the power bloc.

Dominant commercial and financial interests

The mercantile–financial bourgeoisie quickly claimed a leading role in shaping the economic and political future of the independent Republic of Lebanon.[7] Its interests moulded the state's adoption of outward-oriented policies that favoured Lebanon's triangular trade, international finance and services, and a regional intermediary role. The horizons of this elite were greatly expanded after 1946 with the ousting of the French and the assumption of political control by Bishara al-Khoury and his *Hizb al-Destour*[8] and 'New Phoenician' associates.

The 'New Phoenicians' were born out of a group of mainly Christian and Beirut merchants, bankers and economists. Dedicated to promoting *laissez-faire* in Lebanon, this group was organised as the *Société libanaise d'économie politique* (SLEP), whose ideological mentor was economist Gabriel Menassa and whose influential members included Michel Chiha, Henri Pharaon and Alfred Kettaneh. By styling themselves the 'New Phoenicians', they indicated their political and economic philosophy which looked towards the pre-Arab and pre-Muslim commercial city-state of ancient Phoenicia as the model for Lebanon's independent future. At the inaugural banquet of SLEP in June 1943, its president, Gabriel Menassa, made clear its determination to transform Lebanon's wartime, heavily-regulated inward orientation to its former model, which he characterised as economic liberalism:

> *D'autrepart, Messieurs, l'état de guerre a imposé à ce pays un régime économique nouveau, provisoire, restreignant forcément les libertés, dirigeant les activités, écartant les principes de libéralisme économique, si nécessaires pourtant pour un petit pays comme le Liban, centre de négoce et de transit, et carrefour de toutes commerciales du Proche-Orient.*[9]

Soon after the transfer of power from the French to the independent Lebanese government, and influenced by the recommendations of the commercial and financial elite, the Khoury administration began to dismantle wartime economic controls. However, this was not unopposed, nor was it a 'natural' postwar development. Many aspects of deregulation were rejected by Lebanese industrialists and the labour movement. Some French interests also opposed liberalisation, which clashed with old colonial economic relations. Their attitude was important because of French influence in Lebanon's financial system and large investment in strategic industries — namely utilities, infrastructure and large manufacturing firms. Furthermore, liberalisation was not a logical outcome of postwar international conditions. Even a convinced liberal like Philippe Taqla posited that Lebanon could not survive under 'free enterprise' when most of the world's economies were planned and regulated.[10] Nevertheless, given the influence of the mercantile-financial bourgeoisie, bolstered by the political and ideological inclinations of other powerful elements, Lebanon's early policy-makers moved quickly to dismantle bureaucratic controls over the economy, to reduce industrial protection, and to establish conditions that favoured the expansion of foreign-oriented tertiary economic activities.

Positive expectations for an open economy

Positive expectations about the long-run sustainability of this model were based on four important domestic, regional and international economic factors. First, it was building on a foundation of an outward-looking environment laid in Mount Lebanon and Beirut from the nineteenth century. Such expectations were based on an 'evident' path-dependent evolution of Lebanese outward-oriented institutions and economic structures. Furthermore, many in the power bloc also expected that with the destruction of Arab Palestine in 1948, Lebanon's major commercial rival had been eliminated.

Second, large sources of domestic private capital were available to finance commercial and other tertiary economic activities. As discussed earlier, merchants and other private entrepreneurs had amassed large savings during the war. Given the expectations of very high rates of profit and comparatively low risks on triangular trade and financial services, as opposed to high uncertainty about profits and growth in manufacturing and agriculture, large investment would flow into the tertiary sector. Moreover, the question of an exchange constraint or trade gap did not emerge at this time because of Lebanon's sizeable sterling and French franc balances in London and elsewhere.

Third, changing regional conditions, in particular the growth of regional capital and goods markets, provided a favourable environment for the development of an intermediary role for Lebanon. Satisfying pent-up regional demand for imports after the Second World War was a first step towards expanding this position. This strategy was reinforced over the next 25 years, as petroleum revenues multiplied in a region that did not have the economic and financial infrastructure and capacity to absorb them.

Finally, the postwar international economy opened new avenues and opportunities for the Lebanese elite; and the economic outcomes would be determined by the success or failure of emerging institutions and organisations in the newly-independent country. Reflecting this movement was the shifting roles of Lebanese economic agents: agents became principals, and intermediaries were transformed into investors or *vice versa*. International trade and services would be open to this elite, as never before.

Politics and ideology: minimalist, non-activist state

Lebanon's power brokers placed a premium on a minimalist state with few interventionist powers. This was a result of their own inclinations, as well as fears of an opposition turning a highly-developed bureaucratic apparatus against themselves. While rent-seeking and *wasta* (connections) were common forms of bureaucratic behaviour, a powerful activist bureaucracy was never created to permit broad state intervention. A major proponent of this position was Michel Chiha, an intellectual champion of the idea of 'Greater Lebanon'. He argued in *Politique intérieure* that Lebanon's national survival depended on harmony among its numerous confessional sects.[11] Confessional harmony could best be maintained by a weak state which would at least theoretically limit political interference in confessional affairs. In a similar vein, Chiha argued that the state had little to do with the functioning of a healthy Lebanese economy. Thus, he supported the ideal of Lebanese *laissez-faire* based on its intermediary role between east and west, necessitating a free flow of capital, ideas and people. In an often-told story, Chiha illustrated his view of how the Lebanese economy functioned: a Lebanese merchant buys goods in South America, sells them in Stockholm, and earns £L 68,000 profit without the goods ever coming near Lebanon.[12]

Chiha's ideas were transformed into political reality by the 1943 elections that brought Lebanese nationalist, Bishara al-Khoury, and pan-Arabist, Riad al-Solh, to power as the first president and prime minister of an independent Republic of Lebanon. Their formulation of the 1943 National Pact, composed of speeches and writings of Khoury and Solh, heralded a tacit acceptance of power-sharing between Lebanon's two largest communities, the Maronite Christians and the Sunni Muslims, and created the groundwork for their agreement on the prevailing 'rules of the game'. Though the National Pact called for the elimination of confessionalism, the Khoury–Solh alliance actually permitted the institutionalisation of a sectarian system: the spoils of the state (public-sector spending, top political offices and employment in the bureaucracy) were allocated on the basis of confessional affiliation. The emerging Lebanese system, which reinforced historical suspicions, perpetuated divisive politics and augmented patron–client relations, was best served by a weak state. Thus, the leadership established a minimalist state apparatus, which was often immobilised by small challenges as well as major crises.

Content of the Lebanese model

Lebanon's postwar economic model was composed of three fundamental elements:

- the adoption of an open economy strategy: the liberalisation of the movement of goods and capital in its economy and the use of foreign economic relations to support Lebanon's intermediary role, both of which were institutional measures that aimed at creating an enabling economic environment for its commercially-oriented private sector;[13]
- the establishment of *laissez-faire* policies and institutions in a non-activist state that did not intervene in the affairs of its economic agents, yet instilled international confidence through credible macroeconomic management, *inter alia*;
- the creation of a market environment that made the survival of domestic industry and agriculture dependent on their comparative and competitive advantages in Middle Eastern markets.

Open economy: free trade and exchange, shifting economic relations, and stabilisation

In contrast to typical primary-outward or secondary-outward trade strategies that emphasise export promotion of primary or manufactured commodities, Lebanon's strategy comprised tertiary-outwardness, a service-oriented open economy.[14] This strategy promoted import and triangular trade and financial and international services that made Lebanon the principal intermediary between the industrialised countries and the Middle East. In terms of the three main elements of an economic development strategy — demand source, supply source, inward-outward orientation — Lebanon adopted an export demand-led, service-growth strategy with an outward orientation.[15]

An open-economy strategy is based on the notion that international trade in goods and services stimulates economic growth: a widened market promotes productivity and technical progress.[16] The strategy has become associated with the post-1950s' secondary-outward model of Japan and the Asian newly industrialising economies — for example Taiwan, South Korea, Hong Kong, Singapore — most of which utilised industrial and other statist policies to promote manufactured exports and to stimulate rapid growth and structural change.[17] By contrast, Lebanon's open economy rejected *dirigisme* and neglected industry. Lebanon's focus on service exports is unusual compared with the strategies of other (primary and secondary) outward-looking developing countries for three main reasons. First, Lebanese policies did not aim to develop the country's productive economic forces based on industrialisation and structural/technical change, an objective that is normally associated with outward-looking strategies such as EOI. Second, the promotion of service exports is associated with a low level of merchandise exports, which negates much of the traditional *raison d'être* of an open economy strategy.[18] Third, an open economy strategy is often viewed as effective in dealing with the foreign exchange constraint on development by implementing policies to expand exports and to devalue the currency, which make exports cheaper and consumer imports prohibitively expensive. Conversely, Lebanon's policy-makers took extraordinary measures to establish a strong currency to facilitate import and *entrepôt* trade.[19] While Lebanon's over-valued currency was partially a result of inconsistent policy targets, it was also viewed positively as a support for an increased level of imports and domestic consumption; and there was little concern over the rise of a foreign exchange constraint.

In short, the objectives of an open economy in Lebanon did not include industrialising rapidly, strengthening the role of the state, or increasing efficiency through market mechanisms. Rather, they aimed at developing an external service economy, which required greater international confidence, and second, sustaining its agricultural and industrial sectors by expanding exports to the region. As planning was not part of this strategy, the issues of promoting long-run economic growth, structural change, equity, among others, were avoided.

Deregulation of the economy: free trade and exchange objectives

The Lebanese economy emerged from the Second World War saddled with a panoply of regulations concerning the movement of goods and capital and intervening in supply and demand. After the British and French troops left Lebanon at the end of 1946, Lebanon's newly-independent government began to dismantle regulations, to rescind autarkic wartime economic policies and to establish an open economy. Indeed, deregulation and liberalisation were made the highest of priorities by some of Khoury's closest associates. Reflecting this position was Michel Chiha's *Le Jour,* which published an editorial that the bureaucratically-controlled trade and financial regimes should be abandoned because they had created an import monopoly that was inefficient, price-setting and discriminatory.[20] While the government was forced to continue a number of import/exchange regulations because of the inadequate allocation of foreign exchange by France and an enormous surge in local and regional demand for imports — a growing amount of the latter being supplied by Lebanese trading houses — it moved quickly towards the ideal of a liberal trade and exchange regime.

Liberalisation of foreign exchange and the capital account

Given the economic imperatives of this model, the Khoury regime argued that the government must liberalise the exchange regime. This argument ultimately prevailed, even as Lebanon faced a temporary exchange constraint in 1947 caused by rapidly growing imports and inadequate allocation of foreign exchange by France. Hence, Minister of National Economy Suleiman Naufal was forced to retreat on liberalisation when he signed decrees in July and August 1947 that regulated the allocation of hard currency.[21] This temporary move, however, proved no more successful than policies initiated the previous year to tighten controls over imports requiring exchange that was in short supply (notably, dollars). Economic liberals strongly opposed Naufal's move. Michel Chiha's *Le Jour* wrote of the new decree:

> The favoured importers, those who have accumulated hard currency and licences from the National Economy, will certainly become the masters of the market. Up to August 28th, they had the privilege of benefiting from the difference between the official rate and the open market rate. A real import monopoly is now instituted in their favour. . . . The merchants, much as other citizens, know quite well that the country is not governed for the profit of the community and that the Lebanese do not all share the benefits of independence. They likewise know that the relatives of the relatives, the friends of the friends, and all those who participate directly or indirectly in the 'firm' form a separate class; that the decrees issued by General Naufal will only be applied to the common herd.[22]

The scepticism over the restrictions proved justifiable. By August 1948, the exchange situation had deteriorated further and Naufal had announced that hard currencies would be reserved exclusively for urgent governmental needs.[23] With the overvaluation of the Lebanese pound in terms of purchasing power parity *vis-à-vis* the US dollar by an estimated 154 to 226 per cent,[24] and the dwindling of Lebanon's exchange reserves, the government argued that its only remaining option was to liberalise the exchange regime. Minister of Finance Hussein al-Oueini told the US commercial attaché that the establishment of a free exchange market was the government's main hope of eliminating the flourishing black-market operations and of relieving the precarious currency situation.[25] On 17 November 1948, the Lebanese government liberalised the exchange market and allowed Lebanese capital to move throughout the world.[26] The government lifted most remaining restrictions on currency and financial transactions in sequenced stages between 1949 and 1952 to ensure the government's exchange requirements, to protect the Lebanese balance of payments and to support international trade and finance.[27] Financial liberalisation was later reinforced by the enactment of the

Banking Secrecy Law of 1956, which attracted large foreign capital inflows from the Arab world and elsewhere.

Liberalisation of trade: challenge by protectionists

Restrictions on hard currency lay at the heart of import control in Lebanon. Hence, after the government liberalised the exchange market from 1948 to 1952, it found it increasingly difficult to enforce trade restrictions such as the May 1949 Ministry of National Economy's decrees establishing import quotas and price controls on specific import commodities that competed with locally-produced goods.[28] Furthermore, the impact of tariffs and quotas was diluted by a wide range of exemptions and exclusions on imported goods.[29] Finally, the ultimate goal of the Khoury administration was to free trade of all bureaucratic regulation.

Protectionist interests challenged the dilution of measures that had sheltered Lebanon's domestic market from foreign competition. The battle pitted two powerful interest groups against each other: international traders and bankers, on the one side, opposing industrialists, organised in the Association of Lebanese Industrialists, and workers, on the other. However, because of the diversification of their interests, these lines were frequently blurred. For example, entrepreneurs with both commercial and industrial interests often chose to subordinate their manufacturing interests to the more profitable trading activities. Moreover, as previously mentioned, Lebanese agents, principals, intermediaries and investors were shifting their economic roles and activities during this early postwar period. The weakness of the industrialists compared with the merchants and bankers became increasingly evident as their interests began to clash directly.[30] The industrialists, led by the influential Christian textile owners, the Aridas and Asseilys, fought hard to win extensive tariff and non-tariff protection for domestic manufacturing.[31] Meanwhile, the merchants launched a campaign in which the industrialists were painted as wartime profiteers, who could not operate profitably under competitive market conditions. As the government liberalised the economy and internal economic conditions worsened, the split between the free traders and protectionists widened. The industrialists pressed their points forcefully by staging lockouts and threatening to close their factories, something that would have thrown thousands of labourers out of work in a period when unemployment was rapidly accelerating. Not to be outdone by the industrialists in playing 'political hardball', the merchants also threatened the government with strikes and forcing Lebanon into economic chaos, if it did not proceed with the liberalisation process.[32] This threat was probably unnecessary considering the prevailing environment. Although the government feared the tactics of the industrialists, it sided fundamentally with commercial interests.

Throughout the period between 1947 and 1952, the government vacillated between supporting temporarily expedient measures that favoured first trade and then industry.[33] Pressures from competing interests forced the government to enact *ad hoc* policies to deal with successive crises. These measures were indecisive, short-term, and weakly enforced. Ultimately, they satisfied few, as an *Al-Hayat* editorial pointed out: '[the government] followed the system of settlement, procrastination and improvisation ... gratifying the merchants and then the industrialists, while actually gratifying none, except a few individuals.'[34] After the critical year of 1950 when the Syro-Lebanese Customs Union was dissolved, Lebanon's trade regime was further liberalised. Subsequently, Lebanese policy aimed at maintaining a liberal trade and tariff regime,[35] even though the governments were forced from time to time to enact restrictions to meet first, the requirements of the economy's current account position and, second, the demands of influential industrialists. Furthermore, Lebanon's economic turnaround supported liberalisation. By the first half of the 1950s, the open economy strategy appeared to be producing a 'Lebanese economic miracle', as gauged by the sheer growth of foreign trade, the even greater expansion of international services, and rising per-capita income.

Open economy: shifting foreign economic relations

Lebanon's open economy strategy was best served by severing intrusive ties with an economic nationalist Syria, maintaining proper relations with the former mandatory power, France, and developing flexible commercial links with Middle Eastern economies. It also required that Lebanon preserve close economic and political relations with Britain and the USA: both were principal suppliers of Lebanon, and as Great Powers with interests in that country, they exerted great influence. While some of the elite retained an affinity for France, many, such as the 'New Phoenicians', believed that Lebanon's economic interests lay with the USA. The US minister in Lebanon characterised the 'New Phoenicians': 'Here are vigorous exponents of the capitalist system who now look only to the USA for ideas and encouragement.'[36]

Lebanese policies towards the USA and Britain will not be analysed here because relationships were developed largely according to considerations of security and political arrangements, which are beyond the scope of this discussion. However, US Point IV development assistance to Lebanon, which was established to deter communism in Third World countries, will be discussed, given its importance to Lebanese development policy at that time.

Dissolution of the Syro-Lebanese Customs Union: promoting Lebanon's openness and independence in the Arab world

A key turning point in the liberalisation of Lebanon's trade and financial regime came with the dissolution of the Syro-Lebanese Customs Union in 1950. The bifurcating paths of Syria and Lebanon had begun with formal independence from France in 1943 and the termination of the *de facto* Syro-Lebanese economic union in 1944. Conflict between the two countries involved a wide range of political and ideological issues; and the continuation of the Syro-Lebanese Customs Union after 1944 prevented each government from implementing separate tariff and trade policies to promote its disparate economic philosophies.

Antagonism between the two grew as their interests and policies diverged: Lebanon was characterised by outward-looking and non-activist state policies; in opposition was Syrian industrial and agrarian interests, which combined with military-backed state economic nationalism, favoured protectionism and interventionism. The Lebanese suspected the motives of Syrian government encouragement of its merchants to assert control over Syria's import trade, thus cutting into the Lebanese middlemen's market in Syria. Lebanese merchants also denounced the proposed development of Latakia port which, with Jordan's Aqaba port, threatened to rival Beirut. Syria countered that it had been forced to take these defensive measures because its economy was being destroyed by foreign competition. In 1949, many Syrian textile enterprises were forced to close while others, such as those in the sugar and glass sectors, established only in 1947, had to reduce output.[37] Similarly, because Beirut merchants had cornered foreign trade in Syria, many Syrian commercial houses transferred their offices from Damascus or Aleppo to Beirut to take advantage of its conditions.[38]

The Syrian government was also piqued about the adverse consequences of the 1948 Franco-Lebanese Monetary Accord on its own unsettled financial relations with France.[39] Under the Franco-Syrian Monetary Accord of 1949, Syria was obligated to meet a share of the combined Syro-Lebanese trade deficit by settlement in scarce sterling, while Lebanon paid in relatively abundant French francs. The Syrian government was increasingly annoyed by the 'insouciant attitude' taken by the Lebanese government towards Lebanese merchants who flooded Syrian markets with foreign goods paid for by Syria's dwindling exchange.[40]

Most prominent Lebanese economic liberals preferred to break with Syria rather than accept its economic perspective and what they viewed as national arrogance. Lebanon's governing and economic elite also feared Syria's economic nationalism and military intervention in politics, both of which had moved the Syrian government towards greater control over the movement of its capital, goods and people. Lebanese industrial interests were not united with those in Syria because of growing competition between their respective industries.[41] Moreover, the economic conflict was reinforced by the political attitudes of Lebanese isolationists,[42] no matter how the issue might have been couched in economic language by Gabriel Menassa and others. SLEP bluntly stated that Syria should not interfere in Lebanon's economic affairs.[43] However, its understanding of non-interference and 'brotherly friendship' between the two countries included policy recommendations by which Lebanon would receive a higher share of customs revenues than its partner, and Syria would reduce its price of wheat sold to Lebanon. SLEP went on to condemn Syrian economic nationalism, protectionism and, ultimately, the continuation of the Customs Union. Furthermore, its president, Gabriel Menassa, argued for the dissolution of the Customs Union to be replaced by what SLEP advocated as the basis of all relationships with Arab countries — namely free-trade zones for Lebanese goods.[44]

Although leaders in both countries hoped to work out their differences, they were negotiating at cross purposes. The Lebanese government wanted to avoid direct confrontation with Syria because most members realised that Lebanon was the larger beneficiary of the relationship with Syria. However, they wished to maintain or expand their benefits without giving into any Syrian nationalist demands. At the same time, Syria did not want to force the issue, as it hoped to persuade the Lebanese to accept economic union, an objective that was clearly unrealistic. After three years of political brinkmanship, threats, counter threats and intermittent negotiations, Syria's Prime Minister Khaled al-Azm presented the Lebanese government on 7 March 1950 with a virtual ultimatum, calling for complete economic union between the two countries, which included the unification of trade and financial regimes and the pursuit of identical economic policies. The Lebanese government, which had anticipated the dissolution of the union for at least a year,[45] refused to submit to what it labelled economic blackmail. Furthermore, it argued that total economic unity would prejudice Lebanon's political sovereignty. Consequently, the two states severed their remaining economic ties by dissolving the Customs Union on 15 March 1950.

Though Lebanon was now able to pursue its own policies without restraint, its economy was disrupted by the severed relations. It lost its right to conduct triangular trading operations for the Syrian market. Smaller Lebanese merchants, particularly those in Tripoli, suffered greatly from this loss, while the large Lebanese merchants were able to evade the new restrictions. Lebanese producers were hit even harder. Some 60 per cent of Lebanon's manufactured goods were marketed in Syria before the dissolution of the Customs Union.[46] Such Lebanese commodities as cotton yarn, beer and matches were largely dependent on the Syrian market.[47] With the closure of this market, many industries were forced to reduce output by between 35 and 75 per cent, thus depressing revenues and profits, reducing economies of scale and dampening expectations about the future of

Lebanese manufacturing.[48] Lebanese industry was also impeded by the loss of Syrian raw materials which had to be replaced by higher priced foreign inputs. With the separation, Joseph Donato, an official of the Ministry of Social Affairs, called for government protection of Lebanese industry, which was operating at an average of 50 per cent capacity, by establishing a 'customs defence policy'.[49] However, such a policy was never executed. Lebanon's agricultural sector was also negatively affected by the loss of the Syrian market. As fruit producers could not obtain substitute markets quickly, they were forced to flood the domestic market, sending prices through the floor. In addition, the ban on Syrian wheat exports (which had supplied about 60 per cent of Lebanon's wheat requirements) forced the Lebanese government to buy wheat at higher prices on the international market.[50] Nor did the service sector escape the consequences of separation. Previously, Lebanon had benefited from income on joint Syro-Lebanese administrative services in Beirut; and it also stood to lose revenues from Syrian visitors.

On balance, large Lebanese mercantile interests benefited from the separation. Although the merchants were concerned about the redoubling of efforts by the Syrian government to develop Latakia port and the restrictions placed on Syrian businessmen who were not allowed to visit Beirut without a special permit, a large share of Syria's 1950 and 1951 imports continued to travel via Beirut commercial houses;[51] and that share did not decline significantly until the later 1950s. The short-term impact on large Lebanese commercial interests was limited mainly because they were able to evade Syrian restrictions by establishing offices in Damascus or Aleppo and utilising transit trade mechanisms. Alternatively, they smuggled: Lebanese merchants paid a smuggling fee of 10 per cent of the merchandise value to deliver goods to Damascus.[52] Hence, these interests could continue to operate in Syria, and at the same time, they enjoyed a more favourable economic environment, thereby allowing them to expand their role in regional trade.

A comprehensive agreement on Syro-Lebanese economic relations was reached almost two years after the dissolution of the union. It was based on nine substantive points, permitting free trade of agriproducts, initiating export duties on some Syrian raw material inputs used in Lebanese industry, and favouring Syria's manufactured exports in Lebanon over Lebanese manufactures in the Syrian market.[53] However, it did not solve underlying contentious issues: the Syrian government moved to 'Syrianise' foreign agencies and representative offices in Syria, 90 per cent of which were controlled by Lebanese merchants;[54] and the newly elected Chamoun regime responded with a call for ill-defined 'economic unity' with Syria and broader Arab unity schemes. Because Syria's threat was not serious and Lebanon's proposals were no more than talk, Syro-Lebanese economic relations remained normal, but not cordial. Lebanon's main policy objective of maintaining a market environment favourable to international trade and services was, however, bolstered.

Perpetuation of French economic influence

Despite its volatile dealings with France during the war, the Khoury administration established amicable relations with the former mandatory power. In the early postwar years, France attempted to recoup some of its wartime losses in Lebanon by establishing binding economic and political relationships with the independent government.[55] In support of these efforts, French capital continued to exert influence on important sectors (banking, utilities and public enterprises such as the Port of Beirut); and Lebanon agreed to honour French concessions until their contracted expiration dates. Perhaps France's most important tool in regaining influence in Lebanon was its control of Lebanon's bank of issue, the BSL.

The BSL was headed by the powerful René Busson, who had also advised and represented the high commissioners on foreign affairs and finance.[56] With his dual wartime role (as director of the BSL and representative of the *CFLN Caisse Centrale*), Busson was able to forge an alliance between previous rivals, the two major French financial groups in Lebanon, which were under the leadership of Maurice Bérard and P. Philippar.[57] This feat consolidated French interests, and Busson gained even greater influence in postwar Beirut. Busson, dubbed 'the economic dictator over Lebanon',[58] reinforced his position by a close association with the Khoury entourage and Hussein Oueini; and he was known to intervene in BSL lending by favouring friends and discriminating against anti-French interests.[59] More importantly, he used his power as head of the BSL to influence monetary and credit policies, and to establish an array of organisations to bolster French prestige, for example the semi-official trading company, *Société d'études et de réalisations industrielles, agricoles et commerciales* (SERIAC),[60] and its business centre, the Jesuit College of Jamhour, and the workmen's city at Ashrafiyyah. With his clout, Busson was instrumental in persuading the Lebanese government to maintain monetary ties with France and to increase gold coverage of the Lebanese pound. Finally, Busson's influence in Lebanon was magnified because his grand vision and interests reinforced those of the dominant Lebanese elite. His image of Lebanon's future revealed a small Christian enclave, whose liberal economy would be 'a "sort of Singapore" in the Middle East'.[61] As an outspoken critic of Syrian economic nationalism, he argued that Syria and Lebanon would eventually have to abolish the Customs Union and go their separate economic ways.

An initial idea bearing Busson's stamp was to make SERIAC a successor to the French-controlled OEG, which had wielded bureaucratic influence within Lebanese industry during the war. By expanding SERIAC's mandate, the French hoped to develop their markets in the Middle East: it would assist French firms in

Lebanon and promote the association of French and Lebanese capital.[62] To increase their share of business in Lebanon, Syria and the Middle East, French firms worked through SERIAC to build on their expertise, information and networks. Because the French government owned a little over 25 per cent of its equity, SERIAC could negotiate deals with the appearance of French governmental support; or it could claim independence, as the government owned only a minority of shares.

Even though key members of the Khoury administration (including Khoury, Henri Pharaon and Hamid Frangiyyeh) accepted SERIAC's operation in Lebanon,[63] Minister of National Economy Kamal Jumblatt opposed it, due to its potential political and economic interference. Many influential Beirut merchants also objected to SERIAC because, with its semi-official status, they feared that it would be able to monopolise French trade with the Middle East and thereby exclude them. Even before SERIAC had been formally established, a delegation of Lebanese merchants met with French delegate-general Général Beynet, threatening, albeit idly, to sever Lebanese–French relations if SERIAC were established.[64] Because of the hostility of some influential Lebanese towards SERIAC and principally because Jumblatt refused to register it as a corporation, it was forced to operate extra-legally.[65] However, after Jumblatt left his post, SERIAC gained its registration with the assistance of other Lebanese officials who shared in its profits.[66] It became a major commercial player in Beirut and fought aggressively to win contracts for French interests and to minimise other foreign competition. The Lebanese government was forced to take action against SERIAC for the tactics it employed to gain a contract parallel to that awarded to the British firm of Gibb & Partners for the execution of a major economic and financial survey of Lebanon.[67]

Developing economic relations with the Arab world

Both the Khoury and Chamoun administrations wished to establish close commercial and financial ties with the Arab world: well-regulated economic, but politically independent, relationships with Arab neighbours. Such *realpolitik* was in stark contrast to isolationist rivals, who opposed closer Lebanese–Arab relations. Practically, Lebanon could not survive without the Arab world. Its strategy to become the intermediary between the Middle East and the West obviously depended on cordial economic relations with the region. Another by-product of Lebanon's economic model, that of export production for neighbouring markets, was even more dependent on Lebanon maintaining good relations with the Arab world. Even with declining Lebanese access to Palestinian and Syrian markets in the late 1940s and early 1950s, Lebanon continued to maintain a favourable balance of trade within the region. In the 1950s, about 40 per cent of Lebanon's exports was destined for neighbouring countries.[68] In 1951, the Middle East region imported about 70 per cent of Lebanese citrus and other fruits.[69] To expand Lebanese trade in the region, which was a fundamental objective of Lebanese regional economic policy, the groundwork was laid for Lebanon's most important multilateral trade agreement with four other Arab League members (Iraq, Egypt, Syria and Jordan); it was signed by the Chamoun administration on 7 September 1953.

As Lebanon remained in a state of war with Israel after 1948, it benefited economically from the demise of Arab Palestine. In addition to the millions of dollars of refugee aid flowing into Lebanon,[70] Palestinians transferred an estimated £L 60 million to Lebanon.[71] The exodus also brought skilled and educated labour, as well as a vast pool of unskilled labour, subsidised by international aid and prepared to work for almost any wages to survive. The Lebanese economy was also the beneficiary of the wholesale transfer of the IPC refinery and administrative apparatus from Haifa to Tripoli and Beirut. With the boycott of Haifa port by Arab countries, the port of Beirut expanded greatly, and the increased income from trade, services, taxes and fees also helped Lebanon's external payments.[72] Last, many enterprises were transferred from Palestine to Lebanon, generating new economic activities and growth.

Lebanese *laissez-faire*

The Lebanese strategy also featured a non-activist state and a free private sector, which was relied upon to expand and transform the economy. While at times the Lebanese model approached *laissez-faire*, perhaps its actual behaviour was better characterised as *laissez-aller*.

The theme of economic liberalism was strongly and cogently argued by the 'New Phoenician' ideologue, Gabriel Menassa, in his *Le plan de reconstruction de l'économie libanaise et de réforme de l'état* published by SLEP in 1948. This work advocated a totally free regime of capitalism. In it, Menassa praised the liberal economic policies of Jordan, which at that time were attracting some of the region's entrepreneurial talent and capital to Amman. Implicit in his argument was that Lebanon should emulate Jordan's example and, hence, must further deregulate its economy. Because domestic industry could not provide the quantity, quality and competitively-priced goods necessary to meet internal demand, SLEP argued that Lebanon should increase the market share of imports. It excoriated attempts by industrialists to force the government to institute protectionist policies, claiming that Lebanese industry was relegated to a slow steady growth by modernisation and reorganisation of its technologies and only limited state assistance.

The discourse surrounding *laissez-faire* focused on an outward-looking private sector. As argued previously, it did not feature the ideas of competition, efficiency or 'getting prices right'. In fact, while powerful merchants and bankers hailed the

Smithian invisible hand, they were also engaging in price-fixing and manipulation made possible by their market power. As the Shehabist Charles Rizk correctly observed, their '*laissez-faire*' was a cue word for a particular type of economic development based on Lebanon's intermediary role and the domination of mercantile-financial interests and the quasi city-state of Beirut.[73] These ideas were bolstered by changes within the Middle East, as Lebanon attracted investment and entrepreneurial talent with the fall of Palestine and the establishment of nationalist interventionist regimes in Syria, Egypt, and Iraq.

Lebanon's *laissez-faire* was realised through the activities, policies and institutions of those representing commercial-financial interests, fighting to return to what they claimed was Lebanon's historical role. Such forces reinforced a path dependent evolution of Lebanon's outward-looking capitalist economy. Henri Pharaon, a powerful banker, MP and member of the Khoury inner circle, personified this position. Pharaon argued that if social reform could be implemented only at the expense of free enterprise, the former would have to be delayed.[74] While others fought for greater state intervention, for example the influential Association of Lebanese Industrialists,[75] both the Khoury and Chamoun administrations favoured a highly deregulated economy. This was achieved through both active and passive policies.[76] Active policies included those on currency reform and financial stabilisation; many other policy areas, such as fiscal management and socio-economic development, were as much, or more, a result of neglect or inertia.

Monetary reform and stabilisation

Monetary reform and stabilisation policies in Lebanon from 1948 to 1958 were specifically targeted to achieve a strong convertible currency that would expand Lebanon's international intermediary role and attract foreign capital. Monetary policy, which was constrained by the absence of a Lebanese central bank until 1964, was not directed towards gaining control over Lebanon's money supply or credit mechanisms. Nor did stabilisation policies seek to reduce its large current account deficits, which were typically offset by invisible exports and capital inflows. Finally, the government recognised that it did not have the will or the means to stabilise the currency by intervention in the financial markets. Due to its small reserves, the Exchange Stabilisation Fund (established by the government in October 1949) intervened to stabilise the Lebanese pound in only three extraordinary cases: the 1953 post-Korean War recession, the 1956 Suez crisis, and the 1958 civil war.

Three fundamental institutions reformed and stabilised Lebanon's financial system between 1948 and 1958: the Franco-Lebanese Monetary Accord of 1948, the Monetary Law of 1949, and legislation requiring high gold coverage of the Lebanese pound.

Despite the numerous economic and political drawbacks of the 1948 Franco-Lebanese Monetary Accord,[77] the Khoury regime made it a cornerstone of a policy aimed at creating a strong, fully convertible currency in which international markets had confidence. While the terms of the accord overwhelmingly favoured France, Khoury's partisans emphasised that the agreement would stabilise Lebanon's financial system, which had been volatile and underdeveloped throughout the mandatory period. Under the accord, the French central bank guaranteed the convertibility of 67 per cent of Lebanon's French franc balances — namely the French franc cover of the note issue — at a fixed pound sterling/French franc exchange rate until 1958;[78] it also freed Lebanon from *de jure* monetary dependence on France. Echoing the importance that the Khoury administration attached to achieving these goals, Minister of Foreign Affairs Hamid Frangiyyeh argued that Lebanon had no choice but to sign this agreement because Lebanon had solicited guarantees to cover Lebanese currency from the USA, Britain, Saudi Arabia and Egypt, all of whom had refused.[79] Minister of Finance Hussein al-Oueini adopted the same position and declared that were the accord not to be ratified, Lebanon would greatly suffer from a drop in the value of the Lebanese pound and a loss of international financial confidence:[80] 'I believe that this agreement is prejudicial to Lebanon, but do we have a better one? We have sought the lesser evil.'[81]

From this point of view, the advantages of the accord outweighed its disadvantages. One serious flaw was that a third of French-held Lebanese franc balances (FF 4000 million) were not guaranteed under this agreement. They lost almost 45 per cent of their value after the devaluation of the French franc on 26 January 1948, one day after the accord went into effect.[82] The agreement also specified that Lebanese capital could freely flow to the French Union, while French capital transfers to Lebanon were subject to French exchange control. At the time, the restriction was not a serious constraint on the Lebanese economy, given Lebanon's relatively large reserves and its access to foreign capital. Further, by the terms of this accord, Lebanon agreed to purchase French-abandoned property in Lebanon for £L 20 million[83] and to honour the continuation of French concessions in Lebanon until their expiration dates.

A subsequent and companion policy of the ratified 1948 accord, the 24 May 1949 Monetary Law, was promulgated. It provided for the establishment of the Lebanese pound as an independent national legal tender with 100 per cent coverage of all notes issued by the BSL. This law and another decree passed on 3 June 1949 defined the pound's parity with gold, and it stipulated that 50 per cent of the cover consist of gold and foreign exchange with the other half to be composed of government debt.[84] The impetus for passing the monetary law was above all to boost the credibility and stability of Lebanon's currency by reducing dependence on the French franc. A principal defect of the new law was that it did not deal directly with the absence of a Lebanese-controlled monetary authority, and concomitantly, the shortage of basic monetary instruments needed to regulate a market economy.

Table 5. 1: *Note issue and cover of the Lebanese pound, 1948–58*

December	Notes in circulation (£Lm)	Gold cover (%)	Foreign assets (%)	Lebanese assets (%)
1948	185	2	67	31
1949	168	25	23	52
1950	196	36	14	50
1951	208	45	6	49
1952	200	55	0	45
1953	205	62	3	35
1954	242	90	0	10
1955	266	95	0	5
1956	333	79	0	21
1957	356	87	0	13
1958	399	78	0	22

Source: George Medawar, *Monetary Problems in Lebanon*, Ph.D. dissertation (Cornell University, 1963) Table 24, p. 102.

A third and related policy was initiated to implement the 1949 Monetary Law, namely the creation of a gold-backed Lebanese currency freeing it from *de facto* dependence on the French franc and, ultimately, on French financial policies. The 'gold buying' policy, designed principally by René Busson, president of the BSL, and Hussein al-Oueini, greatly enhanced the economic elite's objective of establishing Beirut as the financial and commercial centre of the Middle East.[85] In particular, this policy would discipline the financial system, as the Lebanese pound was roughly pegged to gold. There were also allegations that rent-seeking interests swayed the government's decision to adopt the policy.[86] Subsequently, the government requested the BSL to buy gold on the open market in Beirut and abroad by converting its reserves of French francs and dollars into gold.[87] In 1949, foreign exchange held at the BSL and most of the Lebanese government's oil transit royalties from TAPLINE went towards purchasing the gold cover;[88] and the policy was executed over the next six years. As shown in Table 5.1, gold coverage increased from 2 per cent to 95 per cent of note circulation from 1948 to 1955, while coverage by foreign assets was eliminated.

Managing inflation and stabilising price levels

After the war, Lebanon continued to face the problems of high price levels and inflationary pressures. Inflation was a complex problem and the government did not have adequate instruments with which to tackle it. However, a significant share of the elite supported a large expansion of imports to contract the money supply, which, they argued, would reduce consumer prices.[89] Justifying this position, they argued that alternative policies would not work in Lebanon: public borrowing and tax increases were impracticable; and, without a Lebanese-controlled monetary authority, the government's influence in monetary policy was slight. Moreover, Lebanon had sufficient reserves to import on a massive scale, which many claimed would drive down prices. This solution was fraught with problems. As Lebanese trading houses tended to favour high-quality consumer and luxury imports (because of their commercial networks and higher margins), prices of necessities would remain relatively high; and the solution did nothing to reduce high-cost production and low productivity in the Lebanese economy.

A second position was taken by a small group of technocrats and opposition forces who proposed devaluation of the Lebanese pound as a means of addressing Lebanon's high price levels. Sa'id Himadeh, a main proponent of this viewpoint, argued that devaluation would promote manufacturing and agricultural export production and tourism.[90] The power elite countered by stating the obvious that Lebanon imported more than it exported. Thus, devaluation would lower the price level of Lebanese goods externally, but it would increase import and domestic prices; and they underscored its detrimental effect on the poor and middle classes who were on fixed wages.[91]

A third and decisive standpoint was taken by the BSL, which implemented a direct approach to monetary contraction: it tightened credit and bought gold, thereby reducing bank notes in circulation by 18.5 per cent from £L 205 million in February 1948 to £L 167 million in December 1949.[92] The BSL, which relaxed this policy in 1950, slowed the rapid growth of imports as it contracted the money supply. With the BSL's actions, the issue of government anti-inflationary policies was postponed.

Primarily due to economic fundamentals rather than policy prescriptions, price levels in Lebanon tended to fall between 1947 and 1952, except during the Korean War when wholesale prices rose by about 11 per cent annually; afterwards, they increased by an average of 2.3 per cent per annum for the remainder of the decade. Given that prices had risen so greatly during the war, however, the general price level remained elevated, as compared with that in neighbouring economies.

Fiscal policies: revenue production and surplus budgets

The Lebanese government continued to follow fiscal policies established by mandatory authorities that aimed at revenue generation and prudent management. Lebanon's policy-makers typically did not use fiscal policy to further objectives of economic management or development; instead, they sought to generate

Table 5.2: *Capital expenditure/current expenditure, 1948–58*

Year	Capital expenditure (extraordinary budget) (£Lm)	Current expenditure (ordinary budget) (£Lm)	Ratio
1948	18.5	70.1	0.26
1949	9.0	83.4	0.11
1950	19.6	84.5	0.23
1951	–	90.1	–
1952	4.4	88.5	0.05
1953	6.3	96.3	0.06
1954	15.8	111.2	0.14
1955	15.8	132.4	0.12
1956	40.0	161.3	0.25
1957	44.0	192.5	0.23
1958	17.2	181.6	0.09

Source: Raymond Mallat, *70 Years of Money Muddling in Lebanon, 1900–1970* (Beirut, 1970) Table 5.

budgetary surpluses, regardless of the economic climate, by underestimating state revenues and underspending on capital works.[93] The government rarely employed Keynesian fiscal prescriptions to adjust the economy. Throughout this period, it twice used expansionary fiscal tools to stimulate the economy: the government created state projects financed by deficit extraordinary expenditures once after Suez in 1956 and again in 1958 after the civil war. In general, the Lebanese government adjusted capital expenditures in the ordinary budget to the flow of revenues; and it maintained or expanded the levels of expenditures on administration and security (around 80 per cent). The ratio of capital expenditure (extraordinary budget) to current expenditure (ordinary budget) in this period was low, ranging from 5 per cent to 26 per cent (see Table 5.2).

With the implementation of policies that promoted surplus budgets, only one deficit in the ordinary budget was recorded between 1948 and 1959: a deficit of £L 1.1 million in 1950. As surplus budgets accumulated, by 1959 the reserve account[94] held £L 125 million (see Table 5.3). In terms of revenue generation,

Table 5. 3: *Ordinary budgets, 1948–59 (£Lm)*

Year	Revenues	Expenditures	Surplus/deficit	Reserve account
1948	78.8	70.1	8.7	44.1
1949	87.4	83.4	4.0	39.1
1950	83.3	84.4	–1.1	18.3
1951	105.3	90.1	15.2	33.5
1952	124.9	88.5	36.4	65.5
1953	141.2	96.3	44.9	76.9
1954	157.4	112.2	46.2	88.7
1955	178.9	132.4	46.5	111.1
1956	192.0	161.3	30.7	69.6
1957	209.9	192.5	17.4	79.8
1958	225.5	181.6	43.9	92.6
1959	250.9	198.6	52.3	125.0

Source: Medawar, *Monetary Problems in Lebanon*, Appendix F, p. 275.

indirect taxes generated the greatest share of state revenues. Indirect taxes consisted mainly of customs duties and comparatively low-rate levies on goods with inelastic demand — for example, cigarettes and petrol. Between 1947 and 1958, indirect taxes constituted 60 to 70 per cent of total taxes, while taxes comprised 80 to 85 per cent of total state revenues. The tax base (revenues/NNP) rose from 9 per cent in the early 1950s to 12 per cent in the mid-1960s.[95] The government relied on indirect taxes to finance the state budget for a pragmatic reason: they were relatively easy to collect. It also supported the economic interests and philosophy of decision-makers: they preferred to tax broad-based consumption than upper income groups' profits and savings. Speaking before the *Cénacle libanaise* in May 1950, André Tuéni, director-general of the Ministry of Finance, reiterated the government's position that it would not raise direct taxes because it refused 'to over-tax the proprietor and to increase the burden on people engaged in commerce which is the pillar of the economy of Lebanon'.[96] Consequently, direct taxes played a very small role in Lebanon's fiscal regime and revenue base.[97] The most far-reaching 'tax reform' the Lebanese government instituted before the post-1958 Shehabist period was the imposition of direct taxes during the Second World War, levied on war profits, income and property. However, the government was able to collect only a tiny fraction of anticipated tax revenues on war profits and income; and outdated and inaccurate assessments on buildings resulted in gross underpayment of taxes. In fact, these tax regulations only contributed to a makeshift fiscal system, which, because it had never undergone comprehensive reform, continued to resemble the systems operating during the Ottoman and mandatory periods.

Development policy

The government's fiscal policies placed the responsibility of investment and economic transformation onto the private sector: at least 80 per cent of all capital formation in the 1947–58 period was private. The preferred means to finance large capital projects was foreign direct investment. Foreign capital was very prominent in the development of Lebanese transport and communications, utilities, hotels, and energy resources, particularly oil.

Lebanese policy-makers avoided incurring state debt to finance public works.[98] Thus, to acquire the necessary financing of infrastructure and projects that the domestic private sector could not or would not undertake, the Lebanese government sought private foreign investment and official assistance from countries that did not threaten Lebanon's political or economic position, for example Saudi Arabia. The Lebanese government also solicited development grants and loans from western countries, the most important of which was US Point IV assistance.[99]

In 1949, President Harry Truman proposed a Point IV programme for developing countries, consisting of US technical assistance and government guarantees for private US investment. However, as the US Congress did not approve government guarantees for private investors in the developing economies, the assistance was reduced to a programme of technical aid with promises of development finance. Through Point IV, the US government proposed to assist Lebanon by training Lebanese in the USA and sending US advisers to assist the Lebanese government; but its concept as applied to Lebanon was ambiguous, floating between technical assistance and large-scale grant aid.[100] Despite a very heated debate over many aspects of Point IV, the Lebanese Chamber ratified the programme. Lebanon's government optimistically held that the USA would be generous in its Point IV aid, which would save Lebanon from its economic decline.[101] Eventually, the US government allocated US$ 34.5 million to Lebanon.[102] But the structure of this programme militated against significant local expenditure in favour of building a large US bureaucracy (consisting of 50 persons, one of the largest Point IV administrations in the world) to carry out quite a modest programme. Consequently, the Lebanese government reduced its nominal development goals, eliminating much of the proposed investment for agriculture, human resources and social welfare.

Foreign direct investment in Lebanon's petroleum industry: locating ARAMCO's TAPLINE oil terminus and refinery in Tripoli

For a number of economic and strategic reasons, ARAMCO (Arabian-American Oil Company) and the United States government supported the location of the TAPLINE oil terminus and refinery in Tripoli. After the decision was taken by ARAMCO to implement its plans in Lebanon, negotiations began with the Lebanese government, which ratified the convention for the TAPLINE concession in 1947. Ratification was rapid, as it benefited influential Lebanese interests; and the government hoped that the projected creation of 15,000 TAPLINE jobs would offer some relief to the stagnating national economy. However, Syria delayed ratifying the convention, which greatly angered President Khoury. Khoury told an ARAMCO representative that he was prepared to break all economic ties with Syria should Syria continue to refuse to sign the agreement — if ARAMCO could arrange for the pipeline to bypass Syria by going through northern Palestine to Lebanon. Because Syria eventually ratified the convention, Khoury never had to make good this threat. In 1952, the government of Lebanon renegotiated its convention with TAPLINE. TAPLINE agreed to pay an extra US$ 600,000 per annum and to supply 50 per cent of domestic crude requirements for four major products refined in Lebanon. In return the government acknowledged the right of TAPLINE to deal in the free exchange market, which, based on its 1951 exports, would save TAPLINE an estimated US$ 1 million per annum. The Lebanese government stood to lose considerable revenues by this provision, but overall, the net impact of the new measures was an increase of payments to the Lebanese government of about £L 3 million per annum, making a total of £L 4.5 million. TAPLINE agreed (informally through a letter of understanding given to Sami al-Solh) to employ as many Lebanese as feasible. US diplomats in Beirut commented that Syria, which also renegotiated its convention with TAPLINE, obtained a better agreement with TAPLINE than did Lebanon, but that TAPLINE would extend the same conditions to the Lebanese government, if demanded.

It is difficult to determine Lebanese public development expenditures because of the inexact and changing categorisation of expenditures and, more importantly, because there was no single authority that was responsible for executing development programmes, nor even one single budget that financed development — public capital projects were financed by the ordinary, extraordinary and special autonomous budgets. In general, however, public works were financed from two separate budgets, the ordinary budget and the Development Works Fund, which was primarily financed by the reserve account. Analysis of the various budgets shows that during the 1948–58 period, the largest state capital expenditures were allocated to the Beirut International Airport; the second most important projects were water and irrigation schemes — for example, the Litani River projects; and finally highways and roads.[103] Given this structure of spending, development policy in Lebanon was 'conducive to the promotion of trade, tourism and other services'.[104] In fact, over 60 per cent of public development expenditures between 1945 and 1954 went towards improving communications and transport infrastructure: roads, ports, the Khaldeh Airport and the automatic telephone system.[105]

Table 5.4: *Lebanese fuel consumption, 1948–52 (tons)*

Year	Benzine	Kerosene	Gas oil	Fuel oil	Diesel oil
1948	29 976	10 943	8 610	71 669	2 004
1949	28 626	11 380	11 263	87 029	50
1950	52 887	28 127	30 483	92 819	n.a.
1951	61 824	25 007	34 855	91 093	n.a.
1952	56 429	27 186	34 443	92 823	n.a.

Note: n.a. = not available.

Source: Ministère de l'économie national, *Bulletin statistique trimestriel*, 1952.

During this period, expenditures allocated from the ordinary budget for roads, buildings and ports were worth £L 113 million out of a total of £L 173 million (or 65 per cent).[106] Actual expenditures of the Development Works Fund on roads, buildings, ports and airports between 1945 and 1954 amounted to some £L 69 million out of total expenditures of £L 100 million (or 69 per cent) (see Appendix Table A9). Between 1948 and 1954, the government spent £L 38.6 million out of a total £L 76 million (or 51 per cent) of the Development Works Fund on the Beirut Khaldeh Airport complex, which replaced the small airport at Bir Hassan in 1952. In two years from its partial opening in 1950, the number of passengers using the new airport almost tripled. Clearly, it was the most important and ambitious project undertaken by the state, and it made Beirut an international and regional air hub. Furthermore, the state improved the transport network by linking the port of Beirut with roads and railways. Reflecting the important growth in physical infrastructure and accompanying economic effects was a large rise in Lebanese fuel consumption (see Table 5.4). In addition to the advances in transport, the government undertook the installation of a new advanced telephone network, with an initial capacity of 15,000 telephone lines, expandable to between 35,000 and 40,000;[107] and it linked Beirut with the West by providing a direct circuit to Paris and extended communications to most of western Europe and the USA.

Another feature of development spending was rent-seeking, by which funds were channelled into favourite projects of the governing bloc. Associates and relatives of President Khoury were widely accused of illegally profiting from contracts to build the airport and automatic telephone system.[108] The greatly needed development of water resources often turned out to be pork-barrel projects, which enhanced the value of holdings of large landlords. *Al-Haya*t condemned the proposed irrigation of 5000 hectares of land by one project. 'But who owns this land? Not more than 200 persons! Thus, the government has spent £L 11m for the interests of 200 persons. The country is heading towards many hydraulic projects, the direct interests of which might be limited to the landowners, who are few in proportion to the peasants.'[109]

While the government emphasised policies to expand physical infrastructure, it neglected human resource development and social welfare. The government promised to build more public schools, hospitals and housing, but actual state expenditures were negligible. During these years, the Development Works Fund expenditures on schools amounted to £L 509,000 out of total expenditures of more than £L 100 million (or about 0.5 per cent). In October 1949, only 1446 public and private schools existed;[110] of these, there were about 800 state primary schools in which 2000 teachers taught 70,000 pupils.[111] In 1951, for the first time, government schools educated more primary school pupils (83,295) than the private schools (75,475).[112] But at the same time, over half of the children applying to state schools in Beirut were turned away because of insufficient facilities; and of these, between 30 and 35 per cent were unable to attend school at all.[113] Moreover, as the Ministry of Education supported no schools above the primary level, all secondary and tertiary education was private and generally available only to the middle and upper classes.

Comparative advantage of Lebanese industry and agriculture in regional export markets

The final component of Lebanon's economic model was a *de facto* reliance upon market principles for the development of industry and agriculture. Unlike many of the issues discussed above, this evolved more from neglect and a lack of consensus than policy. Consequently, the forces of a Smithian 'invisible hand', Ricardian static comparative advantage, and various competitive advantages — based on Lebanon's economic and geographical position in the Middle East and its lead in industrialisation — prevailed in the development of Lebanon's manufacturing sector and to a lesser extent in agriculture.

Laissez-faire as applied to Lebanon's industry can only be explained by the dominant commercial–financial interests in the economy, which would have been hurt by protectionism and typical import-substitution measures. This position was not grounded on efficiency and optimisation concepts, given that there were no serious efforts to remove the numerous market distortions in the economy. Nor was it an outcome of a view that manufacturing could not develop further in Lebanon; many recognised that it could build on its base of 'early' (for example, textiles, food-processing) and 'middle' (for example, cement) industries.[114] Moreover, it is apparent that policy-makers recognised the important role that industrialisation could play in employment creation for a population that was growing at an estimated annual rate of between 2.3 and 2.7 per cent.[115] Clearly, labour-intensive manufacturing had greater potential than trade and services for absorbing surplus labour in agriculture and the natural growth of the labour force.

Only a minimum of state assistance was offered to industry between 1948 and 1958. The little that was offered, to placate influential industrialists or to preserve labour relations, consisted mainly of indirect measures advocated by economic liberals such as Gabriel Menassa — for example, the establishment of bilateral trade agreements.[116] This was in stark contrast to strong policies that supported the open service economy.

Lebanon's post-independence free trade strategy eliminated effective protection for Lebanese industry. The ensuing economic liberalisation process required great structural adjustment within industry; and initially, an enormous increase in foreign competition almost destroyed Lebanon's market for locally-manufactured goods. However, in the longer run, liberalisation forced industry to become more competitive through modernisation and reorganisation, which was facilitated by new investments amounting to £L 147 million between 1950 and 1957. Moreover, postwar conditions promoted the development of regional export markets for Lebanese manufactured products, which was essential given Lebanon's small domestic market. This factor may have saved Lebanese postwar industry. Specifically, Lebanese manufacturing was forced to build on its regional comparative and competitive advantages, which had been gained through Lebanon's early industrialisation in the Middle East and its increasingly influential position in the region as regards commerce, finance and services. Lebanese industry further benefited from regional changes that increased its competitive advantages: the end of competition from Palestine; the inflow of Arab capital; and the infusion of oil wealth in the Middle East, which was responsible for the creation of new markets in the region.[117] By the 1960s, it was estimated that between 20 and 25 per cent of Lebanon's total exports were manufactured goods, most of which were destined for Arab markets.[118] In brief, beyond the costs it incurred, deregulation reaped benefits for postwar manufacturing.[119]

Emerging from these changes was a greater interdependence between the economies of Lebanon and the Arab world. Lebanon exported manufactured and agricultural goods to satisfy low- to medium-income consumers in Arab markets in return for Arab exports of oil and primary commodities; and at the same time, Lebanese merchants acted as intermediaries between western suppliers and high-income Arab consumers. Nor did Lebanese industry benefit only from direct exports to the region. Additional internal demand in Lebanon was created through a growing foreign sector of tourism, international business, education and refugee aid.

Table 5.5: *Loans by the* Office du crédit agricole, industriel et hôtelier, *1950–2*

Muhafazats	Year	Agricultural loans Number	Agricultural loans £L	Industrial loans	Hotel loans Number	Hotel loans £L
Beirut*	1950	–	–	–	1	17 000
	1951	8	35 700	–	–	–
	1952	42	151 500	–	–	–
Beka'a	1950	–	–	–	1	40 000
	1951	270	554 950	–	2	12 500
	1952	90	167 100	–	–	–
North Lebanon	1950	–	–	–	4	61 700
	1951	193	475 000	–	7	118 000
	1952	76	210 450	–	–	–
South Lebanon	1950	–	–	–	2	40 800
	1951	196	510 600	–	–	–
	1952	46	89 400	–	–	–
Mount Lebanon	1950	–	–	–	29	467 100
	1951	553	1 297 350	–	21	341 400
	1952	87	180 650	–	16	163 200
TOTAL	1950	–	–	–	37	626 600
	1951	1 120	2 873 600	–	30	471 900
	1952	341	799 100	–	16	163 300

Note: *Loans made to rural landowners living in Beirut.

Source: Ministère de l'économie national, *Bulletin statistique trimestriel*, 1952.

Because of the political power of the large landowners and the high share of labour dependent upon agriculture, the government was more active in the development of the primary sector. The early governments paid more attention to agrarian matters, mainly by investing in (or securing finance for) irrigation and drainage projects: the state spent £L 31 million on irrigation projects between 1945 and 1954.[120] Further, the public *Office du crédit agricole, industriel et hôtelier* extended credit to agriculture (see Table 5.5). However, most progress in agriculture was due to private initiative, which was clearly the dynamic force behind growth and change in the sector.[121] In fact, large private capital, which expanded and modernised fruit and vegetable production in the 1950s,[122] was responsible for transforming agriculture from small subsistence farming to larger modern production for both internal and export markets. With rising investment and growing concentration during the 1940s and 1950s, Lebanon's modern capitalist sector of agriculture survived, then prospered, by export production of fruits and vegetables.

Conclusion

Immediately after the end of the Anglo-French occupation of Lebanon in late 1946, the independent Lebanese government began to deregulate its war economy and create a path of progressive liberalisation of goods and capital. This strategy, which began to reopen the economy, forged the Lebanese Merchant Republic model that achieved its golden age in the 1950s and survived numerous challenges until the beginning of the civil war in 1975. As a consequence of Lebanon's deregulated economic environment, its early-start competitive advantages, and political and economic changes taking place in the Middle East, Lebanese trade, finance and services flourished. The tertiary sector grew rapidly and, by the end of the period under examination, it comprised at least two-thirds of national income. The same forces that promoted international services relegated Lebanese manufacturing and agriculture to secondary and tertiary positions in the economy. Nevertheless, with their advantages in the region, they were able to survive and even expand in the long run. While this chapter has concentrated on the strategy and policy formulation that established the Republic of Lebanon's economic order, the following chapter will marshal additional data to analyse in greater detail the evolution of the Lebanese model.

CHAPTER SIX

Outward-oriented Economic Growth and Change, 1946–58

Wartime conditions, which reduced international trade, transport and communications and created new markets for domestic production, had temporarily reshaped the Lebanese economy. Unemployment was virtually eliminated; physical infrastructure was improved; and wide-ranging regulatory policies were imposed. At the same time, rising price levels dissipated significant purchasing power of Lebanese consumers and diminished the future competitiveness of Lebanese industrial enterprises. Finally, with extraordinary Allied expenditures in the region, Lebanon's foreign reserves and domestic savings grew substantially.

The return to civilian conditions and the effective transfer of power to an independent government between 1945 and 1947 once more reoriented Lebanon's economy. Consumption increased several fold, following seven years of suppression and accumulated savings and foreign exchange. The end of a closed economy reversed the foreign/domestic supply and demand relationship prevailing from 1939 to 1945: demand for domestic goods declined as the supply of foreign goods was greatly increased. Along with increased consumption, came depressed demand for locally-produced goods because consumers frequently substituted imported for domestic commodities. Unemployment followed soon after.

Unemployment and underemployment in Lebanon's early postwar economy rose due to both conjunctural and structural problems. A downward cycle was triggered as Allied forces left Lebanon: with falling demand for locally-produced goods and renewed foreign competition, production was reduced and labour retrenched. With the reorientation of the Lebanese economy, tertiary activities replaced labour-intensive commodity production as the economy's engine of growth. The need for robust adjustment was heightened by the loss of, or reduced access to, Palestinian and Syrian markets. Under these conditions, the growth of labour force participants exceeded Lebanon's employment absorptive capacity, exacerbating the problem of surplus labour. In the early postwar period, Lebanon's unemployed workers were estimated at between 30,000 and 75,000 in the active labour force of between 600,000 and 650,000.[1] Table 6.1 shows the distribution of labour in this period.

Table 6.1: *Distribution of Lebanon's labour force, 1949*

Employment category	Share (%)
Farmers	57.5
Service and industrial workers	22.8
Landowners	3.5
Merchants	3.2
Unemployed	5–12.5
TOTAL	92–99.5
Total labour force participants (number)	600 000–650 000

Source: USNA, RG59, 883A.06/3–3050, 1949, 'Annual Labor Report'.

With a decline in employment opportunities and the reopening of transport, emigration resumed.[2] Lebanese emigration, however, had only a small effect on the relatively large labour supply, as more than 135,000 Palestinian refugees had fled to Lebanon in 1948 and 1949.[3] By contrast, the long-run impact of emigration on Lebanon's savings-investment rates and balance of payments was significant. In 1948, Lebanese emigrés, estimated at 1.2 million, remitted approximately £L 60 million, equivalent to 7 per cent of NNP in that year, also an important source of hard currency.[4] In addition to their stimulating effects on consumption, they provided a major source of capital for enterprises,[5] and created additional demand for employment.

Deregulation and openness comprised the most fundamental policy and institutional shifts in the early postwar period, as was discussed at length in Chapter 5. Fused with Lebanon's historical commercial role and the altered postwar global and regional economic conditions, deregulation and openness put Lebanon on a path of unprecedented growth, particularly in the foreign-oriented tertiary sector.

With the reopening of the economy, import, re-export and transit trade soared; only export trade lagged behind, a situation worsened by declining world prices for primary and low-end commodities that constituted the majority of Lebanese export merchandise. Consequently, trade deficits mounted. An initial response to rising deficits after the dissolution of the Syro-Lebanese Customs Union in 1950 was a call by merchants and the *Bloc national* to make Lebanon one large free-trade zone. This was vehemently opposed by Lebanese industrialists and others in the power elite. In a compromise move to expand exports, the government pushed for commercial agreements with major trading partners, such as the September 1953 multilateral agreement with Egypt, Syria, Iraq and Jordan. While much debate arose over the issue of climbing merchandise trade deficits, their effect on the current account was reduced due to rising service exports.

Postwar deregulation provided a strong stimulus to Lebanon's private sector. Dominant domestic private investment was mobilised primarily from enterprise war profits and highly-concentrated upper-income family savings. The largest share of private investments flowed into tertiary activities, followed by industry and agriculture. In contrast to direct investments, passive investments in equities and gold declined; and the equities index of the Beirut stock exchange fell from a high of 620 in 1943 to 310 in 1951; and gold from an indexed high of 319 in 1945 to 244 in 1950.[6] Supporting domestic private investment was the growth of foreign direct investment, as Lebanon became a regional hub: foreign firms established representative and branch offices in Beirut to service the region. Public investment focused on physical infrastructure. As the largest share of state capital flowed into non-self-liquidating projects in transport and communications, state investment supported the expansion of the service economy.

Trade

The Lebanese economy grew at a robust pace between 1948 and 1957, but it was services, particularly in the foreign sector, that was characterised by high growth and restructuring. Trade, finance and related services attracted a growing share of private domestic capital; and with their high and rapid returns on investment, they became the most dynamic sectors in the economy. In 1952, value-added in the tertiary sector comprised 57 per cent of NNP as compared with 19 per cent in agriculture and 14 per cent in industry; by 1958, it composed 62 per cent of NNP. Trade alone — estimated to have generated about 30 per cent of national income in 1939, dropping significantly during the Second World War — rebounded to 30 per cent of NNP in 1946; and it averaged 29.5 per cent of annual NNP between 1948 and 1958. Although there are no comparative data for financial services, it is evident that their weight in national income multiplied: they grew at an annual average compounded rate of 13.1 per cent between 1948 and 1957 as compared with 5.5 per cent for industry and 7.3 per cent for all services and aggregate NNP during that period. About two-thirds of commerce and a large share of financial services were international in character. Commerce and related services supported somewhat less than half of the population in 1949, and workers in this sector earned higher incomes on average than those in industry or agriculture.[7]

The reorganisation and concentration of merchant capital contributed to a restructuring of the tertiary sector as a whole. Larger trading houses in Beirut were able to increase their market power in import trade; smaller firms were unable to compete due to meagre internal funds, limited access to capital and networks, and practices that excluded smaller merchants. Not only was large commercial market power translated into greater influence over supply and prices of imports in the wholesale and retail markets, but it also affected local industry by discouraging the production of goods that competed with imports.[8]

Economic life was further concentrated in Beirut after the war. Spatially, Beirut was the centre of domestic economic activities. More significantly, it became a hub of regional services and an *entrepôt* for much of the Middle East. Beirut's regional position was enhanced by several important changes in the Middle East.

First was an expansion of links between the elites in Lebanon and those in oil-producing Arab countries such as Kuwait, Saudi Arabia and Iraq.[9] Ties between Beirut and Kuwait were tightened when the Sheikh of Kuwait appointed a Lebanese, Izzat Bey Jaffar, as his chief adviser. At this time, Izzat Bey became instrumental in organising a dominant position for Beirut interests in Kuwait's growing goods and services markets. Supporting this trend was a flourishing gold trade between Beirut and Kuwait. Similarly, in Saudi Arabia, most gold, fresh foods and many other commodities were air-freighted via Beirut on (Lebanese-controlled) Middle East Airlines. This link was buttressed by a rise in Saudi tourism in Beirut and Mount Lebanon and expanded TAPLINE operations. The Iraq–Beirut connection intensified after 1948, as Jewish merchants, who had previously dominated Iraqi commerce, emigrated to Israel and elsewhere. The Iraqis turned to Beirut middlemen to help fill this void. Moreover, Lebanese involvement in Iraqi trade was facilitated by Beirut's foreign exchange market: Iraqis could obtain hard currency for Iraqi dinars in the Beirut market, enabling them to pay for large orders from the USA, Italy and France. Furthermore, the Lebanese Levant Express Transport Company controlled 75 per cent of all lorry transport between Beirut and Baghdad in the early 1950s, transporting a large share of Iraqi merchandise trade to and from the West via Beirut.[10]

Other factors that strengthened Beirut's position in Lebanon's foreign service economy included improvements in its air, sea and land transport networks; tie-ups between foreign and Lebanese capital in services, finance and the international petroleum industry; and large capital transfers from Middle East oil-producing and/or unstable countries to Beirut banks. A final and sometimes underestimated factor was the growth of Arab tourism in Beirut and Mount Lebanon. Tourism and *estivage* expanded Lebanese personal networks and organisational links in the region. Domestic demand and opportunities were also augmented: Arab tourists spent millions of Lebanese pounds on all types of goods and services; and opportunities for Lebanese entrepreneurs in other areas of the economy were created.

Direction of trade

The direction of trade reverted to a modified prewar pattern. In 1938, European goods represented 57 per cent of total Lebanese imports; in 1949, they composed 49 per cent, with another 10 per cent originating from the USA. While western imports regained their prewar share, Lebanese exports to Europe and the USA did not bounce back. This was a major contributing factor to growing deficits in Lebanon's merchandise trade account, which more than quadrupled in nominal

Table 6.2: *Geographical distribution of Lebanon's exports, 1950 (%)*

Country	First quarter 1950 (Syro-Lebanese Customs Union)	April–December 1950 (after separation)
Syria	–	32.0
Saudi Arabia	3.0	14.4
USA	6.0	8.0
Britain	9.0	7.7
Egypt	4.2	7.0
France	29.0	5.7
Belgium	1.3	5.0
Jordan	9.5	4.5
Italy	5.5	1.9

Source: Ministère de l'économie national, *Bulletin statistique trimestriel*, 1951.

terms from £SL 40,773,000 in 1938 to £SL 187,466,000 in 1946. Almost 35 per cent of the merchandise trade deficit in 1951 was derived from the large imbalances between Lebanon and Britain, France, Italy and Germany. Particularly favoured were French imports because Lebanese merchants had greater access to francs than sterling (due to France's contravention of the Catroux Accord) and dollars.[11] Thus, French exporters regained an important share of Lebanon's market, as France rose to become the economy's third most important supplier in 1946 from its twelfth place the year before. Lebanon also increased trade with east European countries, such as Yugoslavia, Czechoslovakia, Hungary and Romania, all of which exported more to Lebanon than they imported; but the differential was smaller than that between Lebanon and the major European capitalist economies.

Another factor underlying this redirection was the substantial growth of trade with the USA, which became Lebanon's primary supplier in 1946.

A growing share of Lebanese exports was destined for Middle Eastern markets, which absorbed its surplus fruits, vegetables and manufactured goods (see Table 6.2). Reflecting this shift was Lebanon's trade surplus in the Middle East. In 1951, Lebanon held a surplus trade account with only five partners: Egypt, Saudi Arabia, Jordan, Cyprus and Palestine. Beyond the growth in recorded regional trade, unofficial border trade was on the rise, particularly between Lebanon, on the one hand, and Israel and Syria on the other. In 1950, an estimated £L 60 million was smuggled to Israel and other neighbouring countries.[12]

Import and triangular trade

The sudden end of war in 1945 caught Beirut importers by surprise. They had begun to stockpile high-priced imports in late 1944 and early 1945, after the Allied supply situation improved, but before an end to the war was certain. They were then saddled with imports that could not be sold at the large premium they commanded during the war. Because the government feared major commercial bankruptcies and to 'cushion the effect on domestic trade of a sharp decline in local prices', in June 1945, the Ministry of Supply fixed profits on imports at 10 per cent from neighbouring countries and 40 per cent from overseas.[13] However, this policy did not eliminate price-gouging on products that were in short supply: profits often reached 400–600 per cent.[14] Nor did it shore up the position of smaller merchants who had neither the cash to clear imports warehoused at the port of Beirut nor the staying power of the larger commercial houses. Partially because it wanted to clear Beirut's congested port, the government responded by abolishing the supply tax on imports and permitting limited re-exportation, although it feared its effect on inflationary pressures. In any event, the policy had little impact at the time, as most of the ports in the Middle East were in the same congested condition as Beirut.

This situation was only a temporary setback. Though trade continued to be regulated in the early postwar period, import licences being allocated on a priority basis for capital goods and consumer necessities, imports in 1946 quickly surpassed their 1938 level (while export tonnage remained less than a third of that of 1938); and they quadrupled in value between 1945 and 1949. Due to Lebanese commercial networks and foreign supply forces, luxury imports exceeded domestic demand, while basic consumer imports were in short supply, assuring continued high prices for essentials.

Manufactures continued to be dominant in import share, while exports were largely primary goods and foodstuffs. Table 6.3 shows the commodity structure of trade between 1950 and 1958.

Table 6.3: *Commodity structure of Lebanese trade, 1950–8 (%)*

Goods	Imports	Exports
Manufactures	44	28
Gold	9	–
Primary goods	18	35
Foodstuffs	22	30

Source: Ministère de l'économie national, *Bulletin statistique trimestriel*; IRFED, *Besoins et possibilités*, vols 1 and 2.

Transit trade was an important growth area during the early postwar period. It increased from a little over £L 128 million in 1945 to over £L 500 million in the last quarters of 1950 (after the separation of Lebanon from the Syro-Lebanese Customs Union); and it reached its zenith in the 1945–58 period in 1951 at £L 1970.5 million (at a free market rate of exchange). It consisted primarily of crude oil from Iraq and Saudi Arabia destined for pipeline terminals and refineries in Lebanon on its way to the West, and of merchandise and gold transported from the USA and western Europe to Lebanon and on to the Arab world and the Far East. In 1952, crude oil comprised 45 per cent of the value of transit trade; gold and other merchandise comprised 23 per cent and 32 per cent respectively.[15] From 1951 to 1958, the value of transit trade equalled £L 8745 million or 85 per cent of Lebanon's NNP in those years. Its profits were estimated at £L 49 million in 1951, or almost 5 per cent of NNP in that year.[16]

Data show that trade grew at an annual average compounded rate of 8.5 per cent between 1948 and 1957, as compared with the NNP's 7.3 per cent. The trade subsectors showed the following annual average growth rates between 1951 and 1958: re-exports +22.9 per cent; transit –3.9 per cent; imports +5.7 per cent; and exports +3.6 per cent.

Expansion of financial services

Accompanying commercial growth was an expansion of financial services. With a market-based exchange regime, a dynamic trade sector, a modernising telecommunications network and growing gold and foreign exchange operations, Beirut became a centre of regional and international finance. At this time, Lebanon's financiers established links with global money centres; and the increasing share of international financial transactions in Lebanon's economy reflected Beirut's aggressive expansion. In the early 1950s, it was estimated that about £L 1000 million of foreign exchange transactions were executed annually for foreigners.[17]

Profits on foreign exchange operations averaged £L 11 million in 1951 and 1952 or over 1 per cent of NNP annually.[18]

Table 6.4: *Lebanon's gold transit trade, 1946–52*

Year	Gold in transit (kg)*
1946	335
1947	12 500
1948	19 500
1949	29 500
1950	57 000
1951	89 000
1952	67 000

Note: *rounded to the nearest 500 units, 1947–52.

Source: USNA, RG59, 883A.2531/3–653, 'Beirut as a Gold Market'.

As political stability declined in Palestine, Syria, Egypt, Iran and Iraq and as oil income grew in developing Middle East economies, capital flowed into Beirut. The net movement of capital into Lebanon, a large share of which was short-term deposits, amounted to more than £L 438 million between 1951 and 1957 (equivalent to almost 5 per cent of NNP in those years). With Lebanon's favourable economic climate, the number of foreign and domestic banks increased and by 1951 a total of 41 financial institutions in Lebanon held an aggregate capitalisation of FF 9000 million.[19] The total number of incorporated banks operating in Beirut tripled from seven in 1945 to 21 in 1954, with a greater increase in Lebanese than foreign banks in international finance.[20]

Lebanon expanded its position in the international gold market after the war. Privately held gold in Syria and Lebanon in 1946 was estimated at some £L 540 million or £12 million sterling.[21] However, more important was the growing international transit trade in gold. Beirut's position in the world gold market was due to its role as an *entrepôt*, facilitated by its strategic geographical location (particularly with its good east–west airline routes with direct connections to Kuwait) and the liberal economic conditions prevailing in postwar Lebanon. Before the Second World War, Beirut's gold transit trade was small, and records in 1938 did not even differentiate between import and transit gold; 3089 kilograms of gold coins entered the country that year.[22] After the war, Beirut's gold transit trade increased sharply from transactions involving 335 kilograms in 1946 to 89,293 kilograms in 1951 and 67,276 kilograms in 1952 (see Table 6.4); and transit trade accounted for 75 per cent of all gold operations in Lebanon.[23] Beirut ranked high in the international market along with Montevideo, Paris, Zurich and Macau; its only regional rivals were Tangiers (which had about a quarter of the volume of Beirut's transactions) and Kuwait (actually an extension of the Beirut gold market). Gold moved mainly from west to east: 95 per cent of Beirut's transit trade originated from western Europe and the western hemisphere and was destined for eastern locations, the Arab Gulf, India and China. By 1951, over 30 per cent of private transactions on the free international gold market went through Beirut;[24] and profits amounted to £L 76.2 million.[25] This return was very high in a sector dominated by 100 financiers, who employed 100 workers and operated with a capital base of £L 45–60 million.[26]

Growth of other services

After the war, growing numbers of multinational companies established branches and representative offices in Beirut, mainly to service expanding Middle Eastern markets. These and other activities discussed elsewhere stimulated large capital flows to Lebanon. It is difficult to estimate the share of external transfers that flowed into long-term investments, in contrast to hot capital seeking higher interest rates or a safe haven. Longer-term capital was invested primarily in real estate, and the remainder in trade, finance, other services and industry.[27] According to Lebanon's balance of payments, earnings on foreign investments in Lebanon amounted to £L 68.6 million between 1951 and 1957. At the same time, the Lebanese earned £L 232.2 million on their investments abroad.

The real-estate sector, which contributed an annual average of 9.4 per cent to the NNP in the 1948–52 period, declining to about 6 per cent in the second half of the 1950s, was linked to the development of tourism and *estivage*. In 1950, Michel Touma, director of tourism, estimated that capital investment in Lebanese tourist-related operations amounted to £L 250 million, which added £L 25 million (2 per cent) to the NNP per annum.[28] Tourism comprised the single most important invisible export in 1952, earning more than half of the value of all exported merchandise.[29] Estimates of direct tourist expenditures in Lebanon between 1951 and 1958 amounted to £L 537.1 million. The government assisted this growing industry by liberalising currency regulations in favour of tourists, subsidising the transport costs of Arab summer visitors,[30] investing in public infrastructure, and by making available government-guaranteed loans to the hotel industry through SCAIL. Finally, the government legalised gambling in resort areas in 1950[31] to attract mainly Egyptian, Iraqi and Saudi tourists, known to spend large sums in establishments that provided gaming facilities.[32] With government encouragement and ready sources of private capital, the number of hotels, restaurants and other touristic amusements expanded. The number of tourists visiting Lebanon grew from fewer than 30,000 in 1937[33] to 60,000 in 1949, 216,000 in 1952, 901,464 in 1955 and declining to 549,593 in 1957.[34] Tourism generated income estimated at £L 17.8 million in 1951, £L 107 million in 1955, dropping to £L 48 million in the 1958 crisis year.

Within Lebanon's service sector, the weight of hotel and education activities, which were highly sensitive to foreign expenditure trends, was large. From 1948 to 1950, these two branches generated about half of all income arising in the service sector, excluding trade and finance; and they were responsible for three-quarters of service wages and two-thirds of service employees.[35] The number of hotels grew from 486 in 1948 to 585 in 1952, while investment in hotels in 1952 was estimated at £L 145 million, more than the aggregate investment in the principal branches of industry in that year.[36]

Evolution of postwar industry

Probably the largest loser in Lebanon's early postwar open economy was industry. Domestic manufacturing was unable to maintain its previous share of the local market; and its average annual growth in the 1948–57 period of 5.5 per cent compared unfavourably with the 7.3 per cent in services. Commercial domination of the economy was also reflected by a large differential in the relative contribution of the industrial and service sectors to NNP: from 1948 to 1958, industry contributed on average 13.5 per cent to the NNP, as against services' 61 per cent. As Lebanon's economic policies and institutions advanced outward orientation, industry was increasingly in conflict with import trade that again dominated domestic markets. With these changes, industrial survival, and then growth and competitiveness, was sustained by its shift to greater export production for Middle East markets.

Industrial structure

Between 1930 and 1945, a modern consumer manufacturing base, consisting of foods and beverages, textiles, cement, wood and leather products, had been established in Lebanon. Extrapolating from industrial data on the early postwar period (1948–52), 1300 industrial enterprises produced on average over 40 per cent of total output of Lebanese goods and contributed 14 per cent to NNP; they also employed 25,000 workers with average annual wages of £L 50 million and generated net profits of almost £L 100 million on revenues of some £L 220 million and capital of about £L 150 million.[37]

Manufacturing was concentrated in eight major sectors: non-metallic minerals, food, beverages, textiles, printing, chemicals, furniture and leather (see Tables 6.6 and 6.7). The three largest sectors were food, textiles and non-metallic minerals, which represented about two-thirds of all industrial capital in the late 1940s.[38]

From 1946 to 1952, of these eight, investment in seven grew, and only leather goods declined (see Table 6.6). In 1950, most industrial enterprises were small: more than half of all manufacturing enterprises were capitalised at between £L 5000 and £L 25,000; fewer than 5 per cent had investment valued at more than £L 500,000; and the average was £L 115,000 (see Tables 6.5 and 6.9).

Table 6.5: *Lebanese industry: capital and enterprises, 1950*

Capital (£L)	Number of enterprises
5000–10 000	249
10 000–25 000	381
25 000–50 000	165
50 000–100 000	130
100 000–250 000	120
250 000–500 000	45
500 000–1 000 000	29
1 000 000 and over	25
TOTAL	1144

Source: Ministère de l'économie national, *Bulletin statistique trimestriel*, 1951.

Table 6.6: *Capitalisation of selected branches of Lebanese industry, 1946–52*

Industry branch	Capital investment (£Lm)			
	1946	1948	1950	1952
Food processing	6.7	20.4	25.0	27.8
Beverages	5.3	7.9	10.7	13.9
Textiles	14.8	23.2	32.6	38.2
Non-metallic minerals	32.9	26.3	35.5	45.5
Chemicals	3.0	4.9	5.9	3.7
Wood products	2.7	4.0	4.6	5.7
Printing	1.1	5.2	8.6	4.5
Leather	5.1	3.4	4.6	4.0
TOTAL	71.6	95.3	127.5	143.3

Source: Ministry of National Economy as cited by UN, Département des questions économique, *L'évolution économique au Moyen-Orient, 1945 à 1954* (New York, 1955); Albert Badre and As'ad Nasr, 'Income arising in the industrial sector', *National Income of Lebanon* (Beirut, 1953) monograph 3.

Table 6.7: *Labour, capital and output in Lebanese industry, 1950*

Industry	E (No)	L (No)	C (£L 000)	GO (£L 000)	NO (£L 000)	Income (£L 000)
Manufacturing:						
Food	455	5 404	24 934	61 684	31 619	30 123
Beverages	123	1 292	10 654	12 196	6 242	5 603
Textiles	60	5 040	32 587	39 545	19 657	17 702
Wearing apparel	15	1 036	3 281	2 309	1 390	1 193
Wood and cork	48	241	1 410	3 792	1 725	1 640
Furniture	95	1 211	4 593	10 324	6 508	6 232
Paper	9	91	475	914	576	548
Printing	100	855	8 606	5 780	3 236	2 720
Leather	64	737	4 554	14 203	6 502	6 229
Rubber	6	447	965	2 094	1 492	1 434
Chemicals	64	1 014	5 937	16 409	8 297	7 941
Non-metallic minerals	156	2 768	35 530	21 533	15 593	13 461
Metal products	30	639	2 649	11 060	6 655	6 496
Machinery	27	590	3 237	3 565	2 133	1 939
Electrical	4	217	1 560	1 915	909	815
Miscellaneous	29	367	6 462	2 720	2 162	1 774
Concessions/public utilities				38 740	15 452	13 862
TOTAL	1 285	22 039	147 434	248 783	130 148	119 712
Handicrafts:						
Carpenters						6 458
Shoemakers						5 010
Tailors						5 355
Other						806
Total						17 629
GRAND TOTAL						137 341

Notes: E = enterprises; L = labour; C = capital; GO = gross output; NO = net output; Income = income at factor cost.

Source: Badre and Nasr, 'Income arising in the industrial sector', Tables 6 and 15.

Table 6.8: *Comparison of industry in selected countries*

Selected variables	Lebanon (1948)	Egypt (1947)	Palestine (1942)	USA (1947)
Employees/establishment	17	14	14	59
Capital/establishment (£L 000)	84.7	57.4	47.8	1 400
Gross output/estbl. (£L 000)	146.6	64.6	90.2	2 950
Capital/worker (£L)	4 900	4 100	3 400	23 700
Gross output/worker (£L)	8 600	4 700	6 400	50 000
Net output/worker (£L)	4 800	2 200	2 600	20 300
Gross output/capital (%)	173	115	189	210

Source: Badre and Nasr, NIL, Industry, Table 21.

Table 6.9: *Capital and labour productivity in Lebanese industry, 1950*

Industry	L/E	C/L (£L)	C/E (£L)	Net O/L (£L)	C/Net O
Food	12	4 600	54 800	5 200	0.79
Beverages	11	8 200	86 600	3 900	1.71
Textiles	84	6 500	543 100	3 800	1.66
Wearing apparel	69	3 200	218 700	1 300	2.36
Wood and cork	5	5 900	29 400	6 100	0.82
Furniture	13	3 800	48 300	5 000	0.71
Paper	10	5 200	52 800	5 800	0.82
Printing	9	10 100	86 100	3 400	2.66
Leather	12	6 200	71 200	8 100	0.70
Rubber	75	2 200	160 800	3 300	0.65
Chemicals	17	5 400	92 800	7 100	0.72
Non-metallic minerals	18	12 800	227 800	5 300	2.28
Metal products	21	4 100	88 300	9 900	0.40
Machinery	22	5 500	119 900	3 500	1.52
Electrical	54	7 200	390 000	4 100	1.72
Miscellaneous	13	17 600	222 800	5 500	2.99
Average	17	6 700	114 700	4 900	1.41

Notes: L/E = labour per enterprise; C/L = capital per labour; C/E = capital per enterprise; Net O/L = net output per labour; C/Net O = capital-net output ratio.

Source: Table 6.7.

Employment in the top eight sectors of industry expanded from a little more than 8000 in 1946 to almost 13,000 in 1952.[39] Lebanese industry compared favourably with Egyptian and Palestinian industry in terms of investment, output and productivity; but the data in Table 6.8 speak for themselves when comparing industry in Lebanon with an advanced economy such as that of the USA.

In Lebanon's top eight manufacturing sectors, the largest share of capital was found in non-metallic minerals, the least in the paper industry. Productivity varied significantly among the sectors. For example, the capital-labour ratio in textiles was similar to the average of all industries, but its net output per worker was lower than average. By contrast, the leather and metal products industries, which had a below average capital–labour ratio, enjoyed a very high net output per worker. The capital–output productivity ratio varied from 40 per cent in metal products to 266 per cent in printing, reflecting large differences in technical requirements, efficiency and over-capacity (see Table 6.9).

Of the larger modern industries, textiles were probably the hardest hit by the end of sheltered markets. The textile owners spearheaded a battle to preserve government protection, which was largely unsuccessful. Despite their failure to win wide tariff protection, however, they reinvested a share of their large war profits in renovating and expanding productive capacity of their plants. In fact, the largest share of early postwar industrial capital flowed into textiles to replace and upgrade technology and plant facilities. Coinciding with a large investment programme in the spinning and weaving industries was an economic downturn, thereby affecting their short-term prospects.

The number of Lebanese spinning mills had increased from two establishments before the war to seven in 1948. Production of cotton yarn and cloth peaked in the years of 1948 and 1949 and then fell in 1950 under pressure from foreign imports. In 1949, Asseily purchased new machinery, expanding the factory's production capacity, which at full utilisation required between 2000 and 2500 employees.[40] In January 1950, it employed 1200; in December 1950, 800.[41] In 1948, 77,000 spindles were utilised throughout the sector; this declined to 54,000 in 1951[42] (see Table 6.10). Meanwhile, Lebanon's weaving industry was undergoing technical change: for example, the use of power looms doubled from 1946 to 1951.[43] With a large increase in productive capacity, accompanied by contracting demand as a result of greater foreign competition, this industry was producing between two and three times the amount of textiles demanded by domestic consumers in the early 1950s; and it did not have a realistic expectation of rapidly acquiring export outlets to absorb the excess. Stagnation led to a period of readjustment, encompassing lowered output, labour retrenchment, and new efforts to develop export markets. With restructuring, the textile branch was able to survive the crisis and, thereafter, it grew moderately.

Table 6.10: *Spindle utilisation in the Lebanese textiles sector, pre-Second World War and 1944–51 (number)*

Enterprise	Prewar	1944	1946	End 1948	1951
Arida Frères	10 000	8 360	–	20 000	–
Asseily	5 600	6 000	–	18 000	–
Kassas, Sadate, Dweik & Cie	–	–	–	16 000	–
Rafik Sa'id Reda	–	–	–	4 000	–
Jabre	–	–	–	10 000	–
Massabni Frères	–	–	–	6 000	–
Mouzannar	–	–	–	3 000	–
Total–Beirut mills	5 600	–	28 000	57 000	–
Total–Tripoli mills	10 000	–	8 000	20 000	–
TOTAL	15 600	28 000	36 000	77 000	54 000

Source: Gabriel Menassa, *Plan de reconstruction de l'économie libanaise et de réforme de l'état* (Beirut, 1948) pp. 356–7; Kurt Grunwald, *The Government Finances of the Mandated Territories in the Near East* (Tel Aviv, 1932) Table 6, p. 151 and Table 16, p. 167; PRO, FO921/175, Industry; FO922 IP 04500/Syria, 1944–5, Textiles.

The evolution of competition and market conditions for most Lebanese industry was very volatile in the 1948–58 period. The events of 1951/2 are instructive. In 1951, the textile branch survived declining internal market conditions by penetrating new markets in the Arab world, Pakistan and a few European countries. This recovery was further facilitated by a reduction in production costs, mainly achieved by slashing the wage bill through a shift to low-cost piece-rate contracts, thereby depressing the whole wage scale in the industry to slightly more than the minimum wage.[44] During this year, the industry was operating at 80 per cent capacity, and 50 per cent of its output was exported.[45] However, only one year later, in 1952, the industry again faced problems due to the tightening of import controls in Pakistan, North Africa and southern Africa (major markets for Lebanon's cotton goods), the continued problems of readjusting to the loss of the Syrian market, and the general volatility of export markets.[46] In that year, one mill was shut down, another struggled to survive and two others operated at reduced capacity.

Moderate growth occurred in many branches of food-processing, which employed the largest number of workers and generated the highest gross revenues of all Lebanese industries. It also held the third largest share of industrial capital, increasing its total stock of capital from £L 6.7 million in 1946, to £L 27.8 million in 1952.[47] During the same years, all branches of this industry, except sugar, enjoyed moderate growth. However, it operated under stiff foreign competition, not only in luxury goods, but also in basics such as jams, confectioneries and pasta. This situation, however, was ameliorated by a growing popularity of its goods with Lebanese consumers, expanded export markets such as Jordan, Iraq, Saudi Arabia and Pakistan, and some tariff protection. Though export production was viewed as the key to growth, this sector was dependent upon domestic markets throughout this period. Table 6.14 shows that its imports greatly exceeded exports in the 1950s.

Table 6.11: *Lebanese textiles production, 1947–51*

Year	Cotton yarn (tons)	Cotton cloth (millions of square metres)	Total textile production value (£L 000)
1947	1 840	3.2*	–
1948	6 000	5.1	20 701
1949	5 000	5.3	19 669
1950	1 550	4.9	17 702
1951	2 050	–	–

Note: *1946 output.

Source: Grunwald, *Government Finances*, p. 167; *Bulletin statistique trimestriel*, 1950–2.

Table 6.12: *Trade of Syro-Lebanese textiles, 1947–52*

Area	Year	Imports		Exports	
		(tons)	(value, £L 000)	(tons)	(value, £L 000)
Syria and Lebanon	1947	19 451	99 349	6 506	25 867
	1948	19 863	87 977	6 492	21 823
	1949	28 478	89 768	6 407	24 462
(before separation)	1950	5 103	15 115	5 667	13 531
(after separation)	1950	7 331	28 303	6 107	13 570
Lebanon	1951	12 814	56 958	8 024	35 453
	1952	12 397	46 094	7 055	20 534

Source: Ministère de l'économie national, *Bulletin statistique trimestriel*, 1950–2.

Lebanon's non-metallic minerals branch was dominated by the Chekka cement firm, which increased output from 148,000 tons in 1945 to 280,000 tons in 1952.[48] High domestic demand for cement and related products was stimulated by large investment in physical infrastructure and a booming construction industry.[49] Besides favourable demand conditions, the cement industry was supported by positive supply forces: most importantly, it was protected by the high costs of transport for imported cement, offsetting the higher prices of Chekka. With large demand and sheltered internal markets, Chekka invested over US$ 100,000 in

Table 6.13: *Mechanisation of the Lebanese weaving industry, 1946 and 1951*

Year	Power looms	Hand looms
1946	694	300
1951	1000	300*

Note: *1949.

Source: UN, Department of Economic and Social Affairs, *Review of Economic Conditions in the Middle East* (New York), supplements to World Economic Report, 1949, p. 55 and 1951, p. 129; and Gibb, *The Economic Development of Lebanon*, Table 34.

Table 6.14: *Imports and exports of processed foods in Lebanon, 1951 and 1955 (tons)*

Category	1951		1955	
	Imports	Exports	Imports	Exports
Canned vegetables	327	10	393	13
Tomato paste and products	358	1	641	30
Fruit jams and jellies	206	1	230	84
Fruit juices	120	13	148	20
Dried fruits	56	201	608	457
Canned fruits	82	9	518	21

Source: Raja Tannous, ‘Food and technology, a developing industry in Lebanon’, in T. S. Stickley, J. A. Asmar, A-R. Sagher, N. Atallah and P. L. Pellet (eds) *Man, Food and Agriculture in the Middle East* (Beirut, 1969) Table 2, p. 677.

new equipment in 1949; and investment in the industry grew by over £L 10 million between 1946 and 1952.[50] Export production was not particularly important for this industry because it enjoyed a domestic sellers’ market, not typical for most Lebanese domestic manufactures. However, Chekka also benefited from high regional demand for its commodities. Under trade controls during the early post-war period, Chekka was forbidden to export; but the regulations were frequently violated, for Lebanese suppliers could command higher prices for cement in neighbouring countries.[51] When cement exports were again permitted in the early 1950s, Chekka exported between 20,000 and 60,000 tons per annum during that period.[52]

Industrial renovation and expansion: incentives and constraints

The two largest incentives to industrial renovation and expansion in the early postwar period were positive expectations and large internal funds of industrial enterprises. Immediately after the war, many entrepreneurs believed that some form of market protection of industry would continue, thereby preserving domestic manufacturing share with its high revenues and profits. Acting on these expectations, they invested in an unprecedented expansion of plant, renovation of equipment and innovation of processes between 1945 and 1948, although capital goods were very expensive and required scarce hard currency from areas such as the USA and Britain.[53] This evolving trend was not deterred even as highly-competitive markets emerged: during the rapid growth of competitive consumer imports between 1948 and 1950, investment increased by £L 38 million or 34 per cent;[54] and in the readjustment period of 1950–2, capital increased by £L 53 million (about 12 per cent of industrial added value in that year).[55] It has been argued that Lebanese industrialists were risk-averse in investment behaviour and 'patrimonial' managers who focused on short-term profits.[56] These characteristics, however, were not dominant during the early postwar years, even after the emergence of greater uncertainty about markets and the long-term competitive position of Lebanese industry.[57] Nevertheless, with the surge of capital formation in other sectors of the economy, the share of industry in total net investment declined from over 14 per cent in 1950 to slightly less than 12 per cent in 1957.

Despite the early optimism, constraints on industrial expansion were significant. They included high costs, low productivity, a shortage of management skills, significant influence of concessionary companies in utilities and strategic areas of the economy and, most importantly, a narrowed internal market for domestic manufacturers. The high-cost structure within Lebanese manufacturing — derived from comparatively high-priced energy and labour (even though wages were falling) and its high dependence on costly imported raw materials — contributed to reduced competitiveness of industry. Moreover, high costs were combined with low productivity, as compared with more advanced industrial economies with which Lebanese products were frequently competing in domestic and regional markets. Although lower worker productivity was partially offset by wage differentials, these were not sufficient to reduce final prices to levels permitting Lebanese goods to compete on price advantage alone.

Table 6.15: *Lebanese industrial capacity, utilisation and consumption, 1949–50*

No. of enterprises, commodity and unit	Productive capacity	Productive utilisation	Domestic market consumption
2 Glue (tons)	350	120	150
4 Alcohol (tons)	2 000	800	600
4 Matches (boxes of 5000)	27 000	12 000	5 000
5 Cardboard (tons)	1 000	300	500
85 Printing (tons)	3 500	1 450	2 000
2 Aluminium ware (tons)	365	40	100
2 Radio sets (units)	15 000	1 431	3 500
2 Brush (units)	500 000	66 450	200 000
2 Spiral spring (tons)	500	210	250
4 Hardware (tons)	500	300	400
6 Nails and screws (tons)	1 925	879	750
2 Wire mills (tons)	1 200	132	1 200
41 Foundries (tons)	5 000	2 050	2 500
4 Boot lasts (pieces)	100 000	23 000	12 000
8 Wooden chairs (pieces)	350 000	100 000	60 000
3 Walnut sheets (sq. meters)	150 000	49 900	75 000
8 Paints (tons)	1 000	423	500
2 Calcium carbonate (tons)	1 000	500	350
53 Tanning (tons)	5 000	2 456	2 000
6 Cotton weaving (tons)	2 400	540	3 000
8 Cotton spinning (tons)	11 340	3 762	1 000
2 Wool weaving Tons)	250	70	350
17 Silk and rayon (tons)	2 500	1 000	2 000
35 Wine (litres)	1m	569 000	500 000
101 Arak (litres)	3m	1 163 000	1m
1 Sugar (tons)	18 000	3 100	18 000
141 Sweets (tons)	9 000	5 500	5 000
4 Chocolates (tons)	1 260	340	600
6 Macaroni (tons)	7 500	2 010	1 500
2 Jams (tons)	5 000	420	400
3 Biscuits (tons)	1 500	287	350
18 Vegetable oils (tons)	25 000	3 200	4 500
12 Perfumeries (litres)	450 000	100 000	250 000
50 Soap (tons)	18 000	6 500	6 000

Source: Association of Lebanese Industrialists, *Guide to Lebanon's Industries, 1949–50* (Beirut, 1950).

The greatest problem facing Lebanon's postwar industry, however, was a slackening internal demand for Lebanese manufactures, a sector that had organised itself around domestic production. With the increase in consumer imports, buyers' markets emerged in some goods that directly competed with local production. Other Lebanese products were severely hit by the loss or reduction of export markets to Palestine after 1948 and Syria after 1950. Lebanese industry required several years of adjustment to recover from these external shocks.

The loss of a large part of its common market, the Syrian hinterland, after the dissolution of the Customs Union in 1950, had a particularly negative impact on Lebanese industry, as suggested by anecdotal evidence from several Lebanese enterprises. In the pre-1950 period, Jabre Company (which produced processed foods, matches and candles), Abro Abroyan (producer of knitwear) and the National Underwear and Socks Company sold over half of their output in Syria; after separation in 1950, Syrian firms imported little from them, which had an immediate effect. They were forced to slash output, rapidly reorient production towards new markets and diversify their product lines. Another company, which fared slightly better, was Tchatalbashian, established in 1936 at Dora (outside Beirut), which manufactured box leather and soles. It was producing at full capacity in the years after the war; but after March 1950, with the loss of its primary market, Syria, it had to reduce production to one-third of capacity.[58] The majority of Lebanese manufacturers appear to have experienced similar declining conditions. Before the dissolution of the Customs Union, approximately 60 per cent of Lebanese manufactured goods were marketed in Syria.[59] At the same time, about 85 per cent of Lebanese cotton yarn was sold to Syria.[60] However, after 1950, many Lebanese industries were forced to lower output by between 35 and 75 per cent because of the closure of the Syrian market coming soon after the loss of the important Palestinian market.[61] As a result, in the early 1950s many industries were fighting for their very survival: they produced at losses in order to maintain their established markets, capital infrastructure and experienced workers until they could find new markets.

Industrialists consistently cited low capacity utilisation caused by market limitations as the number one problem of Lebanese industry in the early 1950s.[62] The nature of this constraint is readily illustrated by Table 6.15, showing the 1949–50 productive capacity and utilisation of Lebanese manufacturers of 34 important consumer goods; this is contrasted with Lebanese consumption of the products. For the overwhelming majority of these commodities, domestic productive capacity and utilisation exceeded domestic consumption. Hence, even without foreign competition, it would have been difficult to expand Lebanon's tiny consumer markets to levels required by Lebanon's industries.

Shift from import-substitution to export production for Middle East markets

With the narrowing of Lebanon's markets for domestic manufactures and the growth of manufacturing capacity, Lebanese industry had little choice but to reorient itself towards export production. Under these conditions, and in Lebanon's liberalised economic era of the 1950s, domestic manufacturers developed new export markets. Given Lebanon's competitive advantages in the region, based on growing networks and relationships among Lebanon's highly-skilled economic agents and regional counterparts and an economy that had achieved greater industrial, technical and economic progress than many of its neighbours, Middle East markets were an obvious partial solution. The infusion of oil income that created rising average incomes and new effective demand in many Middle East economies was a major stimulus to the growth of regional markets. Consequently, Lebanon was able to forge a new regional role by which it exchanged its higher value-added manufactures (and agriproducts) for raw materials and semi-finished goods; and at the same time it was expanding its function as an intermediary of goods and provider of services. In 1951, while Lebanon purchased about 32 per cent of its imports from the Middle East, a large share of which was oil and primary goods, it sold half of its exports to the region, including most of its manufactured exports, as well as processed foods, fresh fruits and vegetables.

Slow movement in traditional agriculture

Due to backward technical conditions, a high share of subsistence production and surplus labour in agriculture, the primary sector continued to decline in economic importance in relation to services and industry. At the same time, the primary sector supported almost half of the population. With a comparatively small capital base and low revenues and returns, particularly in traditional agriculture (comprising the largest share of the sector), it remained the weakest of the sectors by any criteria. However, a number of incentives, which will be discussed below, stimulated both private investment in an emerging modern agriculture and public agro-infrastructure investment, causing a surge in capital formation in this sector during the first decade after the war. Investment expanded production and improved cultivation techniques and technology; and productive and marketing organisation targeted export markets, especially for fruits and citrus. Nevertheless, growth in output and earnings on investment trailed the restructuring process due to time-lags and to high capital requirements to increase output and productivity (reflected by a rising capital–output ratio). Moreover, modernisation and reorganisation shifted the demand for labour, and at least initially, reduced growth in employment creation, thereby showing few positive effects on surplus labour and average worker incomes.

Table 6.16: *Income arising from agriculture, 1949 (£L)*

Gross agriculture income in national economy	178m
Net agriculture income in national economy	141m
Per-capita income of worker and family	500
Per-capita deficit of worker and family	580
Total per-capita expenditures of worker and family	1080
Per-capita income of landlord and family	5000

Source: Joseph Donato, 'Lebanon and its labour legislation', *International Labour Review*, vol. 55 (January 1952) pp. 66, 71.

Lebanon's Ministry of Agriculture estimates show that agriculture in 1946 contributed between 16 and 20 per cent to national income and that in 1947 approximately 600,000 persons or an estimated 50 per cent of the population were dependent upon agriculture for their livelihood.[63] This situation reflected high surplus labour in the most traditional sector of the economy: the productivity of small agricultural owners and workers farming about 300,000 hectares of land (of which 30,000 hectares were irrigated) was very low; and the situation was exacerbated by an annual growth in the rural population of an estimated 15,000 persons.[64] Moreover, as Table 6.16 highlights, the actual distribution of agricultural income was highly unequal: landowners earned ten times the amount of agricultural workers. Finally, income for both workers and owners in agriculture compared unfavourably with that derived from industry or commerce. In 1949, income in the trade sector exceeded by about £L 120 million that in agriculture with fewer dependent on trade than on agriculture. In the same year, the contribution of agriculture to NNP exceeded that of industry by only £L 23 million, although the sector supported 40 to 50 per cent of the population, compared with industry's 10 per cent. In 1951, the per-capita income in agriculture of £L 650 compared unfavourably with the £L 1400 in industry.[65]

Technical progress in agriculture lagged behind that in industry and the tertiary sector. Reflecting this state, agriculture was subjugated to natural forces of climate, weather and topography. Output fluctuated greatly from year to year, and some crops enjoyed good productive seasons only every other year — for example olives — because of the limited use of fertilisers and modern techniques. On the whole, agricultural methods and equipment remained primitive, as farmers followed centuries-old traditions; and a movement towards productive renovation was slow (see Figure 6.1).

Figure 6.1: *Farm machinery and the technical organisation of agriculture, 1951 (number)*

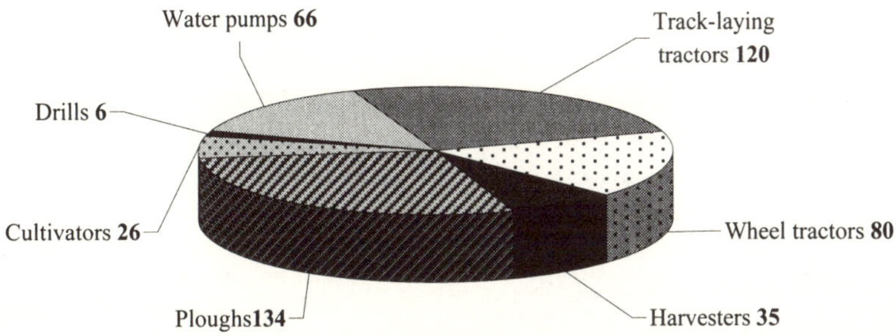

Source: USNA, RG59, 883A.3312/5–2451, 'Farm Machinery, Lebanon'.

The slow transformation of agriculture in Lebanon was due to two fundamental factors. First, there was a low investment–worker ratio: the majority of small owners–workers did not have access to credit at moderate interest rates, even if they had sufficient incentives to make long-term improvements. Thus, the production of grains, which were in high demand in the Lebanese domestic market, could have been tripled by mechanisation and other technical improvements.[66] But credit and incentive constraints impeded large investments. Second, there was the long time-lag before agricultural investments came on stream.

It is difficult to compare investment credit in agriculture with that flowing into other sectors because of the paucity of data. The *Report on Agricultural Credit in Lebanon* points out that competition among the sectors for credit was keen and that trade was favoured, as it required only short-term finance with its quick turnover and high profits. Industrialists also had greater access to capital because of their large war profits. Nevertheless, it is evident that only a very small share of total banking credit, £L 267 million at the end of 1952, flowed into the agrarian sector.[67] Reliable estimates of agricultural credit advanced by private sources such as landlords, moneylenders and merchants are also hard to come by, but the *Report on Agricultural Credit in Lebanon* cites a survey sample of 146 farms in the south Beka'a, which presents an interesting picture of loan capital and debt portfolios in this cereal growing region, as shown in Table 6.17.

This survey shows that private sources of working capital, mainly from moneylenders and landlords, provided the largest supply of agricultural credit. The *Report* also mentions that 'other banks' comprised essentially moneylenders, as indicated by the high rates of interest they charged. After compensating for the biases of this sample, it is possible to estimate that the amount of total debt of Lebanese farmers was between £L 30 million and £L 70 million. The upper limit would represent over a third of the annual income from agriculture. The survey also points out that less than a fifth of the farmers, a large proportion of whom worked holdings of between two and ten hectares, were not in debt, perhaps indicating that these holders had no access to credit at all.

The large and medium landowners benefited most from preferential credit extended by official institutions, such as the state-backed SCAIL. The south Beka'a sample shows that 60 per cent of total loan value extended by SCAIL was made to farmers who owned plots of land greater than 20 hectares. In general, the size of absolute debt correlated positively with the size of holdings. Larger and richer owners, with greater economic security and political influence, could typically obtain cheaper formal credit and larger loans than could a smaller farmer. In brief, a large share of state credit funds went to the large landowners.[68] While this might appear to be justified on commercial grounds — larger landowners would be most able to make repayments — in reality this was not always the case. Some powerful landlords had a record of defaulting on the loans because the government did not enforce repayment.[69] Thus, the system was weakened as revolving credit was not always replenished.[70]

Table 6.17: *Agricultural credit in the south Beka'a**

Source	Number of loans	Total value of loans (£L 000)	Share of total loans (%)	Average rate of interest (%)
Official banks	24	56.7	11.5	6.9
Other banks	42	195.9	40.0	18.5
Moneylenders	90	210.9	43.1	22.4**
Landlords	5	18.1	3.7	24.0**
Family and friends	17	8.1	1.7	3.3
TOTAL	178	489.7	100.0	–

Notes: *This is based on a survey of 146 farms in eight villages in south Beka'a. The report notes that this area might be unrepresentative of other agricultural regions, that these figures might exaggerate the degree of indebtedness and that the loans advanced by official banks in this survey are higher than for the rest of Lebanon. **Indicates that surveyors found significant numbers of cases in which the interest rate was much higher than this average.

Source: AUB, Economic Research Institute, *Report on Agricultural Credit in Lebanon*, Conference on Agricultural Credit (Beirut, 12–14 October 1953) Table VII.

The survey also shows that smaller holders paid much higher rates of interest, on average, than larger owners. Though the legal maximum rate of interest was 9 per cent per annum, actual rates fluctuated greatly and generally exceeded that limit many times. An estimated 80 to 90 per cent of all loans were extended by private banks, moneylenders, merchants and landlords; the private banks charged 18 per cent per annum interest, and the moneylenders, merchants and landlords 25–30 per cent and more.[71] In contrast, a government-guaranteed loan cost 4.8 per cent per annum, and credit from SCAIL and the BSL 8.5 per cent and 7–9 per cent respectively.[72] Borrowers increasingly repaid loans in cash, as repayment in kind was generally far more costly and often fraught with hidden charges. As the Agricultural Credit Conference attested, the small owner of less than ten hectares constituted the heart of Lebanon's agricultural credit problem.[73] Because the small owner represented a very large and problematic part of agriculture, restructuring this sector could only be slow and difficult. Specifically, with limited availability of long-term credit, farmers tended to borrow only for current operations. The impact of this was to retard the expansion of irrigation projects, terracing of slopes and mechanisation. In addition, because the farmers could not normally repay one-year loans out of their current incomes, they tended to renew their loans, thus increasing their total debt burden. In effect, they used medium-term loans to finance short-term needs. This only perpetuated a vicious cycle of underdevelopment.

The second factor affecting agricultural transformation was the long time required for investments to come on stream and become profitable. Large and medium Lebanese rural landowners invested in export-oriented fruit and vegetable production; but tree cultivation, irrigation and the introduction of modern methods to produce fruits and vegetables comprised long-term investments. Many owners did not see results in increased output, revenues and profits for a decade or more. The long time-lag between investment and project maturation affected investment behaviour: the Keynesian problem of short-run conditions determining long-run investment decisions was clearly operative in this situation.

For the analyst, this gap distorts the picture of the state of Lebanese agriculture and its pace of change. Nevertheless, it is evident that despite the many constraints, a modern sector of agriculture was emerging in Lebanon by the early 1950s. Based on expectations of good revenues and profits — stimulated by the success of California fruit imports and aggressive Italian marketing of fruit trees — the Lebanese had begun to invest in the fruit industry even before the Second World War.[74] Although the introduction of new fruit varieties such as peaches, cherries, pears and apples was experimental, fruit production increasingly replaced traditional crops such as cereals and mulberry tree cultivation. Citrus fruits, vegetables and bananas (which were cultivated as quick cash crops) dominated coastal agricultural regions.[75] After the war, relatively large investment flowed into irrigation projects and the building or repairing of mountain terraces. This facilitated the expansion of fruits and vegetables in comparison with cereals and legumes, which did not require such attention. As a result of the thousands of fruit trees that were planted each year after the war, by 1948/9, fruit production had become economically important in southern Lebanon, Mount Lebanon, the Beka'a and the coastal regions; and it represented 40 to 50 per cent of total agricultural production.[76] As irrigation projects were extended, crops such as citrus fruits, bananas, apples and pears, grown on the fertile coastal plain, were to double their output in future years.

Agro-export production for regional markets

Similar to manufacturing, the expansion of Lebanon's fruit and vegetable industries depended on high penetration of neighbouring markets. With market development, Egypt imported significant quantities of Lebanese fruits, and Syria and the Arab Gulf purchased large amounts of both fruits and vegetables.[77] Lebanon's agricultural dependence on neighbouring markets was underlined during the customs separation from Syria. The Lebanese fruit industry was hard hit by the loss of the Syrian market, causing the ruin of large quantities of fruit, a decline in prices and a difficult period of adjustment. In fact, in 1950 and 1951 the government was forced to subsidise exports of surplus fruit. By 1952, the market had adjusted to these conditions, and the majority of Lebanese citrus was temporarily exported to France and Czechoslovakia. Just as the cultivation of potatoes, onions and legumes in the Beka'a and Mount Lebanon had been encouraged during the war by profitable Allied military contracts, regional demand for these products sustained their production after the war.

Conclusion

This chapter has presented empirical data on the effects of Lebanon's open and deregulated institutional environment on its postwar economic order. In an open environment with expanded regional opportunities that offered on average higher profits and lower risks than either domestic industry or agriculture, Lebanese merchants, bankers and intermediaries rapidly resumed, and then greatly expanded, what they knew best — trade, finance and services. Under these conditions in which Lebanon's service economy thrived, industry and agriculture were able to grow and make important structural changes. On the whole, however, they lagged behind the tertiary sector.

Building what came to be known as the Merchant Republic — based on an idealised version of the Swiss model — was a strategic objective of a small power bloc consisting of the mercantile–financial bourgeoisie, much of the governing elite and intellectual economic liberals. In this model, the state assumed little responsibility for development: Lebanese economic growth and change was achieved primarily through private domestic and foreign capital. The state assumed greater obligations for physical infrastructure and activities, which the private sector could not or would not undertake.

Arising from this environment was rapid growth in financial, commercial and other services, which dominated the Lebanese economy for more than a decade. In the decade of building and realising the Merchant Republic (1948 to 1958) on an annualised average basis, tertiary activities contributed 61 per cent to national income. Moreover, exported services and imported capital greatly reduced the impact of Lebanon's large merchandise trade deficit and averted the development of an exchange constraint. From 1951 to 1957, when Lebanon's trade deficits were in excess of £L 4300 million, exported services, capital inflows, emigrants' remittances and charitable private donations more than offset the commercial deficit. With the wide ranging opportunities presented to Lebanon's economic agents, the Merchant Republic flourished in its golden age of the 1950s, only to be abruptly halted in 1958 by the first of many crises. The 1958 civil war gave greater credence to a challenging position that questioned the sustainability of Lebanon's outward-looking economic order, providing the means and will to modify that order in the following Shehabist years.

CHAPTER SEVEN

The Lebanese Economic Model: An Evaluation

Throughout this work, it has been argued that a constellation of internal and external forces evolving in Lebanon since the nineteenth century created an outward-looking environment, which initiated its future path. After the establishment of an independent Lebanese state, this environment shaped an economic model that achieved its ultimate expression in the 1950s' Merchant Republic. We have emphasised the roles of economic agents, institutions and organisations in the creation of this environment; and, in turn, they influenced and interacted with the dynamics of growth and structural change in the Lebanese economy. Building on a real and imagined past, an outward-looking Lebanese elite assumed control of the political economy in 1947. It set out to develop an economic order based on free trade, minimum regulatory institutions and private sector activities concentrated around Beirut's *entrepôt* and regional intermediary positions. Despite opposition to and temporary reversals of this economic path, the Merchant Republic became a reality, and to some a 'Lebanese miracle', in the 1950s.

This work will be concluded with an assessment of the strategy used to achieve Lebanon's open service-oriented economy in its golden age, 1948 to 1958. Due to weak economic data and the lack of comparable cross-sectional data, simple criteria will be used in this evaluation. First, policy performance will be examined: how well the strategy performed according to its own internal logic and objectives. Second, the effects of the model on economic performance, namely on growth, structural change and macroeconomic stability, will be summarised.

Policy assessment

Embracing the vision expounded by Lebanon's 'New Phoenicians' of developing a mercantile capitalist economy, Lebanon's leadership had little choice but to establish economic policies that would support a strong currency, mobilise domestic private capital and attract foreign investment, promote a growing variety of service exports and maintain healthy fiscal and external accounts. From 1947 to 1957, both the Khoury and Chamoun administrations adopted policies based on these general principles. Consequently, macroeconomic fundamentals improved, as policies and institutions sustained a strong gold-backed currency, a market-based exchange rate, low (if repressed) inflation, and surplus fiscal budgets. Further, this economic environment instilled international confidence in Lebanon. These guiding policies did not aim at promoting socio-political stability in the new nation-state, nor at executing public development programmes. Instead, the power bloc attempted to counter opposition to negative economic outcomes by a generous application of patron-client politics and pork-barrel projects.

Financial stabilisation

In terms of one very high priority, the establishment of a strong and stable Lebanese currency that facilitated international trade, finance and services, policy formulation and execution was highly successful. From a position during the mandatory years of 1920 to 1939 when the Lebanese pound was depreciated by about 82 per cent *vis-à-vis* the dollar,[1] it was stabilised between 1950 and 1958 around a target rate of £L 3 = US$ 1; it fluctuated from an average low free market value of £L 3.80 = US$ 1 in 1951 to an average high free market rate of £L 3.16 = US$ 1 in 1958. Beyond creating greater currency stability, these policies attracted large capital inflows, which contributed to large surpluses in Lebanon's capital account — as shown in Table 7.1. The growth of surpluses and gold reserves also endowed policy-makers with a higher degree of control over money management.

However, for other reasons, Lebanese financial management was constrained, resulting in what Raymond Mallat characterised as 'money muddling'. A major limitation was the role of the French-controlled BSL, which operated as Lebanon's bank of issue and lender of last resort until 1964 when Lebanon's first central bank was established. The BSL largely determined money supply and credit policies in Lebanon; but its primary role as a foreign commercial bank often conflicted with its status as Lebanon's quasi-central bank.[2] Reflecting its commercial logic, the BSL did not intervene to counter cyclical effects of the economy: it refused to extend additional credit to the banking system, except in very critical periods, such as the Suez and 1958 crises, when runs on the banks by depositors threatened the solvency of the system.[3] Yet, operating as Lebanon's *de facto* central bank, it interfered in numerous internal matters. For example, during the 1948/9 recession, when local and regional demand for imports (a glut of which were stored at the port of Beirut) was declining and world commodity prices were falling, BSL director-general René Busson unilaterally implemented deflationary policies: he ordered the BSL to contract the money supply by between £L 1 million and £1.5 million per month to force Lebanese speculators to liquidate their large holdings of gold and assets, to pay off their bank loans and to clear warehoused goods at the port of Beirut.[4] By tightening credit to reduce speculative activity in the economy, Busson argued that he was furthering his vision of Lebanon as a 'sort of Singapore' of the Middle East.[5]

Table 7.1: *International balance of payments in selected years, 1951–8 (£Lm)*

	1951	1955	1957	1958
Current account	*–61*	*–176*	*–205*	*–295*
Merchandise	–311	–497	–549	–556
Non-monetary gold	1	–4	–34	–7
Investment revenue	4	40	60	39
Other*	245	285	318	229
Capital account	*80*	*208*	*243*	*309*
Emigrant remittances	54	85	91	72
ODA**	1	24	43	81
Non-governmental assistance	10	19	25	12
Capital movements	15	80	84	144
Balance	*19*	*32*	*38*	*14*

Note: *Other includes foreign travel, transport and insurance, government, and transit and other services (all in surplus); **official government development assistance.

Source: IRFED, *Besoins et possibilités*, vol. 1, Table 223.

With few monetary levers in the hands of the government, repressed inflationary pressures re-emerged in the Lebanese economy. These conditions were essentially a result of (1) a large flow of hot capital into Lebanon, which could not be intermediated into productive investments because of its short-term character and, typically, it was not sterilised through open market operations or other measures; and (2) a real growth rate of NNP which trailed the expansion of the money supply. From 1948 to 1958, the money supply expanded by an annual average compounded rate of 11 per cent, while national income grew by 4.9 per cent

Table 7.2: *Money supply, liquidity, inflation, 1948–58*

Year	MS (£Lm)	MS index[1]	NNP(cp, £Lm)	Lqty (%)[2]	Lqty index[1]	BC index	Ct NNP index[1]	Wp index[3]	Infln index[4]	CoL index[1]
1948	382	100	919	42	100	100	–	–	–	100
1949	347	91	932	37	90	122	–	–	–	94
1950	410	107	1042	39	94	125	100	100	107	87
1951	465	121	1086	43	103	142	79	124	153	94
1952	510	133	1115	46	111	159	90	116	147	94
1953	537	140	1168	46	111	160	109	103	128	88
1954	665	174	1256	53	127	197	126	95	138	84
1955	774	202	1374	56	136	237	137	96	147	85
1956	844	220	1417	59	143	259	135	101	162	90
1957	1008	263	1503	67	162	317	140	103	187	96
1958	1083	282	1325	82	197	313	122	104	231	100

Notes: MS = money supply; cp = current prices; Lqty = liquidity; BC = bank credit; Ct = constant; Wp = wholesale price; Infln = inflation; CoL = cost of living; NNP = net national product; (1) 1948=100; (2) Liquidity = Money supply/Current NNP; (3) 1950 = 100; (4) Inflation index = Money supply index/Constant NNP index.

Source: Mallat, *70 Years of Money Muddling*, Tables 1, 2, 3, pp. 198–200; Table 1B, p. 186.

Table 7.3: *Compound growth rates of selected variables, 1948–58 (%)*

Year	Money supply	Constant NNP	Liquidity	Bank credit	Wholesale prices
1948	3.5	–	–	110.3	–
1949	–9.1	–	–1.0	22.0	–
1950	18.1	–	–4.4	2.9	–
1951	13.4	–20.8	9.6	13.6	24.0
1952	9.7	13.5	7.8	11.9	–6.4
1953	5.3	20.9	0	0.3	–11.2
1954	23.8	16.4	14.4	22.9	–7.8
1955	16.4	8.3	7.1	20.5	1.0
1956	9.9	–1.8	5.1	9.1	5.2
1957	19.4	3.8	13.3	22.3	2.0
1958	7.4	–12.7	21.6	–1.0	–1.0

Note: NNP = net national product.

Source: Mallat, *70 Years of Money Muddling*, Table 4, p. 201.

and real per-capita income grew at 2.6 per cent. The resulting inflationary pressures in the economy were repressed through Lebanon's continuous external surpluses, a share of which were utilised to build up Lebanon's official gold reserves until 1955 (when the gold cover stood at 95 per cent of note issue), and to supply foreign exchange to meet rising local demand through imports.[6] From this point of view, policies supporting the gold cover and a large volume of imports were essential to maintain financial stability of the system. In particular, legally-mandated gold coverage of the Lebanese pound, which operated through mechanisms similar to the traditional gold standard, disciplined Lebanon's financial system. Nevertheless, latent inflationary pressures remained in the economy, as indicated by the liquidity ratios and inflation indices, both of which more than doubled from 1950 to 1958, as shown in Tables 7.2 and 7.3.

Fiscal policies and development

Lebanon's fiscal policies between 1948 and 1958 can only be described as conservative, deflationary and designed to promote trade and services.[7] Unlike stylised fiscal management in the East Asian export-oriented model, Lebanon's budgetary management was not conducive to industrialisation and employment creation. Although Lebanon's private credit system favoured tertiary over other economic activities, the government did not try to offset negative consequences by employing fiscal policies to develop labour-intensive, export-oriented industry (as in the East Asian model) or to transform traditional agriculture. Given Lebanon's economic model and the primary roles of the private domestic and foreign sectors, public spending was concentrated on meeting the physical infrastructure needs of rapidly growing trade and services. Policy-makers did not seek to fund publicly other (large) supply-side requirements of industrialisation, nor to fill any investment gap in industry and agriculture, which required much larger capital flows and stocks with their higher capital-output ratios than the tertiary sector. Moreover, these expenditure policies were not counterbalanced by tax and other measures to encourage private investment in the neglected sectors. Consequently, as one analyst has argued: 'Commercialisation remains the major source of economic activity, while industry and technology show little advance.'[8]

Employment

While Lebanon's model of an open service-oriented economy was relatively successful in mobilising and intermediating financial capital, it paid little attention to developing human capital and employing its labour force effectively. Typical of underdeveloped economies, surplus labour in Lebanon's traditional agriculture sector was high.[9] Nor was employment creation in other sectors a high priority of the state. Without investment incentives for the expansion of labour-intensive industries, their growth in Lebanon was too slow to absorb more than a fraction of labour in the traditional sector. Furthermore, the fastest growing areas of the economy, finance, transport and trade, simply did not have the job-generating capacity on the scale that was necessary to absorb the unemployed, underemployed and new members of the labour force. Thus, Lebanon's time-honoured method of dealing with this problem, large-scale emigration, continued.

Table 7.4: *Employment and incomes in agriculture, industry and commerce, 1949*[a]

Category	Agriculture	Industry	Commerce
Persons directly engaged in work in sector	250 000[b]	45 000–50 000	130 000[c]
Persons dependent on sector	500 000	140 000	600 000
Per capita income per workers and families (£L)	500	750	1 000
Per capita expenditure per workers and families (£L)	1 080	1 440	1 440
Per capita income/owners, merchants and families (£L)	5 000	17 000	7 000

Notes: (a) Lebanese population in 1949 = 1.4 million; active workforce = 665,000; unemployed and inactive population = 735,000; (b) 160,000 workers + 90,000 landowners; (c) 100,000 clerks, shop assistants and so forth + 30,000 merchants.

Source: Donato, 'Lebanon and its labour legislation'; UN, *Review of Economic Conditions in the Middle East*, 1951–2.

There are no reliable statistics on unemployment during this period, but a number of analysts have estimated the rate at 6–7 per cent.[10] On the surface, this appears moderate, but its actual impact was greater for two main reasons. First, with the high share of youth in the population, labour participation was relatively small, composing about 28 per cent of the total population, compared with 40 per cent in the USA in this period.[11] In absolute numbers, those seeking employment was low; but at the same time, the employed had to support a high ratio of dependants, spreading the effects of unemployment. Second, the greater problem in Lebanon, as in most LDCs, was that of underemployment. Lebanon's traditional agriculture sector (under-) employed a large share of the labour force; but with low productivity, it created a much smaller share of value-added than the other two major sectors. However, Lebanon differed from many other LDCs in that its most rapid and dynamic economic growth was occurring in the non-labour-intensive service and foreign sectors. This model of growth did not promote structural change typical in the industrialisation process, whereby labour is transferred from traditional agriculture into modern industry, and later, as average incomes rise, into services. Instead, agricultural workers, who supplemented their incomes with off-farm activities, remained a large part of the economy. Due to heightened foreign competition, increased capital intensity of the larger, modern and profitable manufacturing sectors (for example cement and textiles) and stagnation of small and technically backward industries (for example soap, glass and leather), employment in manufacturing did not absorb a significant share of the growing labour force.

Figure 7.1: *Distribution of labour force and income, 1959 (%)*

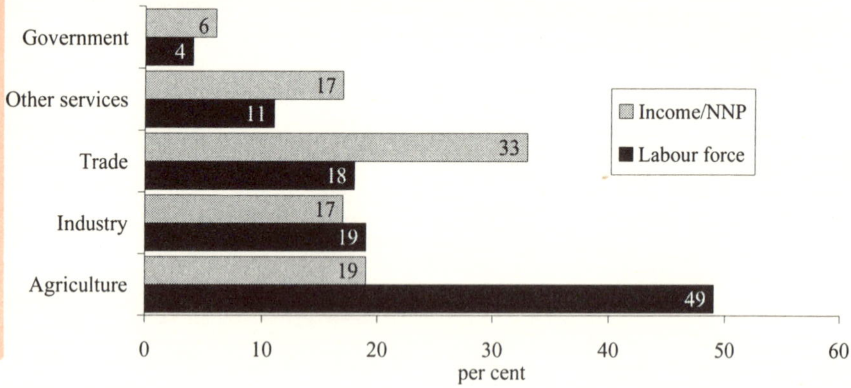

Note: Industry = manufacturing, handicrafts, construction; Trade = internal and external trade, transportation and banking; Other services = tourism, finance and other services.

Source: IRFED, *Besoins et possibilités*, vol. 1, p. 13; Medawar, *Monetary Problems in Lebanon*, Table 3, p. 12.

Table 7.4 provides data on employment and incomes in the three major sectors of the economy in 1949. Figure 7.1, which shows the distribution of Lebanon's labour force and income by sector in 1959, indicates high under-employment and low productivity in the agriculture sector and comparatively low labour intensity in the high-income sectors of trade and services.

Income distribution

Following its economic philosophy and interests, the governing elite neither formulated nor executed policies to reduce income inequality in Lebanon. The impact of income inequality on Lebanese society during this period is difficult to evaluate, but for reasons that went far beyond the economic, it probably contributed significantly to latent instability.

In 1954, the top 4 per cent of Beirut households earned incomes of over £L 25,000, while the bottom 65 per cent earned less than £L 5000, the poverty line set for Beirut households.[12] This pattern of income distribution continued into the next decade. As Table 7.5 shows, in 1960, income distribution in Lebanon was such that the top 5 per cent of the Lebanese population received 35 per cent of national income; the lowest 20 per cent only 7 per cent; and almost 50 per cent of Lebanon's population were under the national poverty line. Lebanon's Gini coefficient ratio of .537 suggests relatively high inequality, comparable, however, to many Latin American and Middle Eastern countries in that period.

Table 7.5: *Income distribution, 1960*

Population share in national income		Gini coefficient
Lowest 20%	Top 5%	
7%	35%	0.537*

Income level (£L)	*Share of population (%)*
1200 or less (destitute)	9
1200–2500 (poor)	40
2500–5000 (average)	30
5000–15 000 (well-off)	14
15 000 or more (rich)	4

Note: *1955–60.

Sources: Issawi, *An Economic History of the Middle East and North Africa* (New York, 1982) Table A. 4, p. 232; B. J. Odeh, *Lebanon Dynamics of Conflict* (London, 1985) Table 15, p. 69.

Although there are no reliable data showing income distribution during the 1940s, it would appear that it became more unequal during and after the Second World War. Several hypotheses may explain this development. First, supply and demand forces were in severe disequilibrium in Lebanon's closed war economy, which favoured producers over consumers and capital over labour, leading to a greater rise of profits than wages in total factor income. This trend was reinforced by consumer inflation that outpaced wage rises. Second, it reflects the nature of the engine of growth in Lebanon's postwar economy — namely, foreign services that permitted high profits and savings by merchants and bankers, but had small effects on employment absorption and average incomes. Both these trends increased profits absolutely and relatively, compared with wages. Thus, while real national and per-capita income increased significantly between 1948 and 1958, the relative shares appear to have shifted in favour of the top 5 per cent of the population, who owned and controlled commercial, financial and industrial enterprises, large landholdings and real estate in Beirut and Mount Lebanon, and against the bottom 20 per cent of the population, who were mainly small agricultural producers and urban workers.

Investment, growth and structural change

The pattern of investment in Lebanon, shown in Table 7.6, helps explain the structure and rate of growth during this period. The data show that average annual net capital formation in Lebanon (NCF/NNP) during the period between 1950 and 1957 was 14.3 per cent, comparing favourably with many low- and middle-income countries attempting to industrialise at that time (but did not approach East Asian NIE rates of between 25 and 30 per cent after the 1960s). The sectoral composition of capital investment was highly concentrated: over two-thirds of investment between 1950 and 1957 flowed into the communications and transport infrastructure and service-oriented activities. While agriculture received about 9 per cent and industry a little over 10 per cent of total investment, more than a third

Table 7.6: *Capital formation, 1950–7 (£Lm)*

Year	NCF	NCF/NNP (%)	NCF/GNP (%)	A	I	T	C&S	PA	RE
1950	160	15.4	20.8	12	23	8	13	30	74
1951	131	12.1	17.8	14	15	15	14	22	69
1952	150	13.5	19.0	15	15	14	14	18	74
1953	155	13.3	19.0	17	15	16	15	23	69
1954	165	13.1	18.8	20	15	18	16	25	71
1955	206	15.0	19.9	15	13	17	14	48	98
1956	225	15.9	21.4	22	24	19	19	49	92
1957	233	15.5	21.0	18	27	15	17	53	103
TOTAL	1425	14.3*	19.7*	133	147	122	122	268	633

Notes: NCF = net capital formation; NNP = net national product; GNP = gross national product; A = agriculture; I = industry; T = transport; C&S = commerce and services; PA = public administration; RE = real estate development; *annual average, 1950–7.

Source: Albert Badre, 'Economic development of Lebanon', in Charles Cooper and Sidney Alexander (eds) *Economic Development and Population Growth in the Middle East* (New York, 1972) Table 4–3, p. 186; IRFED, *Besoins et possibilités*, vol. 1, Table 24 and vol. 2, Table 33.

of all capital was invested in real-estate development, mainly for the construction of hotels in Beirut. Investment categorised as public administration and transport in Table 7.6 is weighted heavily towards infrastructural development that promoted trade, tourism and other services, for example Beirut International Airport, Beirut and Tripoli ports, and a road and highway network centred around Beirut.

Figure 7.2: *Incremental capital–output ratios by sector, 1950–7*

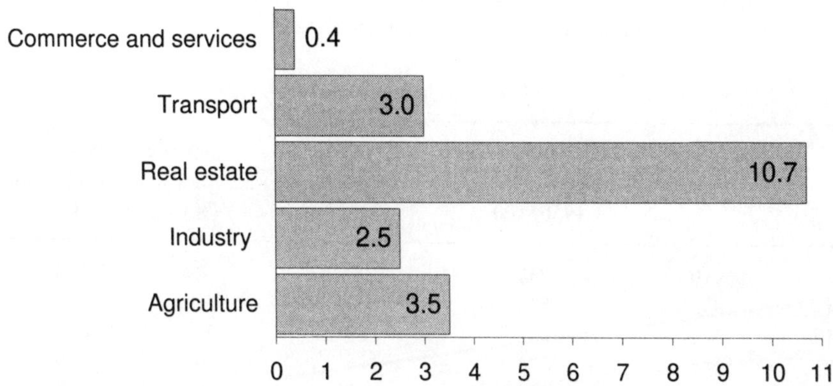

Source: IRFED, *Besoins et possibilités*, vol. 2, Table 33.

The high variation of the incremental capital-output ratios (ICOR) of the economic sectors, as shown in Figure 7.2, exacerbated the constraints of this pattern of investment. Commerce and services with a much lower ICOR of 0.4 were able to expand output with far less investment (and equally, with the same amount of investment, would create between 6.25 and 8.75 times more output) than agriculture and industry with capital-output ratios of 3.5 and 2.5 respectively. Hence, the £L 122 million investment in commerce and services in the 1950–7 period produced an additional output of £L 305 million; the £L 133 million of agriculture an additional £L 38 million; and the £L 147 million in industry an additional £L 59 million. Long-run expectations of high growth and profits in tourism explain the high rate of investment in real-estate development and construction with a capital–output ratio of 10.7. High profits and rapid turnover rates encouraged investment in other services. By contrast, lower incentives, such as lower profits and higher uncertainty, and higher capital requirements in agriculture and manufacturing reduced their attractiveness to potential investors.

From 1948 to 1958, Lebanon experienced strong but variable economic growth, as shown in Table 7.7 and Figure 7.3. The annual average compounded rate of real growth (based on constant 1950 prices) from 1948 to 1958 was 4.9 per cent.

Excluding the crisis year of 1958, the more representative period of 1948 to 1957 shows a rate of 7.3 per cent. These data mask high variance (the coefficient of variation of the compound rate of growth of NNP from 1948 to 1959 is 132 per cent). This is due to the variation between high growth periods of 1949–50 when the economy was favoured by large capital inflows (due primarily to the events in Palestine and Syria) and several years in the 1950s when the stimulating effects of liberalisation began to take hold, on the one hand, and the deflationary years of the post-Customs Union adjustment after March 1950, the post-Korean War recession, the Suez crisis in 1956, and the 1958 civil war, on the other.

Table 7.7: *Growth of net national product, 1948–59*

Year	NNP (current prices, £Lm)	NNP (constant prices, £Lm) 1950=100	Implicit price deflator 1950 = 100	Constant NNP rate of growth (%)	Per-capita real income (£L)
1948	919	747	123	–	618
1949	932	836	108	11.9	697
1950	1042	1042	100	24.6	828
1951	1086	934	116	–10.4	726
1952	1115	994	112	6.4	753
1953	1168	1143	102	15.0	844
1954	1256	1312	96	14.8	915
1955	1374	1417	95	8.0	966
1956	1417	1384	102	–2.3	923
1957	1503	1408	107	1.7	918
1958	1325	1207	109	–14.3	769
1959	1500	1336	112	10.7	832

Note: NNP = net national product.

Source: Medawar, *Monetary Problems in Lebanon*, Table 5.

The variability of economic growth reflects to a large extent external shocks rather than domestic cyclical forces. The growth of income was highly correlated with the inflow of foreign capital (and foreign expenditures concentrated in Beirut). Growth declined sharply during internal political and foreign crises primarily because of their impact on triangular trade and foreign-oriented services such as tourism (see Figure 7.4 and Table 7.8).[13] By the mid-1950s, total trade growth was also affected by a slow decline in transit trade activities due to increasing competition of neighbouring seaports and a number of Syrian restrictions on the use of its transit facilities.[14]

Figure 7.3: *Average annual compounded rate of growth of selected variables, 1948–57* (%)*

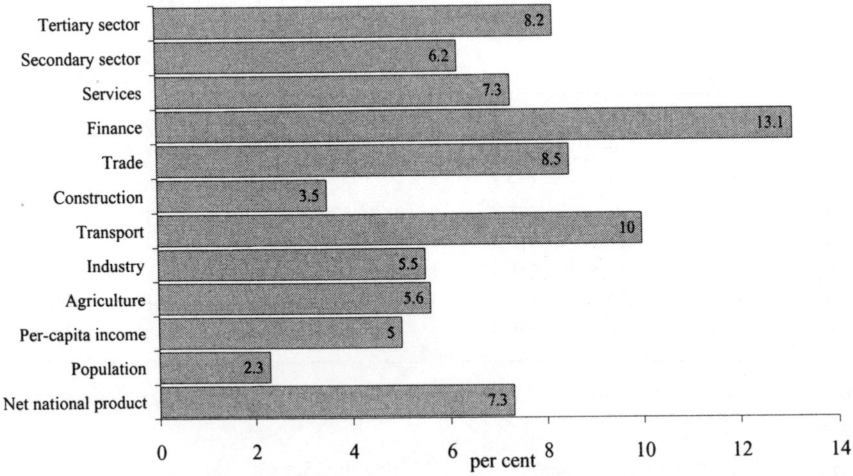

Note: *Based on constant 1950 prices.

Source: Data from IRFED, *Besoins et possibilités*, vol. 1, Table 23; Medawar, *Monetary Problems in Lebanon*, Table 2.

Figure 7.4: *Estimated direct expenditures of tourists, 1951–8 (£Lm)*

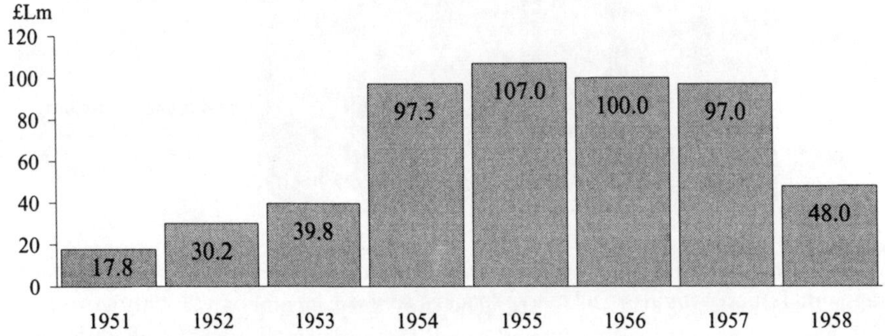

Source: Mallat, *70 Years of Money Muddling*, Table 18, p.45.

Clearly, Lebanon's external services sector was the economy's growth pole in the 1950s: growth was led by foreign-oriented tertiarisation. The ratio of added value in the tertiary sector to total NNP grew from 59 per cent in 1948 to 62.8 per cent in 1958, while similar ratios of agriculture and secondary activities declined from 18.4 per cent to 16.5 per cent and from 22.6 per cent to 20.7 per cent,

Table 7.8: *Evolution of trade, 1951–8 (£Lm)*

Year	Imports	Exports	Deficit	X/M (%)	M/NNP (%)	X/NNP (%)	Re-exports	Transit
1951	514.1	97.6	416.5	19	47	9	14.2	1970.5
1952	531.0	77.6	453.4	15	48	7	36.7	1735.7
1953	511.3	86.7	424.6	17	44	7	19.6	1659.9
1954	651.0	105.6	545.4	16	52	9	20.4	1518.9
1955	733.0	120.6	612.4	16	53	9	24.2	1698.8
1956	762.1	145.8	616.3	19	54	10	21.5	1617.8
1957	857.5	152.3	705.2	18	57	10	37.4	1808.1
1958	719.0	110.5	608.5	15	54	8	23.5	1418.5

Notes: X = Exports; M = Imports; NNP = Net national product. Values are based on the free market exchange rate.

Source: IRFED, *Besoins et possibilités*, vol. 1, Tables 74–75.

Figure 7.5: *Sectoral contribution to net national product, 1948–58 (%)*

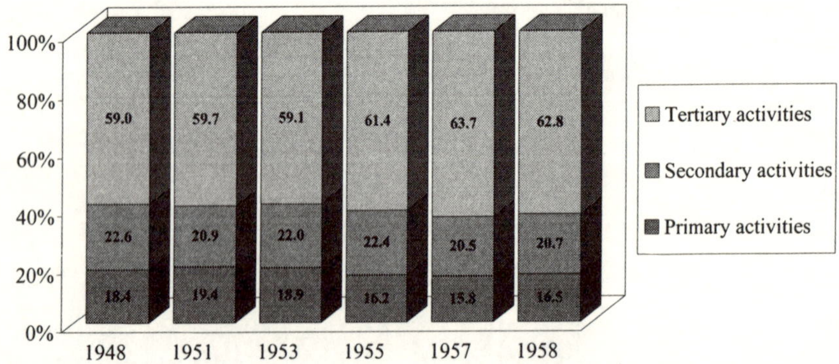

Notes: Primary activities = agriculture; Secondary activities = industry, construction and transport; Tertiary activities = all other economic sectors.

Source: Mallat, *70 Years of Money Muddling*, Table 1, p. 13.

respectively, as shown in Figure 7.5 and Table 7.9. This shift in sectoral composition reflects the higher rate of growth of tertiary activities, as compared with agriculture and industry. Between 1948 and 1957, real income in the tertiary sector grew at a compounded rate of 8.18 per cent per annum, compared with 5.56

Table 7.9: *NNP by industrial sector, 1948–58 (current prices in £Lm and share in total NNP)*

	A	%	I	%	C	%	TD	%	F	%	TN	%	RE	%	S	%	G	%
1948	169	18.4	134	14.5	35	3.8	261	28.4	35	3.8	40	4.3	91	9.9	91	9.9	63	6.9
1949	159	17.1	136	14.6	32	3.4	278	30	35	3.7	41	4.4	93	10	93	10	65	6.9
1950	206	19.7	141	13.5	43	4.1	300	28.8	40	3.8	44	4.1	96	9.2	100	9.6	72	6.9
1951	211	19.4	147	13.5	35	3.2	337	31	46	4.2	46	4.2	97	8.9	103	9.5	64	5.9
1952	216	19.3	155	13.9	48	4.3	333	29.8	50	4.5	45	4	98	8.8	106	9.5	64	5.7
1953	221	18.9	161	13.7	47	4	344	29.4	51	4.3	50	4.3	101	8.6	122	10.5	71	6.1
1954	226	18	166	13.2	60	4.7	368	29.3	57	4.5	60	4.7	112	8.8	134	10.6	73	5.8
1955	223	16.2	175	12.7	60	4.3	407	29.6	70	5.1	75	5.4	116	8.4	165	12	83	6.0
1956	231	16.3	183	12.9	50	3.5	410	28.8	80	5.6	78	5.5	130	9.2	160	11.3	95	6.7
1957	238	15.8	189	12.5	41	2.7	469	31.2	91	6	80	5.3	139	9.2	148	9.8	108	7.2
1958	219	16.5	181	13.6	38	2.8	365	27.5	93	7	57	4.3	155	11.7	104	7.8	113	8.5

Notes: A = agriculture; I = industry; C = construction; TD = trade; F = finance; TN = transport; RE = real estate; S = services; G = government; NNP = net national product.

Source: Albert Badre, American University of Beirut, Economic Research Institute.

Table 7.10: *Growth rates of NNP by sector, 1949–58 (%)*

Year	A	I	C	TD	F	TN	RE	S	G	NNP
1949	–5.9	1.5	–8.6	6.5	0.0	2.5	2.2	2.2	3.2	1.4
1950	29.6	3.7	34.4	7.9	14.3	7.3	3.2	7.5	10.8	11.8
1951	2.4	4.3	–18.6	12.3	15.0	4.5	1.0	3.0	–11.1	4.2
1952	2.4	5.4	37.0	–1.2	8.7	–2.2	1.0	2.9	0.0	2.7
1953	2.3	3.9	–2.1	3.3	2.0	11.1	3.1	15.1	10.9	4.8
1954	2.3	3.1	27.7	7.0	11.8	20.0	10.9	9.8	2.8	7.5
1955	1.3	5.4	0.0	10.6	22.8	25.0	3.6	23.1	13.7	9.4
1956	3.6	4.6	–16.7	0.1	14.3	4.0	12.1	–3.0	9.6	3.1
1957	3.0	3.3	–18	14.4	13.8	2.6	6.9	–7.5	13.7	6.1
1958	–8.0	–3.7	–7.3	–22.2	2.2	–28.8	11.5	–29.7	4.6	–11.8

Notes: A = agriculture; I = industry; C = construction; TD = Trade; F = finance; TN = transport; RE = real estate; S = services; G = government; NNP = net national product.

Source: Data from Table 7.9.

per cent in agriculture and 5.53 per cent in industry. The following data reflect the influential economic role of the foreign and tertiary sectors: even in the crisis year of 1958, net foreign private capital of £L 144 million (much of which flowed into property and services), or almost 11 per cent of NNP, entered Lebanon's economy; Lebanon imported £L 719 million of goods (or 54 per cent of NNP); and the value-added of the trade and financial sectors amounted to £L 458 million, or almost 35 per cent of NNP. The Lebanese miracle was without doubt based on Beirut's intermediary position that made possible the high growth of income in financial and commercial services, construction, transport and communications. It diverged greatly from structural changes normally associated with economic modernisation (industrialisation): that is, a relatively rapid rise in investment, employment and value-added in the manufacturing sector; a decline in the weight of the primary sector; the transfer of surplus labour from the traditional to modern sectors, thereby increasing labour productivity; and a growth in domestic services with the secular rise of internal demand.[15]

Final remarks

Lebanon's choice and implementation of a service-oriented open-economy model was successful in the medium run: in the first decade after the Second World War, it created and institutionalised a 'Merchant Republic' political economy that supported Lebanese sovereignty and material sustainability. Though this economic order had been 'enabled' by an environment that had evolved over a long period of time, its expression during its golden age of 1948–58 bears the distinct stamp of Lebanon's outward-looking economic and political elite of the early post-independence period. Applying a strategy that exploited the shifting conditions of the Middle East, Lebanon's competitive advantages in the region, and information, skills and networks of its dominant economic agents, Lebanon's policy-makers buttressed the country's economic position by establishing institutions that permitted high economic growth, improvement in physical infrastructure and a modicum of technical progress.

Lebanon's open, service-oriented economy furthered the interests of the dominant elite, but it was less successful in contributing to nation-building and to constructing a socio-economy that met the needs of the majority of the population. Although the economy enjoyed high growth, its dependence on the foreign sector made it vulnerable to regional and international shocks and pressures, and its sustainability was always in question.

Did this mode of development, however, have a tangible effect on domestic political and social stability? Although the available evidence shows no tidy relationship between Lebanon's economic model and political stability, conventional wisdom holds that it contributed to socio-political disharmony. Clearly, the

Shehabist successors to the ill-fated Chamoun regime viewed its tendency of promoting extremely uneven socio-economic development[16] as a contributing factor to the 1958 civil war. The model's major contribution to long-term instability was its real or apparent links to potent political and socio-confessional challenges to the system. Majority opinion perceived that the Lebanese state existed for the benefit of a small elite, identified as Christian merchants and bankers in Beirut, and that socio-economic upward mobility was restricted to those from certain classes, sects and regions. Such views, reinforced by rapid socio-cultural changes and the resurfacing of historical tensions, brought about various manifestations of discontent in the 1950s. Given Lebanon's weak state, those who were not part of the political inner circle were able to use the threats of violence and mobilisation of mass support to break the monopoly of power of the Khoury administration in 1952 and then the Chamoun regime in 1958. Hence, it was not the economic mode alone, but the interaction of forces — the economic model, a weak state and festering confessional, cultural and political problems — that jeopardised stability in Lebanon. As the aftermath of 1958 shows, a change in economic and institutional environment, established by the interventionist and developmental Shehabist regime, was not enough to avert the post-1975 conflagration.

Lastly, the Lebanese are now rebuilding their state and economy after 15 years of civil war, which destroyed the old order. While the past might not be a guide for the future, a thorough re-examination of Lebanon's old order can support the difficult task of creating appropriate institutions and structures to underpin a viable political economy. It is hoped that the analysis presented here will contribute to this process.

Notes

Chapter 1

1. Due to the focus of this work, the term 'agents' will refer to economic, in contrast to political, agents in the Lebanese system.
2. The analysis of this work is guided and informed by neo-institutional economics. The use of 'institutions', 'organisations' and related concepts follows this perspective. 'Institutions are the rules of the game in a society or, more formally, are the humanly devised constraints that shape human interaction. In consequence, they structure incentives in human exchange. Institutional change shapes the way societies evolve through time and hence is the key to understanding historical change' (p. 3). By contrast, organisations are 'groups of individuals bound by some common purpose to achieve objectives' (p. 5); Douglass C. North, *Institutions, Institutional Change and Economic Performance* (Cambridge, England, 1990). See also North, 'A transaction cost approach to the historical development of polities and economies', *Journal of Institutional and Theoretical Economics*, 145 (1989) pp. 661-68.
3. This study also draws from the theoretical framework of evolutionary economics; see Richard R. Nelson and Sidney G. Winter, *An Evolutionary Theory of Economic Change* (Cambridge, MA, 1982).
4. However, many of the tigers – notably, Japan, South Korea and Taiwan – shifted from a first stage (post-1945) strategy of ISI to a later stage (post-1950s) of EOI. For more on the East Asian export-oriented model, see for example, World Bank, *The East Asian Miracle, Economic Growth and Public Policy* (New York and Oxford, 1993); Tibor Scitovsky, 'Economic development of Taiwan and South Korea, 1965–1981', in L. J. Lau (ed.) *Models of Development: A Comparative Study of Economic Growth in South Korea and Taiwan* (San Francisco, 1986); Tony Mitchell, 'South Korea: vision of the future for labour surplus economies', in Manfred Bienefeld and Martin Godfrey (eds) *The Struggle for Development: National Strategies in an International Context* (Chichester, 1982); C. H. Kirkpatrick, *Export-led Development, Labour-market Regulation and the Distribution of Income in Asian NICs: the Case of Singapore* (Paris, 1987); I. M. D. Little, 'The experience and causes of rapid labour-intensive development in Korea, Taiwan Province, Hong Kong and Singapore; and the possibilities of emulation', in E. L. H. Lee (ed.) *Export-led Industrialisation and Development* (Bangkok, 1981); William Cline, 'Can the East Asian model of development be generalized?', *World Development* (February 1982); W. S. Jung and G. Lee, 'The effectiveness of export promotion policies: the case of Korea', *Weltwirtschaftliches Archiv*, 122 (1986); R. Leudde-Neurath, *Import Controls and Export Oriented Development: A Re-assessment of the South Korean Case* (Boulder and London, 1986); Robert Wade, *Governing the Market: Economic Theory and Role of Government in East*

Asian Industrialization (Princeton, 1989); Mohamed Ariff and Hal Hill, *Export-oriented Industrialization: the ASEAN Experience* (Sydney, 1985); Alice Amsden, *Asia's Next Giant: South Korea and Late Industrialization* (New York, 1989).

5. Keith Griffin, *Alternative Strategies for Economic Development* (London, 1989) Chapter 5.
6. Raoul Prebisch, 'The economic development of Latin America and its principal problems', *Economic Bulletin for Latin America*, vol. 7, no. 1 (February 1962); Raoul Prebisch, *Towards a New Trade Strategy for Development. Report by the Secretary-General of the UN Conference on Trade and Development* (New York, 1964).
7. Ragnor Nurkse, 'Some international aspects of the problem of economic development', *American Economic Review* (May 1952); Nurkse, 'Patterns of trade and development', *Wicksell Lectures* (Stockholm, 1959).
8. Paul Streeten, 'Trade strategies for development: some themes for the seventies', in Paul Streeten (ed.) *Trade Strategies for Development, Papers of the Ninth Cambridge Conference on Development Problems, September 1972* (London, 1973).
9. Jagdish N. Bhagwati, 'Directly-unproductive, profit-seeking (DUP) activities', *Journal of Political Economy*, vol. 90 (1982) pp. 988–1002.
10. Hollis B. Chenery, S. Shishido and T. Watanabe, 'The pattern of Japanese growth, 1914–1954', *Econometrica*, vol. 30 (1962); Hollis B. Chenery and Moshe Syrquin, *Patterns of Development 1950–1970* (Oxford, 1970); Chenery and Syrquin, *Patterns of Development 1950–1983* (Washington, DC, 1986).
11. Jagdish N. Bhagwati, 'Export-promoting trade strategy: issues and evidence', in Chris Milner (ed.) *Export Promotion Strategies: Theory and Evidence from Developing Countries* (New York, 1991) p. 18.
12. David Ricardo, *Principles of Political Economy and Taxation* (1817, reprinted London, 1957). See also Eli Heckscher, 'The effect of foreign trade on the distribution of income', reprinted in H. Ellis and L. Metzler (eds) *Readings in the Theory of International Trade* (1949); Bertil Ohlin, *Interregional and International Trade* (Cambridge, MA, 1933); Paul Samuelson, 'International trade and equalization of factor prices', *Economic Journal* (June 1948) pp. 163–84. 'New Trade Theory' has also supplemented the notion of comparative advantage with additional determinants of trade patterns and gains, for example product differentiation, increasing returns to scale and conditions of imperfect competition. See, for example, Paul R. Krugman, 'Is free trade passé?', *Journal of Economic Perspectives*, vol. 1 (1987) pp. 131–44.
13. For a summary of the arguments and evidence, see Bhagwati, 'Export-promoting trade strategy', pp. 23–6.
14. Bhagwati, 'Directly-unproductive, profit-seeking (DUP) activities'. See also Anne O. Krueger, 'The political economy of the rent-seeking society', *American Economic Review*, vol. 64 (1974) pp. 291–303.
15. Anne O. Krueger, *Trade and Employment in Developing Countries: Synthesis and Conclusions* (Chicago, 1982).
16. Adam Smith, *The Wealth of Nations* [*An Inquiry into the Nature and Causes of the Wealth of Nations*] edited by Edwin Cannan (New York, 1937). See also Irma Adelman, *Theories of Economic Growth and Development* (Stanford, 1961) Chapter 3.

17. J. S. Mill, *Principles of Political Economy* (London, 1902) especially pp. 350–2.
18. See, for example, Denis O'Hearn, 'TNCs, intervening mechanisms and economic growth in Ireland: a longitudinal test and extension of the Bornschier model', *World Development*, vol. 18, no. 3 (1990) p. 422; Volker Bornschier, 'Multinational corporations and economic growth: a cross-national test of the decapitalization thesis', *Journal of Development Economics*, vol. 7 (1980); Volker Bornschier and Christopher Chase-Dunn, *Transnational Corporations and Under-development* (New York, 1985).
19. On the role of macroeconomic management in economic growth and change, see World Bank, *The East Asian Miracle*, Chapter 3.
20. David Dollar, 'Outward-oriented developing economies really do grow more rapidly: evidence from 95 LDCs, 1976–1985', *Economic Development and Cultural Change*, vol. 40, no. 3 (1992) pp. 523–44.
21. I have extended Paul Streeten's notion of a fourfold division of primary-inward, primary-outward, secondary-inward and secondary-outward orientation ('Trade strategies', p. 4) to include tertiary- or services-outward orientation.
22. H. David Evans, 'Outward orientation: an assessment', in Chris Milner (ed.) *Export Promotion Strategies*, p. 41. See also W. A. Lewis, 'The slowing down of the engine of growth', *American Economic Review*, vol. 70 (1982) pp. 555–64; Irving Kravis, 'Trade as a handmaiden of growth: similarities between the nineteenth and twentieth centuries', *Economic Journal* (December 1970) pp. 850–72; James Riedel, 'Trade as the engine of growth in developing countries, revisited', *Economic Journal*, vol. 84 (1984) pp. 56–73.
23. For more on 'trickle-down' growth in LDCs, see Irma Adelman and Cynthia T. Morris, *Economic Growth and Social Equity in Developing Countries* (Stanford, 1973).
24. Charles Rizk, *Le régime politique libanais* (Paris, 1966).
25. See Carolyn L. Gates, *The Development of the Modern Political Economy of Lebanon: the State and the Economy from Colonialism to Independence, 1939–1952*, D.Phil. thesis (Oxford University, 1985) and *The Historical Role of Political Economy in the Development of Modern Lebanon*, Centre for Lebanese Studies, *Papers on Lebanon*, no. 10 (Oxford, 1989); Nadim Shehadi, *The Idea of Lebanon: Economy and State in the Cénacle Libanais, 1946–1954*, Centre for Lebanese Studies, *Papers on Lebanon*, no. 5 (Oxford, 1987); Claude Dubar and Salim Nasr, *Les classes sociales au Liban* (Paris, 1976); Raymond Mallat, *70 Years of Money Muddling in Lebanon, 1900–1970* (Beirut, 1970); Elizabeth Picard, *Etat de discorde, des fondations aux guerres fratricides* (Paris, 1988).

Chapter 2

1. Lebanon in its present boundaries did not exist until 1920. For the pre-1920 period, 'Lebanon' is defined as Mount Lebanon and the Beirut region. Silk production originated in the Shuf and Kisrawan districts of Mount Lebanon and was exported to Europe via Beirut and Sidon.
2. Charles Issawi, *An Economic History of the Middle East and North Africa* (New York, 1982) p. 1.

3. Irina M. Smilianskaya, 'From subsistence to market economy: the disintegration of feudal relations in Syria and Lebanon in the middle of the nineteenth century', in Charles Issawi (ed.) *The Economic History of the Middle East, 1800–1914* (Chicago, 1966) pp. 227–47.
4. The expansion of Syria's international trade in the nineteenth century can be contrasted with the stagnation or decline of its overland trade, which until the 1840s had been highly important; Charles Issawi, *The Fertile Crescent 1800–1914: A Documentary History* (New York and Oxford, 1988) p. 128.
5. Smilianskaya, 'From subsistence to market economy', p. 229.
6. J. L. Farley, *Two Years in Syria* (London, 1858) p. 372, as cited by Smilianskaya, 'From subsistence to market economy', p. 230. During the second half of the nineteenth century, 75 per cent of all silk production in Greater Syria originated from Lebanese territories, and about 90 per cent of total Syro-Lebanese silk production was exported through Beirut.
7. Boutros Labaki, *Introduction à l'histoire économique du Liban: soie et commerce extérieur en fin de période ottomane (1840–1914)* (Beirut, 1984) p. 28.
8. Dominique Chevallier, *La société du Mont Liban à l'époque de la révolution industrielle en Europe* (Paris, 1971) pp. 196–226; V. Cuinet, *Syrie, Liban et Palestine*, vol. 5 (Paris, 1896) p. 67, cited by Roger Owen, *The Middle East in the World Economy, 1800–1914* (London and New York, 1981) p. 249.
9. Labaki, *Introduction à l'histoire économique*, p. 28; Gaston Ducousso, *L'industrie de la soie en Syrie et au Liban* (Beirut and Paris, 1913) p. 10; Issawi, *The Fertile Crescent*, p. 321.
10. Labaki, *Introduction à l'histoire économique*, pp. 155–6.
11. Ibid., p. 154.
12. Ibid., pp. 371–2.
13. Ibid., pp. 155–6.
14. Omar Celal Sarc, 'The Tanzimat and our industry', Chapter 5, 'Ottoman industrial policy, 1840–1914', in Charles Issawi (ed.) *Economic History of the Middle East, 1800–1914* (Chicago and London, 1966) pp. 48–59. At that time, only two reeling plants were owned by Lebanese.
15. Labaki, *Introduction à l'histoire économique*, p. 89.
16. Ibid., p. 91.
17. Dominique Chevallier, 'Lyon et la Syrie en 1919, les bases d'une intervention', *Revue historique*, vol. 224 (1960) p. 289; Ducousso, *L'Industrie de la soie*, p. 10.
18. Issawi, *Fertile Crescent*, Table III.7, p. 148.
19. European-Levantine commercial control of Lebanon's silk industry produced a 'contradictory movement' in its development: initially, it stimulated the growth of sericulture, but later impeded its modernisation, reorganisation and expansion; Paul Saba, *The Development and Decline of the Lebanese Silk Industry*, B.Litt. thesis (Oxford University, 1977) p. 1.
20. Labaki, *Introduction à l'histoire économique*, pp. 150–1.

21. Jean Ducruet, *Les capitaux européens au Proche-Orient* (Paris, 1964) p. 240. See also Jacques de Monicault, *Le Port de Beyrouth et l'économie des pays du Levant sous le mandat français* (Paris, 1936).
22. Jacques Thobie, *Intérêts et impérialisme français dans l'empire ottoman: 1895–1914* (Paris, 1977).
23. Although international factors were a primary stimulus to the rise of Beirut, three important local and regional factors contributed to Beirut's growing importance. (1) Primary trading routes were moving from the interior to the Mediterranean during the nineteenth century; see Dominique Chevallier, 'Western development and Eastern crisis in the mid-nineteenth century: Syria confronted with the European economy', in William Polk and Richard Chambers (eds) *Beginning of Modernization in the Middle East* (Chicago, 1968). (2) There were local and regional shifts in power relations, making Mount Lebanon and the interior increasingly dependent on Beirut; see Leila Fawaz, *Merchants and Migrants in Nineteenth Century Beirut* (Cambridge, MA, 1983) pp. 3–7. (3) Ottoman military and civil expenditures, which favoured Beirut's development, were rising during this period; see Marwan Buheiry, *Beirut's Role in the Political Economy of the French Mandate, 1919–1939*, Centre for Lebanese Studies, *Papers on Lebanon*, no. 4 (Oxford, 1987) p. 2.
24. Fawaz, *Merchants and Migrants*, Table 1, pp. 127–30.
25. Buheiry, *Beirut's Role*, p. 3; Kamal Salibi, *The Modern History of Lebanon* (New York, 1977) p. 142.
26. Fawaz, *Merchants and Migrants*, p. 73.
27. Nada Sehnaoui, *L'Occidentalisation de la vie quotidienne à Beyrouth, 1860–1914: memoire de maîtrise* (Université de Paris X-Nanterre, 1981).
28. Mas'ud Dahir, *Tarikh lubnan al-ijtima'i: 1914–1926* [The Social History of Lebanon: 1914–1926] (Beirut, 1974) p. 119.
29. Issawi, *An Economic History of the Middle East and North Africa*, p. 17.
30. Dubar and Nasr, *Les classes sociales*, p. 54.
31. M. S. Kalla, *Role of Foreign Trade in the Economic Development of Syria, 1831–1914*, Ph.D. dissertation (American University, Washington, DC, 1969) pp. 68–84.
32. Issawi, *Fertile Crescent*, Table III.7, pp. 148–9. During this period, British export prices fell by about 20 per cent, while the price for cocoons and raw silk almost doubled.
33. The cross exchange rate of the piastre–FF moved from piastre 1 = FF 1.37 in 1800 to piastre 1 = FF 0.22 in 1900; Issawi, *Fertile Crescent*, p. 408.
34. Issawi, *An Economic History of the Middle East and North Africa*, p. 38 and Issawi, *Fertile Crescent*, Table 2, pp. 154–5, respectively.
35. Especially before 1890, French investment in Syria compared with other regions in the Middle East and North Africa was not large. See, Badr al-Din al-Siba'i, *Adwa' 'ala al-rasmal al-ajnabi fi suriyya 1850–1958* [Foreign Capital in Syria 1850–1958] (Damascus, 1968) pp. 35–6. On the eve of the First World War, French capital constituted approximately 45 per cent (almost £T 37 million) of all foreign investment within the Ottoman Empire, and French financiers controlled about 60 per cent (more than £T 52 million) of the Ottoman public debt; Thobie, *Interêts et impérialisme français*,

pp. 306 and 481; Issawi, *An Economic History of the Middle East and North Africa*, Table 4.2, p. 69.

36. Al-Siba'i, *Adwa'*, pp. 34–6 and Noel Verney and George Dambmann, *Les puissances étrangères dans le Levant* (Paris, 1900).
37. For an examination of the vast network of economic, commercial, politico-strategic and ideological interests by which France had built its sphere of influence in the Levant in the nineteenth century, see William Shorrock, *French Imperialism in the Middle East: the Failure of Policy in Syria and Lebanon, 1900–1914* (Madison, 1976) and Stephen Roberts, *History of French Colonial Policy (1870–1925)* vol. 2 (London, 1929).
38. The first French High Commissioner in Lebanon, Henri Gouraud, claimed that French direct control of the Levant 'opened the way to French capital' in the region. See, Henri Gouraud, *La France en Syrie* (Paris, 1922) p. 30.
39. Virginia Thompson and Richard Adloff, 'French economic policy in tropical Africa', in Peter Duignan and Lewis Gann (eds) *Colonialism in Africa, 1870–1960* (Cambridge, 1975) vol. 4, p. 128. Samir Amin argues that the *économie de traité* 'describes analytically the exchange of agricultural commodities provided by a peripheral society . . . for the products of a central capitalist industry, either imported or produced on the spot by European enterprises'. See, Samir Amin, *Unequal Development* (New York and London, 1976) p. 329.
40. Safiuddin Joarder, *Syria under the French Mandate: the Early Phase, 1920–1927* (Dacca, 1977) p. 201; PRO, FO371, E9566/89, dispatch 2916 of 23 August 1922, Damascus, 'French economic policy in Syria' and E11109/274/89, dispatch no. 2390 of 13 October 1922, attachment 'Report from the President of the Union économique de Syrie/Paris to the President of the Damascus Chamber of Commerce', 8 June 1922.
41. Dahir, *Tarikh lubnan*, pp. 136–7; Banque de Syrie et du Liban, *Bulletin annuel de la banque de Syrie et du Liban*, 1939 (Paris, 1939) pp. 64–100.
42. 'Abd Allah Hanna, *Al-haraka al-'ummaliyya fi suriyya wa lubnan, 1900–1945* [The Labour Movement in Syria and Lebanon] (Damascus, 1973) p. 105.
43. George Medawar, *Monetary Problems in Lebanon*, Ph.D. dissertation (Cornell University, 1963) p. 93.
44. Sa'id Himadeh, 'Monetary and banking system', in Sa'id Himadeh (ed.) *Economic Organization of Syria* (Beirut, 1936) p. 287.
45. Sa'id Himadeh, *Monetary and Banking System of Syria and Lebanon* (Beirut, 1935) p. 188.
46. Issawi, *An Economic History of the Middle East and North Africa*, p. 74.
47. B. Aboussouan, *Le problème politique syrien* (Paris, 1924) p. 29, as cited by Dubar and Nasr, *Les classes sociales*, p. 60.
48. Dahir, *Tarikh lubnan*, p. 122.
49. Ibid., p. 126. See also Himadeh, 'Monetary and banking system', p. 284.
50. League of Nations, Permanent Mandates Commission, Minutes, 27th Session, June 1935, p. 100.
51. Stephen Longrigg, *Syria and Lebanon under French Mandate* (London, 1958) p. 281.
52. George Hakim, 'Fiscal system', in Sa'id Himadeh (ed.) *Economic Organization of Syria* (Beirut, 1936) p. 357.

53. Raja Himadeh, *The Fiscal System of Lebanon* (Beirut, 1961) p. 8.
54. MAE, *Syrie-Liban 1930–1940*, vol. 571, 1936/7, Meyrier/Beirut to MAE/Paris, 16 September 1936, telegram no. 725.
55. Great Britain, Department of Overseas Trade, G. T. Havard and F. C. Ogden, *Report on Economic and Commercial Conditions in Syria and the Lebanon* (London, 1936) p. 1.
56. Norman Burns, *The Tariff of Syria*, 1919–1932 (Beirut, 1933) p. 268; Norman Burns and Allen Edwards, 'Foreign trade', in Sa'id Himadeh (ed.) *Economic Organization of Syria* (Beirut, 1936) p. 255.
57. Dubar and Nasr, *Les classes sociales*, p. 54.
58. Albert Badre, 'Economic development of Lebanon', in Charles Cooper and Sidney Alexander (eds) *Economic Development and Population Growth in the Middle East* (New York, 1972) pp. 163–4.
59. Dahir, *Tarikh lubnan*, p. 54.
60. Havard and Ogden, *Report*, p. 18.
61. Calculated from Jacques Weulersse, *Paysans de Syrie et du Proche-Orient* (Paris, 1946) p. 185.
62. See Zvi Hershlag, *Introduction to the Modern Economic History of the Middle East* (Leiden, 1972) pp. 250–2.
63. Prime Minister Khaled Shihab's official policy statement in the *Journal officiel de la république libanaise, débats parlementaires,* Chambre des députes, Quatrième législature, Première session ordinaire, Compte-rendu résumé de la 1ère séance (25 March 1938) annexe au procès verbal, p. 125.
64. Weulersse, *Paysans de Syrie,* pp. 140–1.
65. Albert Khuri, 'Agriculture', in Sa'id Himadeh (ed.) *Economic Organization of Syria* (Beirut, 1936) pp. 90–2.
66. George Hakim, 'Industry', in Sa'id Himadeh (ed.) *Economic Organization of Syria*, p. 119; Hershlag, *Introduction to the Modern Economic History*, p. 225; Dahir, *Tarikh lubnan*, p. 48.
67. Jacques Couland, *Le mouvement syndical au Liban: 1919–1946* (Paris, 1970) pp. 58–9.
68. France, *Rapport à la SDN*, 1929, p. 16; MAE, Guerre 1939–1945, E-Vichy-Levant, vol. 52, Dentz/Beirut to MAE, Levant/Paris, 2 January 1941 (notes 1 and 3 on industrial development in Syria and Lebanon); Mohammed Amine El-Hafez, *La structure et la politique économique en Syrie et au Liban* (Beirut, 1953) p. 46.
69. Couland, *Le mouvement syndical*, p. 132.
70. Ibid., p. 133.
71. Iskandar Riashi, *Al-ayyam al-lubnaniyya* [Lebanese Days] (Beirut, 1957) pp. 337–9.
72. 890e.6476/9–447 American Legation/Beirut to DS, 4 September 1947, 'Cement distribution in Lebanon'; USNA, RG59, 883a.14/6–1351, American Legation to DS, 'Influence of the BSL in the financial system of Lebanon'; USNA, RG59, 890e.6376/8–2947, American Legation/Beirut to DS, 29 August 1947, 'Current cement crisis in Lebanon'.
73. Kurt Grunwald, 'The industrialization of the Lebanon and Syria', *Weltwirtschaftliches Archiv*, vol. 76, no. 1 (1956) p. 147.

74. Mustafa al-Nusuli, 'Min al-hirfa ila al-sina'a' [From craft to industry], in *Muhadarat al-nudwa* [*Les conférences du Cénacle libanais*] (Beirut, 1953) as cited by United Nations, Department of Economic and Social Affairs, *Review of Economic Conditions in the Middle East, 1945 to 1954* (Supplement to World Economic Report, 1953/4) (New York, 1955) n. 1, p. 151. Most data are aggregated for Syria and Lebanon in this period.
75. Grunwald, 'Industrialization', pp. 146–7.
76. Ibid., Table 4, p. 146.
77. Ibid., p. 149.
78. France, *Rapport à la SDN*, 1937, pp. 218–19. This disparity is due to different methodology used by Grunwald and French surveyors to categorise modern and traditional industries in Lebanon. See also *International Labour Review*, vol. 39, no. 4 (April 1939) pp. 513–26.
79. Calculated from France, *Rapport à la SDN*, 1937, pp. 218–19.
80. Hakim, 'Industry', p. 131.
81. France, *Rapport à la SDN*, 1930–1939 and France, Haut-commissariat de la République française en Syrie et au Liban, *Bulletin économique trimestriel des états du Levant sous mandat français, 1930–1938* (Beirut).
82. El-Hafez, *La structure*, p. 56.
83. de Monicault, *Le Port de Beyrouth*, pp. 99–100.
84. France, Haut-commissariat de la République française en Syrie et au Liban, *La Syrie et le Liban en 1922* (Paris, 1923) p. 294.
85. RG84, vol. X (1938) 'Annual Economic Review, 1938'.
86. Burns and Edwards, 'Foreign trade', p. 232.
87. Hershlag, *Introduction to the Modern Economic History*, p. 261.
88. Gabriel Menassa, *Plan de reconstruction de l'économie libanaise et de réforme de l'état* (Beirut, 1948) pp. 347–8.
89. Burns and Edwards, 'Foreign trade', p. 242.
90. Duchâtel, 'Une grande voie internationale: l'avenir d'Alexandrette', *Bulletin de l'union économique de Syrie*, vol. 7, 1982, pp. 97–9 as cited by Buheiry, *Beirut's Role*, p. 8. The other axis was Alexandretta.
91. *L'Orient*, 23 November 1933 and 8 January 1934.
92. MAE, E-Levant, Syrie–Liban, 1930–1940, vol. 587, De Martel/Beirut to MAE (Levant)/Paris, 3 August 1937, no. 750; Le Sous-secrétaire d'état/MAE Levant au Ministre de la marine, no. 969, 9 juin 1937; MAE, E-Levant, Syrie–Liban, 1930–1940, vol. 584, G. de Monicault, Compagnie française du port et des entrepôts de Beyrouth/Paris au Comte de Saint Quentin/MAE/Paris, 17 February 1937.
93. Union des ingénieurs et techniciens de la France combattante (Section du Levant), *Vingt-cinq ans d'efforts français au Levant* (Beirut, 1944) p. 27. See also Edward Nickoley, 'Transportation and communications', in Sa'id Himadeh (ed.) *Economic Organization of Syria* (Beirut, 1936) p. 178.
94. Havard and Ogden, *Report*, 1932, p. 23; Hershlag, *Introduction to the Modern Economic History*, p. 247.
95. USNA, RG84, box 34, file 866, American Legation/Beirut, vol. XII, 1944, 'Relève en tonnage et valeur et par importateur, des pièces de rechange et des accessoires pour

automobiles, importés aux fins de consommation locale durant les années 1938–1939'. See also Negib Moussali, *Etudes économiques sur la Syrie et le Liban* (Beirut, 1957) p. 25.

96. MAE, E-Levant, Syrie-Liban, 1930–40, vol. 587, De Martel/Beirut to MAE (Levant)/Paris, 3 August 1937, no. 750; Le sous-Secrétaire d'état/MAE Levant au Ministre de la marine, no. 969, 9 June 1937; vol. 584, G. de Monicault, Compagnie française du port et des entrepôts de Beyrouth/Paris au Comte de Saint Quentin/MAE/Paris, 17 February 1937.
97. Monicault, *Le Port de Beyrouth*, pp. 41–100.
98. Buheiry, *Beirut's Role*, p. 9.
99. *Bulletin annuel de la BSL*, 1939, p. 56.
100. MAE, Guerre 1939–45, E-Vichy-Levant, vol. 52, Dentz/Beirut to MAE, Levant/Paris, 22 January 1941 (note no. 1). See also Riashi, *Al-ayyam*, pp. 338–89.

Chapter 3

1. MAE, Guerre 1939–1945, E-Vichy-Levant, vol. 52, Paul Baudoin/Vichy to HC Gabriel Puaux/Beirut, 12 July 1940, tel. no. 102, 'Politique économique de la France au Levant'; vol. 54, Puaux/Beirut to MAE/Vichy, 19 July 1940, tel. no. 763–766; vol. 54, Puaux/Beirut to MAE/Vichy, 9 December 1940, tel. no. 1848; vol. 54, Puaux/Beirut to MAE/Vichy, 13 December 1940, 'Lutte contre la hausse des prix et la spéculation'; vol. 54, Puaux/Beirut to MAE/Vichy, 13 December 1940, 'Transport et circulation des céréales'; USNA, RG84, Beirut, vol. xi (1940) box 23, 'Economic Report', 26 September 1940.
2. MAE, Guerre 1939–1945, E-Vichy-Levant, vol. 55, Reuters wire service and MAE commentary.
3. MAE, Guerre 1939–1945, E-Vichy-Levant, vol. 70, Dentz/Beirut to Vichy, 15 February 1941, no. 278–9; and vol. 52, Dentz/Beirut to MAE/Vichy, 23 April 1941.
4. MAE, Guerre 1939–1945, Londres CNF, vol. 55, Politique extérieure du CNF Questions économiques, March–December 1942, pp. 115 ff.
5. Expenditures on public works in Syria and Lebanon fell from £SL 1,741,312 in 1939 to £SL 268,302 in 1940; USNA, RG59, 890e.51/30, enclosure to no. 307, William Witman/Beirut to DS, part III, appendix F, March 1944, 'Financial situation in Syria and Lebanon'.
6. General Sir E. L. Spears was named by Prime Minister Winston Churchill as the head of the Spears Mission to the Gaullist Movement, and after the Allied occupation of the Levant, the Spears Mission to the Levant. The Spears Mission, representing expanded British authority in Syria and Lebanon, intervened in virtually every facet of economy and politics in the Levant. See General Sir Edward Spears, *Fulfilment of a Mission: the Spears Mission to Syria and Lebanon, 1941–1944* (Hamden, CN, 1977).
7. Their research and analysis is compiled in reports to the mission, which are now found at the Public Record Office (PRO) categories FO921 and FO922.
8. Couland, *Le mouvement syndical*, p. 280.

9. The OEG was created by General Georges Catroux, Delegate-General of the Free French Forces to the Levant States, to adapt the local economy to war conditions, also the objective of the Anglo-American MESC. Many claimed that it became 'a little MESC for the states under French control'; MAE, Guerre 1939–1945, Alger CFLN–GPRF, vol. 1024, Captain G. M. Louyot/Damascus, Report of 17 February 1944. Catroux also used the OEG to counter British influence. Many of the well known altercations between Catroux and Spears were played out through rivalries of the two organisations.
10. USNA, RG84, vol. xi (1943) box 1, no. 25, file 850/711.2 Scott/Beirut, 'Office de l'économie de guerre', 14 May 1943, p. 1.
11. MAE, Guerre 1939–1945, Alger CFLN–GPRF, vol. 1023, 'L'économie de guerre dans les états de Syrie et du Liban' (hereafter referred to as 'L'économie de guerre') p. 32.
12. PRO, FO922, S/83/MS/2, Syria and Lebanon, Textiles, part II, 1944–5, R. Canter to Col. R. N. Bruce, MESC/Cairo, 3 May 1945.
13. Initially created as a subcommittee of the Middle East War Council and headed by Minister of State Oliver Lyttelton in Cairo, the MESC was established to implement Allied economic warfare policies in the Middle East.
14. USNA, RG165, G–2 Regional File, Middle East entry 2, box 2869, Board of Economic Warfare, F. Boardman to G. Gilpatric, 13 June 1942; and PRO, FO371, U82/82/71, War Cabinet Offices, SME (42) 100, 28 December 1942, p. 3.
15. USNA, RG165, G–2 Regional File, Middle East, entry 77, box 2869, FEA Special Branch, 'The MESC', unedited report, March 1944.
16. 'L'économie de guerre', deuxième partie, Section II, L'action directe des pouvoirs publics.
17. MAE, Guerre 1939–1945, Londres, CNF, vol. 54, 20 November 1941, Approvisionnement de la Syrie en matières premières.
18. 'L'économie de guerre', Report presented to the Middle East Financial Conference, Cairo, 24–9 April 1944, pp. 26–7.
19. PRO, FO371, U4423/82/71, MESC, *Middle East Economic and Statistical Bulletin,* no. 5, August 1943, pp. 8, 13. See also USNA, RG59, 890e.00/365, 'Monthly Political Review, February 1944', 17 March 1944, no. 317; USNA, RG59, 890e.00/7–1444, 'Monthly Political Review, June 1944', 14 July 1944, no. 442.
20. PRO, FO371, E3998/706/65, Beirut Chancery to Eastern Department, Memo for General Spears, 28 June 1944.
21. PRO, FO371, E7410/3479/89, Spears/Beirut, 18 November 1944, no. 124; see also USNA, RG84, vol. xi (1940) box 23, 'Economic Report (Syria–Lebanon) September 1940'.
22. Conseil supérieur des intérêts communs, Service d'études économiques et de statistiques, *Recueil de statistiques de la Syrie et du Liban* (Beirut, 1948) 1944, 1945–7.
23. H. Durand, *L'expérience d'union économique entre la Syrie et le Liban*, thèse de droit (Université de Grenoble, 1953) p. 109, as cited by Centre d'études et de recherches sur le Moyen-Orient, *Etat et perspectives de l'industrie au Liban* (Beirut, 1978) p. 51.

24. USNA, RG84, vol. xi (1944) box 34, 'Annual Economic and Financial Review (Syria–Lebanon) 1943', enclosure nos 3, 4; and USNA, RG84, vol. xi (1943) box 31, 'Annual Economic and Financial Review (Syria–Lebanon) 1942', enclosure nos 4, 5.
25. PRO, FO921/354, file 82(2) (4613).
26. Félix Rosenfeld, 'Les échanges commerciaux entre la Syrie et le Liban et les autres pays du Proche-Orient', *L'économiste européen*, vol. 98, no. 2, 25 November 1945, p. 333.
27. *The Times*, 25 May 1943, and notes in MAE, *Guerre 1939–1945*, Londres-CNF, vol. 56.
28. PRO, FO921, file no. 54, Spears to Minister of State/Cairo, 2 December 1943.
29. USNA, RG59, 890e.51/30, enclosure to no. 307 of March 1944, Judd Polk Report, p. 9. See also Papiers d'agents, Gabriel Puaux, vol. 35, Dossier affaires financières: Avance de 100ms, Année 1939.
30. USNA, RG84, vol. xi (1940) box 23, file 851/850, Palmer/Beirut, 'Financial Report', completed 18 October 1940.
31. Ibid.
32. MAE, Guerre 1939–1945, E-Vichy-Levant, vol. 68, MAE(Levant)/Vichy to HC/Beirut 14 June 1941, tel no. 808–809; MAE, Guerre 1939–1945, E-Vichy-Levant, vol. 68, Ministry of National Economy and Finance/Vichy to HC/Beirut, 23 June 1941 and vol. 70 HC/Beirut, 30 September 1941, summary report on funds evacuated from the Levant.
33. PRO, FO371, E40/3/89, Spears/Beirut to GOC-in-C, 9th Army, 9 December 1941.
34. MAE, Guerre 1939–1945, Alger CFLN–GPRF, vol. 1016, Convention entre l'Office des changes et la BSL.
35. PRO, WO178, vol. 20, March 1943.
36. PRO, FO922, File 979/07, parts 1 and 2, 1943–4, 'Agricultural development in Syria', report by Najib Alamuddin, 3 January 1943.
37. PRO, FO922, File 979/07, parts 1 and 2, 'Agricultural development in Syria', report by Najib Alamuddin, 3 May 1943.
38. USNA, RG84, vol. XI (1943) box 31, 'Economic and Financial Review (Syria and Lebanon) quarter ending 31 December 1942', p. 3; American University of Beirut, Economic Research Institute, *Report on Agricultural Credit in Lebanon*, Conference on agricultural credit sponsored by the Ford Foundation and organised by the AUB (Beirut, 12–14 October 1953).
39. *Report on Agricultural Credit in Lebanon*, pp. 8–9.
40. PRO, FO922, AP10000/Syrian Agricultural Policy, Syria, Spears Economic Section to Director/Food, 18 December 1944.
41. The total amount of land under cultivation in 1946 was only 230,000 hectares. In 1934, French researchers claimed that Lebanon could potentially cultivate 560,400 hectares; Jewish Agency for Palestine, Economic Research Institute (ERI) *Statistical Handbook of the Middle Eastern Countries* (Jerusalem, 1945) p. 101. Agriculture specialists in 1946 stated that it was possible to bring into cultivation another 180,000 hectares (in addition to the 230,000) mainly through intensive cultivation methods; Sir Alexander Gibb and Partners, *The Economic Development of Lebanon* (London, 1948) p. 42.
42. Gibb, *Economic Development*, Diagram no. 4.

43. USNA, RG319, 'P' file, Lebanon, box 2180, Wadsworth/Beirut to DS, 3 July 1946, no. 1258, transmitting a 'Survey of the economic problems of Lebanon' by the assistant director of the Ministry of National Economy, Na'im Amiouni, pp. 7–8.
44. PRO, FO921/175, Industry, p. 32. Beirut's three glassware factories employed a total of 280 workers in 1943.
45. USNA, RG84, vol. xi (1942) box 28, file 850/851.2, 'Annual Economic and Financial Review (Syria and Lebanon) 1941', Wittman/Beirut, 7 July 1942.
46. The modern and complete Kab Elias (Beirut) was a typical cardboard mill, employing 30 workers and producing in 1943 an average of 25–30 tons of cardboard per month. It had an output capacity of about three to four times that amount; PRO, FO921/175, Industry, p. 18.
47. PRO, FO921/175, p. 4 of Industry in Syria and Lebanon, part 4 (1944–1945) (hereafter referred to as PRO, FO921/175, Industry).
48. PRO, FO921/175, Industry.
49. PRO, FO922, SS734/E, Match Industry/1944.
50. PRO, FO922/file 461, MESC Monthly Letter, February 1945.
51. Longrigg, *Syria and Lebanon*, p. 338; USNA, RG84, vol. XVII (1945) F. A. Kuhn/Beirut, 'Economic and Financial Review, quarter ending 30 September 1945', pp. 4–5. Unemployment statistics do not exist for this time, but French estimates show that at the beginning of 1941, unemployment in Beirut and its suburbs stood at 25,000 people, affecting at least 100,000 inhabitants; MAE, Guerre 1939–1945, Londres–CNF, vol. 55, Travail, p. 108.
52. Kamal Bohsali, 'Contribution à l'étude de la situation de la classe ouvrière au Liban', thèse de droit (Paris, 1951) pp. 300–3 as cited by Couland, *Le mouvement syndical*, p. 283. Reflecting the level of industrial development, union organisation was most extensive in Beirut, followed by Tripoli and Zahlé. See Couland, *Le mouvement syndical*, p. 318. The Lebanese government began to authorise new labour associations, such as the Beirut Electrical Workers and the Railway and Beirut Port Workers and Agents in 1944 and the *Régie des Tabacs* workers and employees in 1946. The British Goodwill Trade Mission reported after its visit to Lebanon in April–May 1946 that the Lebanese government had authorised 37 workers' syndicates; PRO, FO371, E8826/8826/65, 'Report of the British Goodwill Trade Mission to Iraq, Syria, the Lebanon and Cyprus, April–May 1946', part IV, p. 65. Labour associations, whose authorisations were delayed or denied by the Beirut government, established themselves as branches of individual Beirut unions; Couland, *Le mouvement syndical*, p. 337.
53. Great Britain, Department of Overseas Trade, *Iraq, Syria, the Lebanon, Cyprus: British Goodwill Trade Mission* [Davidson Mission], Report, 31 August (London, 1946) p. 38.
54. Ibid.
55. A. R. Prest, *War Economics of Primary Producing Countries* (Cambridge, 1948) p. 23.
56. USNA, RG59, 890d.9111/192, Wadsworth/Beirut to DS, 6 February 1943, no. 43 (Economic and Miscellaneous, part 5).
57. USNA, RG59, 890e.00/371, Wadsworth/Beirut to DS, 'Political Review of March 1944', 21 April 1944 no. 353, p. 3.
58. Dubar and Nasr, *Les classes sociales*, p. 62.

59. James Tobin, 'The interest elasticity of the transactions demand for cash', *Review of Economics and Statistics*, vol. 38 (August 1956); James Tobin, 'Liquidity preference as behavior toward risk', *Review of Economic Studies*, vol. 25 (February 1958). See also William Baumol, 'The transactions demand for cash: an inventory theoretic approach', *Quarterly Journal of Economics*, vol. 66 (November 1952). Fundamental questions exist about why wealthy Lebanese would choose to hold money in £SL: were all three Keynesian motives (transaction, precaution and speculation) operating? Or were they maintaining £SL balances primarily for transactions, as monetarists would argue? Although confidence in the £SL increased greatly during the war, on balance, two facts suggest the latter. First, time deposits/demand deposits between 1939 and 1945 were tiny, on average about 1 per cent, suggesting that bank deposits were used primarily for transactions, rather than speculation and precaution. Furthermore, much investment and speculation during the war was transacted through the medium of gold or foreign currency. Second, even though the Lebanese expected the postwar period to reverse supply/demand conditions, it was rational that accompanying high inflation was a large increase in demand for non-monetary assets. Using the Tobin approach, the characterisation of uncertainty, which Keynes employed in his theory of speculation, is overcome by assuming that a financial investor will assign a range of possible values to the future interest rate of assets that he will hold with certainty, rather than the one value which Keynes assumed.
60. L'économie de guerre', pp. 18–19.
61. Ibid.
62. Ibid.
63. USNA, RG84, Beirut, vol. xi (1944) Scott/Beirut, 'Economic and Financial Review, quarter ending 30 June 1944'.
64. Gibb, *Economic Development*, p. 169.
65. Félix Rosenfeld, 'Variations des prix et de la circulation monétaire en Syrie et au Liban au cours de la deuxième guerre mondiale', *Journal de la société de statistique de Paris*, Berger-Levrault edition (Paris, 1946) p. 6.
66. USNA, RG59, 890e.51/30, 'Study of the financial situation in Lebanon', prepared by William Wittman II, part II, p. 47.
67. PRO, FO371, UE4320/100/53, *Middle East Economic and Statistical Bulletin*, no. 41, January 1941; PRO, FO921, file 79/15, 'Allied military expenditures', 22 December 1945, PAY/5/6/7.
68. USNA, RG59, 890d.51/81, 'Report on measures to check inflation in Syria and the Lebanon', drawn up by British and French financial experts: R. Busson, E. M. H. Lloyd, W. W. Lawson, H. Thomas, Beirut, 4 May 1943, p. 1.
69. 'L'économie de guerre', p. 22.
70. USNA, RG59, 890e.9111.1, Wadsworth/Beirut to DS, 'Political Review, 25 March–8 April 1943', 17 April 1943, p. 6.
71. PRO, WO169/15961, box 172, vol. 41, December 1944, Beirut Consumer Association.
72. 'L'économie de guerre', p. 48.
73. Ibid.

74. PRO, FO371, E1487/23/89, Spears, no. 99, 23 February 1944; E1825/23/89, Spears no. 101, 8 March 1944.
75. USNA, RG84, vol. x (1941) box 25, file 850.102, Engert/Beirut to DS, 26 October 1941, no. 184 and enclosure, Letter from Association des commerçants de Beyrouth, 13 October 1941. See also PRO, FO371, E3977/207/89, Spears/Beirut, 1 July 1942, no. 276.
76. PRO, FO371, E6982/3479/89, Spears/Damascus, 12 November 1944, no. 72.
77. Profits up to £SL 75,000 were assessed at 15–25 per cent and over £SL 75,000 at 33.33 per cent; USNA, RG84, vol. xi (1943) box 31, file 851.2, James Scott/Beirut, 'Excess war profits in the Lebanon', 29 January 1943 no. 3, p. 1.
78. See PRO, FO371, E6344/207/89, Spears/Beirut 28 October 1942, no. 610.
79. El-Hafez, *La structure*, p. 180.
80. PRO, FO922, S86, part I, 1942–3, Anti-Inflation Standing Committee, tel. no. 881, 7 April 1943.
81. PRO, FO921/175, Industry.
82. USNA, RG165, G–2 Regional File, Middle East, entry 77, box 2869, Interview with Lt. Col. Charles M. Belem, general purchasing officer, Economic Division, USAF/ME, 12 August 1943.
83. USNA, RG319, Transmitting a 'Survey of the Economic Problems of Lebanon', p. 9.
84. PRO, FO921/175, IP 94500/Syria, 1944–5, Textiles.
85. Mallat, *70 Years of Money Muddling*, p. 13. The year 1948 is the first one for which there are reliable estimates of national income.
86. Albert Badre and As'ad Nasr, *National Income of Lebanon, Income Arising in the Industrial Sector*, monograph 3 (Beirut, 1953) p. 23. (Henceforth cited as NIL, Industry.)
87. MAE, Guerre 1939–1945, Londres-CNF, vol. 54, CNF/London to Delegation-General/ Beirut, 22 December 1941, tel. no. 3655a/AX/ECO.

Chapter 4

1. PRO, FO921/175, Industry, p. 21.
2. Ibid., p. 22.
3. The remainder was exported to Britain and France; USNA, RG319, 'P' File, G–2, Lebanon, box 2180, George Arnold, 'Raw silk and cocoons, Lebanon', May 1945. Beirut, 23 May 1946.
4. PRO, FO371, E8826/8826/65, 'Report of the British Goodwill Trade Mission', part III, pp. 75–6.
5. Gibb, *Economic Development*, p. 133.
6. PRO, FO921/175, Industry, p. 23. During the war years, the productive capacity of the weaving industry was estimated to be about five times that of the spinning industry.
7. PRO, FO371, E3734/706/65, A. Spero/Ministry of War Transportation to Mr Dundas, 21 July 1944.
8. The largest textile factory was Arida, with between 350 and 400 weaving looms in the late 1930s, followed by the Asseily factory. Following them, the most important

mechanical weavers in Beirut were Paul Minas with 26 looms, 100 workers, producing 650 metres per day; the *Lainière nationale* with 20 operating looms, 50 workers, producing 360 metres per day; *Société libanaise de tissage* with 15 looms, 40 workers, producing 333 metres per day; hand-weaving subcontractors such as the Near East Rug Weaving and Dyeing Industry, which typically employed 45 workers and produced 130 metres per day. All production figures are for 1944–5; PRO, FO922, IP04500/Syria, 1944/5, Textiles Syria.

9. PRO, FO921/175, Industry, p. 22.
10. Ibid.
11. PRO, FO922, File SS744 E, Report by Captain T. Joyce, 1943, TIR/TJ/7 31 December 1942; PRO, FO922, IPO4500/Syria, 1944/5, Textiles, Syria. This factory produced about 108,000 metres per annum in the last years of the war, constituting about a fifth to a sixth of its productive capacity.
12. Gibb, *Economic Development*, pp. 134–5.
13. Two of the more important mechanical knitting factories in 1944/5 were G. Zouighian (Beirut) equipped with 40 stocking machines, employing 48 workers and producing 140 dozen pairs per day; and *Fabrique nationale de bonneterie* with seven stocking machines and nine workers, producing 21 dozen pairs a day; PRO, FO922, IPO4500/ Syria, 1944/45, Textiles, Syria.
14. PRO, FO921/175, Industry, p. 23.
15. At the beginning of 1946, the Syro-Lebanese weaving industry required 12,000 tons of yarn, which was over four times the amount produced by Asseily and Arida in 1946. See Gibb, *Economic Development*, p. 131. Even with additional output of smaller mills, the required domestic yarn inputs for local weavers could not be met.
16. Ibid., p. 133. Some small but effective dyeing houses had been established, such as Nersessian and Yessayan in Jounieh, which were hank and piece dyers of cotton, silk and rayon. The Near East Rug Weaving and Dyeing Industry, located in Beirut and owned by the Alamuddin family, specialised in hand-dyeing and winding, warping and weaving of cotton; PRO, FO922, TIR/TJ/14, File SS744E (1943–1945) MESC.
17. PRO, FO921/175, Industry, p. 26.
18. Gibb, *Economic Development*, p. 131.
19. USNA, RG84, vol. XVII (1945) box 218, 'Economic and Financial Review (Syria and Lebanon) quarter ending 31 March 1945'.
20. PRO, FO921/175, Industry.
21. Ibid., p. 21.
22. *Bulletin annuel de la BSL*, 1939, p. 94.
23. USNA, RG59, 890e.6476/9–447, American Legation/Beirut to DS, 4 September 1947, no. 6.
24. PRO, FO922, file 1982, 'Cement production: 1942–1943'.
25. PRO, FO921/175, Industry, p. 31.
26. PRO, FO922, 'Economic Bulletin, May 1944'.
27. PRO, FO922, file 1982, 'Cement production: 1942–1943'.
28. Gibb, *Economic Development*, p. 137.

29. USNA, RG59, 890e.6376/8–2947, Current Cement Crisis in Lebanon, 29 August 1947, no. 153, enclosure no. 4, 'The cement question' (Memo from the Merchants of Building Materials).
30. *L'Orient*, 2 September 1947.
31. PRO, FO921/175, Industry, p. 19.
32. Ibid.
33. PRO, FO922, MS 18600/Lebanon, Hides, Leather and Manufactures: Lebanon, 1945 (MESC) Report by Major W. S. Kennedy, MESC Hides Officer. (Hereafter referred to as PRO, FO922, MS 18600/Lebanon, Hides.)
34. Ibid.
35. Ibid.
36. Ibid.
37. PRO, FO921/175, Industry, p. 19.
38. Gibb, *Economic Development*, p. 138.
39. PRO, FO922, MS18600/Lebanon, Hides.
40. PRO, FO921/175, Industry, p. 26.
41. PRO, FO922, MS18600/Lebanon, Hides.
42. USNA, RG84, vol. xi (1943) box 31, 'Annual Economic and Financial Review (Syria and Lebanon) 1942', p. 5.
43. PRO, FO922, MS18600/Lebanon, Hides.
44. Gibb, *Economic Development*, p. 138.
45. USNA, RG84, vol. xi (1944) box 34, 'Annual Economic and Financial Review (Syria and Lebanon) 1943', p. 8.
46. Ibid.
47. USNA, RG84, Beirut, 'Annual Economic and Financial Review, 1942', p. 6.
48. The productive capacity of the Syro-Lebanese match industry was between 18,000 and 20,000 cases (5000 boxes per case) per year.
49. PRO, FO921/175, Industry, p. 37.
50. Ibid.
51. Despite import controls, Kettaneh was able to obtain new machinery in Palestine and raw materials; PRO, FO922, SS734/Match Industry, 1944; PRO, FO371 Spears to MESC, 19 December 1944.
52. PRO, FO921/175, Industry, p. 37.
53. PRO, FO921/175, Industry, p. 10.
54. PRO, FO921/175, Industry, pp. 10–11.
55. Ibid.
56. PRO, FO921/175, Industry, pp. 28–9. Beirut Electric Company was also one of Lebanon's largest companies with a legal capital of FF 75 million in 1939. Its concession was established in 1923 for a duration of 99 years by the merger of two Ottoman companies, Beirut Tramways and Electricity and Beirut Gas Company. See *Bulletin annuel de la BSL*, 1939, p. 70.
57. PRO, FO921/175, Industry, p. 29. See also USNA, RG59, 890e.6376/8–2947, American Legation/Beirut to DS, 29 August 1947, no. 153 and 890e.6476/9–447, American Legation/Beirut to DS, 4 September 1947, no. 156.

58. Ibid.

Chapter 5

1. Republished as *The Wealth of Nations* edited by Edwin Cannan (New York, 1937) p. 404.
2. This chapter draws substantially on material from Carolyn L. Gates, 'Choice, content and performance of a "service-oriented open economy" strategy: the case of Lebanon, 1948–1958', paper presented at a conference organised by the University of Texas at Austin and the Centre for Lebanese Studies, Oxford, *A Look Back at Lebanon, 1958* (Austin, September 1992); and Carolyn L. Gates, 'Laissez-faire, outward-orientation, and regional economic disintegration: a case study of the dissolution of the Syro-Lebanese Customs Union', in Youssef Choueiri (ed.) *State and Society in Syria and Lebanon* (Exeter, 1993).
3. Shehadi, *The Idea of Lebanon*; Picard, *Etat de discorde*; Carolyn L. Gates, 'Development strategy, the state and institutional change: the case of Lebanon', paper presented at a conference organised by the Centre for Lebanese Studies, *Current Research on Lebanon* (Oxford, 1986); and Carolyn L. Gates, 'Governance and economic restructuring in Lebanon, 1948–1970', unpublished paper presented at the University of Amsterdam, Faculty of Economics and Econometrics and Department of International Relations, October 1991.
4. USNA, RG59, 690e.006/7–2249, 22 July 1949.
5. PRO, FO371, E2158/1011/88, Boswall/Beirut, 6 February 1949, no. 17, point 9.
6. Jan Tinbergen, *Economic Policy: Principles and Design* (Amsterdam, 1956). According to the 'Tinbergen rule', a government must have at least as many effective policy instruments as it has independent target variables. If it has fewer, then inconsistency in policy targets emerges. This can be resolved by increasing the number of instruments or making explicit the trade-offs between the variables. See also Henri Theil, *Optimal Decision Rules for Government and Industry* (Amsterdam, 1964).
7. See Chevallier, *La société du Mont-Liban*; Fawaz, *Merchants and Migrants*; Irina M. Smilianskaya, *Al-haraka al-fallahiyya fi lubnan, al-nisf al-awwal min al-qarn al-tasi' 'ashar* [The Peasant Movements of Lebanon during the First Half of the Nineteenth Century, translated from the Russian] (Beirut, 1972); Smilianskaya, 'From subsistence'; Buheiry, *Beirut's Role*; and Gates, *Development of the Modern Political Economy of Lebanon*, pp. 58–63.
8. Bishara al-Khoury's *Hizb al-Destour* was a parliamentary bloc party that espoused the idea that Lebanon belonged to the Mediterranean world. As such, it was prepared to build a political coalition based on Lebanese and Arab nationalist interests and Christian and Muslim coexistence. It typically supported liberal economic policies and institutions advocated by the more restricted circles, such as the 'New Phoenicians'.
9. USNA, RG84, Beirut, vol. xl (1943) box 31, Speech by Gabriel Menassa at inaugural banquet of SLEP on 3 June 1943, Beirut. [On the other hand, Gentlemen, wartime conditions have imposed upon this country a new and temporary economic way of life with forceful constraints upon our rights and management of our activities, brushing

aside the principles of economic liberalism which are so essential for a small country like Lebanon, the centre of commerce and entrepôt activities of the Middle East.]

10. USNA, RG84, American Legation (DC Dennett)/Beirut to DS, 29 May 1946, no. 1231, enclosure no. 2, Biographic Data Report on Mr Philippe Taqla.
11. Michel Chiha, *Politique intérieure* (Beirut, 1964) pp. 303–4.
12. USNA, RG84, Beirut, box 230, Memo of conversation with Michel Chiha, the director of the Banque de Syrie, W. D. Brewer and H. Ayoub on Lebanon's monetary crisis, [n.d.].
13. For more on the orthodox view of an 'enabling environment' of a dynamic private sector, see Staffs of the World Bank and the International Monetary Fund, 'The contribution of the private sector to development, and the roles of the Bank Group and the Fund', *Development Issues: Presentations to the Development Committee, May 8, 1990* (Washington, DC, 1990); Review Group on Private Sector Development, *Developing the Private Sector: A Challenge for the World Bank Group* (Washington DC, 1989).
14. Streeten, 'Trade strategies', pp. 3–4. For more on an open economy development strategy, see Griffin, *Alternative Strategies*, Chapter 4.
15. A development strategy can be identified by three main components: demand source of growth, which can be domestic (investment, consumption and government expenditure) or export; supply source of growth (agriculture, industry, services); and inward or outward orientation, which is based on the effective exchange rate defining import-substitution or export orientation; see Ifzal Ali, 'Strategies and policies for structural transformation in Asia', *Asian Development Review*, vol. 8, no. 2 (1990) pp. 1–27.
16. Smith, *Wealth of Nations*; Ricardo, *Principles*.
17. See Paul Streeten, 'A cool look at "outward looking" strategies for development', *World Development*, 1982; Organisation for Economic Cooperation and Development, *The Newly Industrialising Countries* (Paris, 1988); Peter Nolan, 'Assessing economic growth in the Asian NICs', *Journal of Contemporary Asia*, vol. 20, no. 1 (1990); Gordon White (ed.) *Developmental States in East Asia* (London, 1988).
18. Moshe Syrquin and Hollis B. Chenery, 'Patterns of development, 1950 to 1983', *World Bank Discussion Papers*, no. 41, p. 92.
19. See A. M. Kaissouni and Ernest Struc, 'Report of the mission to Syria' (typescript, IMF, Washington, DC, 22 June 1948) p. 5; Elias Saba, *The Foreign Exchange Systems of Lebanon and Syria 1939–1957* (Beirut, 1961) p. 101; Mallat, *70 Years of Money Muddling* , p. 102; Medawar, *Monetary Problems*, p. 100.
20. *Le Jour*, 4 September 1947, transmitted in USNA, RG84, Damascus, 1947, 'Eradicaion of the Lebanese black market', 9 September 1947.
21. USNA, RG59, 890E.5151/7–847, Pinkerton/Beirut to DS, 8 July 1947, no. A–314; RG59, 890E.5151/9–347, Pinkerton/Beirut to DS, 3 September 1947, no. A–399; RG84, Damascus, 1947, box 680, file 850, Curtis Jones/Beirut, 'Eradication of the Lebanese black market', 9 September 1947, no. 41; *Le commerce du levant*, 30 August 1947.
22. *Le Jour*, 4 September 1947, translated in USNA, RG84, Damascus, 1947, 'Eradication of the Lebanese black market', 9 September 1947.

23. USNA, RG59, 890E.5151/9–348, Kuniholm/Beirut to DS, 3 September 1948, no. A–365.
24. Kaissouni and Struc, 'Report of the mission to Syria', p. 101.
25. USNA, RG59, 890E.5151/11–2348, Pinkerton/Beirut to DS, 23 November 1948.
26. Elias Saba, 'Lebanon's liberal foreign exchange system', *Middle East Economic Papers* (1961) pp. 104–5; USNA, RG59, 890E.5151/12–648, Pinkerton/Beirut to DS, 6 December 1948.
27. Exchange policy continued to be liberalised between 1949 and 24 May 1952 when the last of the import restrictions was removed, so that effectively the only buying rate left was the market rate; and on the selling side, the official rate was applied only to government payments. The official conversion rate of the £L was US$ 1 = £L 2.19 (the par value established by the IMF) while the free market rate fluctuated between US$ 1 = £L 3.87 and US$ 1 = £L 3.04, 1949–53.
28. USNA, RG59, 6903.006/5–2649, American Legation/Beirut to DS, 'Import and price control measures', no. 84; USNA, RG59, 890E.60/5–2349, A–169; USNA, RG59, 890E.5017.
29. Himadeh, *Fiscal System*, p. 8.
30. The conflict between the industrialists and merchants was essentially a clash between economic interests, even though sectarian and regional rivalries contributed to the polarisation of the debate. Although the mercantile–financial bourgeoisie was dominated by Beirut Christians, industry provided more entrepreneurial opportunities for Muslims. See Yusif Sayegh, *Entrepreneurs of Lebanon: the Role of the Business Leader in a Developing Country* (Cambridge, MA, 1962) pp. 70–1. However, some of the most important industries, such as textiles and non-metallic minerals, were controlled by prominent Christian families. The regional factor was complicated by the fact that while Beirut was a main beneficiary of industrialisation, Tripoli was far more dependent on industry for jobs and incomes. Its decline, which could be partially offset by a boom in trade and services in Beirut, was a much larger threat to the welfare of Tripoli's population.
31. Marwan Nasr, head of the Association of Lebanese Industrialists, warned that Lebanese industry could be saved only by supportive national industrial policies, which were outlined in eight major points in the Association of Lebanese Industrialists, *Guide to Lebanon's Industries, 1949–1950* (Beirut, 1950).
32. USNA, RG59, 783A.00(W) 2–1050, Military Attaché/Beirut to DS, 10 February 1950.
33. See also *Al-Hayat*, 9 August 1951.
34. *Al-Hayat*, 9 February 1950.
35. Lebanon, Ministère du plan et mission IRFED (1960/1) *Besoins et possibilités de développement du Liban* (Beirut, n.d.) vol. 1, p. 247. (Hereafter, this work is cited as IRFED.)
36. USNA, RG59, 890E.50/8–1947, Pinkerton/Beirut to DS, 19 August 1947, A–385.
37. El-Hafez, *La structure*, p. 203.
38. Ibid.

39. Elias Saba, 'The Syro-Lebanese Customs Union: causes of failure and attempts at reorganization', *Middle East Economic Papers* (1960); Saba, 'Lebanon's liberal foreign exchange system'.
40. Saba, 'The Syro-Lebanese Customs Union', p. 100.
41. Menassa, *Plan de reconstruction*, p. 344.
42. 'Lebanese isolationists' advocated a strict separation of Lebanon from Syria and the Arab world and closer ties with the West.
43. USNA, RG84, Damascus, box 680, file 801, Cairo, August 1948. Memo: Recommendations for Syro-Lebanese Relations, prepared by SLEP; enclosure, Syro-Lebanese Parity by Judd Polk.
44. Menassa, *Plan de reconstruction*, p. 355.
45. USNA, RG59, 711.90e/5–1049, Memo of Conversation between State Department officials Satterthwaite and Clark and Mr Francis Kettaneh, 10 May 1949.
46. *Foreign Commerce Weekly*, 4 September 1950.
47. UN, *Review*, 1950/1, p. 74.
48. El-Hafez, *La structure*, p. 209.
49. Joseph Donato, 'Lebanon and its labour legislation', *International Labour Review*, vol. 55 (January 1952) p. 68.
50. USNA, RG59, 783A.00(W)/1–551, Military Attaché/Beirut to DS, 5 January 1951.
51. UN, *Review*, 1950/1, p. 74; see also IRFED, vol. 1, p. 237.
52. USNA, RG59, 883A.00/3–1753, 'Economic and Financial Review, 1952', Lebanon.
53. USNA, RG59, 783A.00(W)/2–2152, Military Attaché/Beirut to DS, 21 February 1952.
54. USNA, RG59, 883A.00/3–1753, 'Economic and Financial Review, 1952', Lebanon.
55. USNA, RG59, 783A.00/6–1752, Minor/Beirut to DS, 17 June 1952.
56. MAE, Guerre 1939–1945, Londres CNF, vol. 60, Francom/Beirut to de Gaulle/CNF, 12 September 1940, no. 1221.
57. USNA, RG59, 883A.14/6–1351, 'Influence of the French-controlled Banque de Syrie et du Liban in the financial system of Lebanon', 13 June 1951 (henceforth cited as USNA, RG59, 883A.14/6–1351, 'BSL influence').
58. PRO, FO371, E5681/1102/88, Conversation between the British Commercial Secretary and René Busson, Boswell/Beirut, 2 May 1949, no. 51E.
59. USNA, RG59, 883A.14/6–1351, 'BSL influence'.
60. Britain claimed that SERIAC was organised by French intelligence; PRO, FO371, E5321/1106/65, Economic Intelligence Department, 31 January 1949. SERIAC, a semi-official trading company, was organised along lines similar to the British East India Company. The French government owned shares worth FF 12.5 million out of a total capitalisation of FF 44 million. The non-governmental shares were owned by 43 French companies, including nine banks: BSL, Ottoman Bank, *Banque nationale pour le commerce et l'industrie*, *Crédit Lyonnais*, *Banque de Paris et des Pays Bas*, *Banque nationale française de commerce extérieur*, *Banque de l'Indo-Chine*, *Crédit foncier d'Algérie et de Tunisie* and the *Compagnie algérienne*; these nine banks were the majority shareholders, owning FF 25 million of the shares. See USNA, RG319, Lebanon, box 2180, 'P' file, Library file, Functions and Organization of SERIAC, enclosure to 17 July 1947, no. 118. Besides the large governmental and banking

interests, influential companies, such as Air France, held shares in SERIAC. See USNA, RG319, Lebanon, box 2180, 'P' file, Kuniholm/Beirut to DS, 10 September 1946, no. 1224. Most of the founders of SERIAC were French, who had worked and lived in Lebanon for many years, including the dominant figure in the organisation, René Busson; USNA, RG84, Beirut, box 231, file 850.3, Kamal Jumblatt, Minister of National Economy to PM, Beirut, 4 February 1947, no. 269.

61. PRO, FO371, E5681/1102/88, 2 May 1949.
62. USNA, RG319, 'Lebanon, functions and organizations of SERIAC', enclosure to despatch no. 118, 17 July 1947.
63. USNA, RG84, Cairo, box 175, American Embassy General Records/Cairo, US Legation/Beirut to DS, 17 July 1947, no. 118.
64. USNA, RG319, entry 82, box 2179, 10 January 1946.
65. USNA, RG319, 'P' file, box 2180, Kuniholm/Beirut to DS, 10 September 1946, no. 1224.
66. USNA, RG59, 883A.14/6–1351, 'BSL influence'.
67. PRO, FO371, E4306/251/88, Harpham/Beirut, 'Economic Review of April 1947', 6 May 1947, no.CS 16/1–47.
68. Medawar, *Monetary Problems in Lebanon*, p. 43.
69. El-Hafez, *La structure*, p. 118.
70. Amounting to £L 68 million in 1951 and £L 40 million in 1952. See Edward Fei and Paul Klat, *The Balance of Payments of Lebanon, 1951 and 1952* (Beirut, 1954) p. 40.
71. A. Basile, 'La vocation régionale de la place financière de Beyrouth', *Proche-Orient études économiques* (January–December, 1973) p. 146, as cited by Dubar and Nasr, *Les classes sociales*, p. 71.
72. El-Hafez, *La structure*, p. 202. For a contrasting viewpoint, see Albert Badre, 'Economic development', p. 164.
73. Rizk, *Le régime politique libanais*.
74. Michael Hudson, *The Precarious Republic: Political Modernization in Lebanon* (New York, 1968) p. 139.
75. Association of Lebanese Industrialists, *Guide*.
76. Yusif Sayegh and Muhammad Atallah, *Nazra thaniya li al-iqtisad al-lubnaniyya* [A second look at the Lebanese economy] (Beirut, 1966) p. 102.
77. Saba, 'The Syro-Lebanese Customs Union'; Saba, 'Lebanon's liberal foreign exchange system'; and Saba, *The Foreign Exchange Systems*.
78. After the Lebanese signed the accord with France in 1948, the Lebanese pound was set at £L 8.83 = £1 sterling.
79. USNA, RG59, 890e.5151/9–248, McCormick/Beirut to DS, 2 September 1948, no. 239; USNA, RG59, 883A.14/6–1351, 'BSL influence'.
80. USNA, RG59, 890e.5151/8–3148, McCormick/Beirut to DS, 31 August 1948, no. 235.
81. USNA, RG59, 890e.5151/9–148, McCormick/Beirut to DS, 1 September 1948, no. 236.
82. Mallat, *70 Years of Money Muddling*, p. 102.
83. El-Hafez, *La structure*, p. 206.
84. Mallat, *70 Years of Money Muddling*, p. 102; Medawar, *Monetary Problems*, p. 100.

85. PRO, FO371, E5681/1102/88, Conversation between British Commercial Secretary and Busson, Boswall/Beirut, 2 May 1949, no. 51e.
86. See PRO, FO371, EL1113/2, Boswall/Beirut to FO, Ernest Bevin, 14 March 1950, no. 38e. See also USNA, RG59, 883A.14/6-1351, 'BSL influence'.
87. Talha Yaffi, 'La réforme bancaire au Liban', *Le Commerce du Levant*, 24 October 1949.
88. USNA 883a.00/3–850, Lebanon, 'Annual Economic Report, 1949'.
89. USNA, RG84, Damascus 1947, box 680, file 801, 'Report on monetary developments in Syria and Lebanon' by Sa'id Himadeh, submitted to Minister of National Economy, Kamal Jumblatt, 20 April 1947, p. 26.
90. Sa'id Himadeh, 'Mashakil al-iqtisadiyya wa-kayf nu'alijuha' [Economic problems and how we should deal with them], *Les conférences du Cénacle libanais* (Beirut, 1947).
91. USNA, RG84, Damascus, box 680, file 801, Himadeh Report, p. 27.
92. PRO, FO371, EL1113/2, Boswall/Beirut to FO, 14 March 1950, no. 38e.
93. Saba, *Foreign Exchange Systems*, p. 19.
94. The reserve account comprised the cumulative surplus/deficit from the ordinary budgets minus transfers to the Development Works Fund or extraordinary budgets.
95. Badre, 'Economic development', p. 178.
96. Lecture by André Tuéni, 'The budget and the tax system in Lebanon', delivered on 8 May 1950 to the *Cénacle libanais*, published as 'Al-muwazana wa nizam al-dara'ib fi lubnan', *Les Conférences du Cénacle libanais*, vol. 4, nos 5–6 (25 May 1950) pp. 75–99.
97. For a comparison with Egypt during this period, see Mahmoud Abdel-Fadil, *The Political Economy of Nasserism: a Study in Employment and Income Distribution Policies in Urban Egypt, 1952–1972* (Cambridge, 1980) Table 5.1, p. 72.
98. USNA RG84, Cairo, box 235, file 500, enclosure no. 2, Memo from John F. L. Ghiardi to Ambassador Caffery on tentative grant aid programme for Lebanon, 11 January 1951; Saba, *Foreign Exchange Systems.*
99. For more on the application of the Truman doctrine to Lebanon, see USNA, RG59, 883A.00TA/11–3051, Minor/Beirut to DS, 30 November 1951, and 883A.00–TA/8–1952, Secret, Minor/Beirut to Parker Hart/NEA, DS, 19 August 1952.
100. USNA, RG59, 883A.00TA/3–2852, Minor/Beirut to DS, 28 March 1952.
101. USNA, RG59, 883A.00/3–1753, 'Economic and Financial Review, 1952', Lebanon.
102. USNA, RG59, 883A.00–TA/11–350, Pinkerton/Beirut to DS, 3 November 1950.
103. Medawar, *Monetary Problems*, pp. 79–80.
104. UN, FAO, *Mediterranean Development Project, Country Report: Lebanon* (Rome, 1959) pp. I:5–7.
105. Arthur E. Mills, *Private Enterprise in Lebanon* (Beirut, 1959) p. 120.
106. Extrapolated from UN, Département des questions économiques, *L'évolution économique au Moyen-Orient, 1945 à 1954* (Supplément au rapport sur l'économie mondiale, 1953–1954) (New York, 1955) p. 192.
107. USNA, RG59, 783a.00(w)/1–551, Military Attaché/Beirut to DS, 5 January 1951; USNA, RG319, ID file, ID #788589, R–78–51, 25 April 1951; USNA, RG59, 983A.00/12–2750, Basic Telecommunications Report.
108. *L'Orient*, July-September 1952.

109. *Al-Hayat*, 15 December 1949.
110. *L'Orient*, 9 October 1949.
111. USNA, RG59, 783A.02/5–2950, Pinkerton/Beirut to DS, 29 May 1950.
112. USNA, RG59, 883A.413/2–851, Bruins/Beirut to DS, 8 February 1951.
113. USNA, RG59, 883A.00TA/3–2852, Minor/Beirut to DS, 28 March 1952.
114. See Chenery and Syrquin, *Patterns of Development*; Simon Kuznets, *Economic Growth of Nations: Total Output and Production Structure* (Cambridge, MA, 1971).
115. Badre, 'Economic development in Lebanon', pp. 184–5; Medawar, *Monetary Problems in Lebanon*, p. 201; IRFED, vol. 1, Table 23.
116. Menassa, *Plan de reconstruction*, pp. 353–5.
117. Badre, 'Economic development', p. 165.
118. Mustafa al-Nusuli, *Nahwa ghadan afdal li-as-sina'a al-lubnaniyya* [Towards a better tomorrow for Lebanese industry] (Beirut, 1968) p. 4.
119. However, even in the midst of restructuring in 1950, Lebanese industry was profitable: profits amounted to 43 per cent of those generated by the much larger import trade sector; Albert Badre, 'The national income of Lebanon', *Middle East Economic Papers* (1956) Table 7, p. 22.
120 UN, *L'évolution*, 1945–54, p. 190.
121. USNA, RG59, 890e.61/4–958, Note on Agricultural Development Plan, April 1948; UN, *L'évolution*, 1945–54, p. 170.
122. Badre, 'Economic development', p. 185.

Chapter 6

1. UN, *L'évolution économique, 1945–54*, p. 164. For unemployment data, see Donato, 'Lebanon and its labour legislation', p. 72; USNA, RG319 'P' file, Lebanon, box 2180, 'Annual Economic and Financial Review (Syria and Lebanon) 1946', pp. 32–3; *Bayrut al-masa*, 12 March 1952; *L'Orient*, 23 April 1952; USNA, RG59, 783A.001/2–1951 Bruins/Beirut to DS, 19 February 1951.
2. USNA, RG59, 883A.18/3–1152 Minor/Beirut to DS, 11 March 1952.
3. UN, *Review*, 1951–52, p. 114.
4. USNA, RG59, 883A.18/3–1152 Minor/Beirut to DS, 11 March 1952.
5. Ibid.
6. Ministère de l'économie national, Service de statistique générale, *Bulletin statistique trimestriel* (henceforth, this is cited as *BST)* (Beirut) 1952, vol. 3 no. 4. August 1939 = 100.
7. Donato, 'Lebanon and its labour legislation', pp. 65–71.
8. Salim Hoss, 'Economic concentration in Lebanon', *Middle East Economic Papers* (1963) p. 69.
9. USNA, RG59, 883A.00/2–652 'Annual Economic Report, 1951', Lebanon. Unless otherwise noted, the remainder of the paragraph is based on this source.
10. USNA, RG59, 883A.00/3–1753 'Economic and Financial Review, 1952', Lebanon.
11. USNA, RG319, 'Annual Economic and Financial Review, 1946', Lebanon, p. 2.
12. USNA, RG59, 483a.84a/6–1951 Secret File, Bruins/Beirut to DS, 19 June 1951.

13. USNA, RG84, vol. xvii, 1945, box 218, file 850, Scott/Beirut to DS, 7 September 1945, no. 28.
14. USNA, RG59, 690e.006/7–1846 Wadsworth/Beirut to DS, 18 July 1946, no. A–118.
15. *BST*, 1952, vol. 3, no. 4.
16. Ministry of Finance Statement in *Le Commerce du Levant*, 26 December 1951.
17. UN, *L'évolution*, 1945–54, p. 182.
18. International Monetary Fund, *Balance of Payments Yearbook*, vol. 10 (April 1959) Lebanon, p. 1.
19. USNA, RG59, 883A.14/6–1351, 'Influence of the French-controlled BSL'; 883a.00/2–652, 'Annual Economic Report, 1951', Lebanon.
20. UN, *L'évolution,* 1945–54, pp. 184–5.
21. USNA, RG84, Beirut, box 230, file 851, Lane/Beirut, 'Importation of gold from the US to Syria and the Lebanon', 10 July 1946, no. 1265.
22. USNA, RG59, 883A.2531/3–653, 'Beirut as a gold market'.
23. Ibid.
24. *Le commerce du Levant*, 9 February 1952; see also USNA, RG59, 883A.2531/3–653, 'Beirut as a gold market'.
25. Fei and Klat, *Balance of Payments*, p. 43. The UN, *L'évolution*, 1945–54, states that these figures are high. Michel Doumit, the largest gold dealer in Beirut at that time, claimed that profits from the gold trade in 1951 could have been as low as US$ 850,000 and as high as US$ 6 million, if much of the trade involved smuggling; USNA, RG59, 883A.2531/3–653, 'Beirut as a gold market'. Sources also vary on estimates of profit rates on this trade. US officials stated that Lebanese gold dealers earned 77 per cent in profits in 1946 on gold imported from the USA; RG84, box 230 'Importation of gold . . .', 10 July 1946. Another claimed that profits on transit gold amounted to about US$ 1–1.20 per ounce in 1948/9; FO371, EY1103/1 'Notes of Mr G. D. Wilson on Syria and Lebanon'. Still another source claims that profits on transit gold had declined from US$ 5–6 per ounce in 1947/8 to US$ 0.50 per ounce in early 1951 to US$ 0.10 per ounce in early 1952; *International Financial News Survey*, vol. 4, no. 35 (14 May 1952) p. 281.
26. USNA, RG59, 883A.2531/3–653, 'Beirut as a gold market'.
27. Badre, 'Economic development', p. 168.
28. USNA, RG59, 883A.181/11–950 Clifford and Ruff, 'Travel and tourism', Lebanon.
29. USNA, RG59, 883A.00/3–1753 'Economic and Financial Review, 1952', Lebanon.
30. UN, *L'évolution,* 1945–54, n. 44.
31. USNA, RG59, 883A.45/5–1550 Pinkerton/Beirut to DS, 15 May 1950; see also 783A.21/12–2051 Minor/Beirut to DS, 20 December 1951.
32. USNA, RG59, 783a.00(w)/5–1652 Military Attaché/Beirut to DS, 16 May 1952.
33. Havard and Ogden, *Report,* 1936–8, p. 3.
34. *Le Commerce du Levant*, 3 July 1954; Mallat, *70 Years of Money Muddling*, p. 45.
35. Albert Badre and As'ad Nasr, 'Income arising in the services sector', *National Income of Lebanon*, monograph 4 (Beirut, 1953) p. 23 (henceforth, NIL, *Services*).
36. UN, *L'évolution*, 1945–54, p. 182; Badre and Nasr, NIL, *Services*, Table 1, p. 13.
37. Badre and Nasr, NIL, Industry, p. 7; USNA, RG59, 883A.00TA/10–1752 Minor/ Beirut, September 1952, TCS Report, Lebanon; UN, *L'évolution*, 1945–54, pp. 164, 171.

Varying estimates of industrial labour show employment of 25,000 to 50,000 workers between 1945 and 1958, compared with some 20,000 at the beginning of the Second World War. See also UN, *Review*, 1951/2, p. 41; Badre, 'Economic development'; Donato, 'Lebanon and its labour legislation', pp. 67, 69; *BST*, 1951, vol. 2, nos 3–4; Kurt Grunwald, *The Government Finances of the Mandated Territories in the Near East* (Tel Aviv, 1932) p. 163.

38. Badre and Nasr, NIL, Industry, Table 19, p. 24. Unless otherwise noted, all data on the top eight branches of Lebanese industry in 1950 are drawn from the Badre and Nasr survey of industry.
39. UN, *L'évolution*, 1945–54, p. 171.
40. USNA, RG59, 883A.06/12–1550, '1950 Annual Labor Report'.
41. Ibid.
42. Menassa, *Plan de reconstruction*, pp. 356–7; UN, *Review*, 1951–2, p. 129.
43. Grunwald, *Government Finances*, pp. 167–8.
44. USNA, RG59, 883A.06/3–752, '1951 Annual Labor Report'.
45. USNA, RG59, 883A.00/2–652, 'Annual Economic Report, 1951', Lebanon.
46. USNA, RG59, 883A.19/3–1753 Minor/Beirut to DS, 17 March 1953, 'Lebanese industrial production and employment in 1952'.
47. UN, *L'évolution*, 1945–54, p. 171, n. 21.
48. Ibid., p. 173.
49. The area for which Beirut building permits were issued rose from 107,000 square metres in 1945 to over 322,000 square metres in 1952; see *BST*, 1952, vol. 3, no. 4. These figures, however, under-represent actual construction by at least 25 per cent. In 1952, the second largest area of construction was found in Tripoli, which issued permits for less than one-fifth of the area licensed in Beirut. The building boom continued unabated until the outbreak of the Korean War when world market prices for raw materials rose sharply. In 1950, the gross value of construction at cost was estimated at £L 98,716,000; Albert Badre, 'The national income of Lebanon', pp. 18–19; see also Albert Badre and Apogig Altoumian, 'Income arising in the construction sector', *National Income of Lebanon*, monograph 2 (Beirut, 1951)
50. Badre, 'Economic development', pp. 64–6.
51. USNA, RG59, 890e.6476/9–447, American Legation, 'Cement distribution in Lebanon', 4 September 1947, no. 156.
52. UN, *L'évolution*, 1945–54, p. 173.
53. El-Hafez, *La structure*, p. 72.
54. Arthur E. Mills, 'Economic change in Lebanon', *Middle East Economic Papers* (1956) p. 72.
55. Calculated from IRFED, vol. 2, Table 26, p. 379.
56. IRFED, vol. 1, p. 211.
57. Samir Khalaf and Emilie Shwayri, 'Family firms and industrial development: the Lebanese case', *Economic Development and Cultural Change*, vol. 15, no. 1 (October 1966) p. 87; Sayegh, *Entrepreneurs*, p. 87; Frederick Harbison and Charles Myers, *Management in the Industrial World: An International Analysis* (NewYork, 1959) p. 69.
58. USNA, RG59, 883A.332/4–2453 Minor/Beirut to DS, 27 April 1953.

59. *Foreign Commerce Weekly*, 4 September 1950.
60. Menassa, *Plan de reconstruction*, p. 356.
61. El-Hafez, *La structure*, p. 209.
62. USNA, RG59, 883A.19/9–852 Lobenstine/Beirut to DS, 8 September 1952; Badr and Nasr, NIL, Industry.
63. USNA, RG59, 883A.001/7–2254 Hare/Beirut, 'Consumption Patterns in Lebanon'. Estimates on the share of Lebanon's population dependent on agriculture during this period vary from 40 to 70 per cent. See US Department of Agriculture, *Report of the United States–Lebanon Agricultural Mission*, IAG Series, no. 7 (Washington DC, 1948) p. 4; estimates by Lebanon's Ministry of Agriculture and the Lebanese Central Office of Statistics, cited in AUB, *Report on Agricultural Credit*, p. 2, n. 2 and p. 1, n. 3.
64. USNA, RG59, 883A.20/8–1253 Rourk/Beirut to DS, 12 August 1953.
65. UN, *Review*, 1951–2, p. 41.
66. El-Hafez, *La structure*, p. 32. See also C. R. S. Wheeler, 'Large-scale farming in the Northern Djezira of Syria', *Proceedings of the Conference on Middle East Agricultural Development*, p. 67 as cited by Paul Klat, *Land Tenure in Syria and Lebanon and its Economic and Social Effects with Some Suggestions for Reform*, B.Litt. thesis (Oxford University, 1948).
67. *Report on Agricultural Credit*; except where otherwise noted, this section is based on this source, pp. 9–13.
68. USNA, RG319, 'P' file, Lebanon, box 2180, 'Annual Economic and Financial Review (Syria and Lebanon) 1946', p. 15.
69. Agricultural Credit Conference, AUB, 'Agenda, Working Materials and Proceedings', p. 22.
70. Ibid.
71. Ibid., p. 6.
72. Ibid.
73. Ibid.
74. B. A. Keen, *The Agricultural Development of the Middle East* (London, 1946) p. 82.
75. Ibid.
76. UN, *L'évolution*, 1945–54, p. 168.
77. Ibid., p. 167.

Chapter 7

1. Mallat, *70 Years of Money Muddling*, p. 99.
2. See PRO, FO371, E5681/1102/88, Conversation between the British Commercial Secretary and René Busson, 2 May 1949 no. 5le.
3. Medawar, *Monetary Problems*, p. 131.
4. PRO, FO371, E5681/1102/88, 2 May 1949.
5. PRO, FO371, EL1113/2, Boswall/Beirut to FO, March 14th 1950, no. 38e. See also Gates, *Development of the Modern Political Economy of Lebanon*, pp. 246–8.
6. Mallat, *70 Years of Money Muddling*, p. 118; Medawar, *Monetary Problems*, p. 176.
7. FAO, *Mediterranean Development Project, Lebanon*, pp. I:5–7.

8. Medawar, *Monetary Problems*, p. 82.
9. S. Siksek, A. Baaklini and A. Daouk, *Preliminary Assessment of Manpower Resources and Requirements in Lebanon* (Beirut, 1959) pp. 29–30.
10. Medawar, *Monetary Problems*, p. 35; Albert Badre, 'Economic development', pp. 200–1.
11. Medawar, *Monetary Problems*, p. 34.
12. USNA, RG59, 883a.001/7–2254 Hare/Beirut, 'Consumption Patterns in Lebanon', 22 July 1954. Per-capita income in Beirut was between five and six times greater than that in rural areas where two-thirds of all Lebanese lived.
13. The intermittent political crises do not appear to have hit the financial sector, which grew by an average compound rate of 10.3 per cent per annum from 1948 to 1958 without ever experiencing a decline.
14. Medawar, *Monetary Problems*, pp. 43–4.
15. See Simon Kuznets, *Economic Growth and Structure: Selected Essays* (New York, 1965) pp. 94–6.
16. For more on the issue of uneven development in Lebanon, see Kuwait Fund for Arab Economic Development, *Report on the Lebanese Economy and its Development Projects* (1976) and IRFED, vols. 1 and 2. For a general discussion of uneven development, see Kuznets, *Selected Essays*, pp. 61–74 and 94–6.

Appendix

Table A1: *Population density, 1944*

	Area (square km)	Population	Density
Beirut	18	237 000	13 000
Mount Lebanon	1 951	272 000	139
North Lebanon	1 959	227 000	116
South Lebanon	2 045	170 000	83
Beka'a	4 427	158 000	36
TOTAL	10 400	1 064 000	102

Source: Mas'ud Dahir, *Lubnan al-istiqlal, al-mithaq wa sigha* (Beirut, 1977) pp. 9–11.

Table A2: *Land distribution, 1953*

Size of unit	% of land	Number of owners
< 10 hectares	70–75	133 000* (70–75 and 15–20 combined)
10–100 hectares	15–20	
> 100 hectares	10	6 000

Note: *The majority owned less than two hectares.

Source: Lebanese Bureau of Statistics, US Foreign Operations Administration and *Report on Agricultural Credit in Lebanon.*

Table A3: *Formation and capitalisation of companies, 1924–50*

Year of establishment	Number	Total capital (£SL 000)
1924	1	3000.00
1925	1	200.00
1926	–	–
1927	–	–
1928	1	500.00
1929	5	5 573.00
1930	1	220.00
1931	1	20.00
1932	2	200.00
1933	3	442.50
1934	2	510.00
1935	4	5 525.00
1936	1	513.00
1937	1	613.00
1938	2	740.00
1939	3	1 336.00
1940	1	50.00
1041	1	1 400.00
1942	1	300.00
1943	4	1 750.00
1944	6	4 790.00
1945	9	3 200.00
1946	13	7 745.00
1947	4	2 130.00
1948	10	10 482.00
1949	13	14 850.00
1950	8	3 754.00
TOTAL	98	69 843.50

Source: El-Hafez, *La structure et la politique économique en Syrie et au Liban*, p. 55.

Table A4: *Deposits and loans of principal banks, 1939–52 (£L 000)*

December/Year	Time deposits	Demand deposits	Total deposits	Loans and discounted paper
1939	934	26 531	27 465	9 649
1940	674	39 737	40 411	8 082
1941	727	30 285	31 012	12 136
1942	1 633	85 391	87 024	15 140
1943	1 527	164 902	166 429	17 749
1944	1 527	178 374	179 931	31 145
1945	1 302	225 827	227 129	69 763
1946	886	208 798	209 684	67 385
1947	1 481	205 386	206 867	106 380
1948	4 543	194 259	198 802	142 556
1949	4 773	175 783	180 556	168 725
1950	5 514	209 667	215 181	176 587
1951	6 205	253 092	259 297	216 604
1952	11 766	301 456	313 222	263 238

Source: Ministère de l'économie national, *Bulletin statistique trimestriel*, 1953, vol. 4, no. 4.

Table A5: *Monetary circulation, 1939–52 (£L 000)*

31 December/ Year	Bank notes	Silver or gold coins	Coins	Other notes	Total
1939	27 950	687	356	–	28 993
1940	51 600	707	405	–	52 712
1941	59 200	708	406	–	60 314
1942	95 250	710	406	920	97 286
1943	110 750	710	406	2 433	114 299
1944	142 500	710	406	2 594	146 210
1945	168 750	710	406	2 069	171 964
1946	142 500	710	467	1 916	145 593
1947	160 500	710	467	1 834	163 511
1948	185 000	710	467	1 903	188 080
1949	168 000	710	467	2 027	171 204
1950	196 000	710	496	2 750	199 956
1951	208 000	706	493	3 113	212 312
1952	200 000	706	489	3 751	204 946

Source: Ministère de l'économie national, *Bulletin statistique trimestriel*, 1953, vol. 4, no. 4.

Table A6: *Financial indices, 1939–52*

Year	Money supply[1]	Gold[2]	Equities[3]
1939	100	105	105
1940	164	198	122
1941	249	214	220
1942	346	259	426
1943	474	314	620
1944	544	283	444
1945	709	319	458
1946	676	309	486
1947	666	278	443
1948	828	314	421
1949	766	262	345
1950	818	244	317
1951	930	288	310
1952	894	272	344

Notes: (1) Index of bank notes in circulation at the end of the month. Base: 1939=100; (2) Index of average monthly rate of the gold sovereign on the Beirut bourse. Base: August 1938–July 1939=100; (3) Index of average end of month values on the Beirut bourse. Base: August 1938–July 1939=100.

Source: Ministère de l'économie national, *Bulletin statistique trimestriel*, 1952, vol. 3, no. 4.

Table A7: *Cost of living, Beirut, 1940–52**

Month	Year	Food	Housing and water	Heating and lighting	Clothing	Direct taxes	Miscellaneous	General index
January	1940	114	102	n.a.	110	100	116	110
January	1942	334	133	n.a.	260	187	178	233
December	1942	564	166	n.a.	459	187	224	365
"	1943	612	120	345	651	n.a.	311	441
"	1944	663	132	306	1 002	n.a.	435	560
"	1945	732	130	289	1 068	n.a.	483	607
"	1946	662	130	279	909	n.a.	484	553
"	1947	604	130	221	n.a.	739	492	500
"	1948	626	140	229	642	n.a.	485	492
"	1949	569	141	263	620	n.a.	452	461
"	1950	509	141	226	566	n.a.	447	426
"	1951	569	148	228	615	n.a.	463	462
"	1952	586	148	226	599	n.a.	443	462

Note: *Base: June 1939=100; n.a. = not available.

Source: CSIC, *Elements statistiques des Etats de Syrie et du Liban*, no. 20, 3, 1947; *Bulletin statistique trimestriel*, 1952, vol. 4, no. 4.

Table A8a: *Ordinary budgets, 1939–45 (£L 000) receipts*

Receipts	1939	1940	1941	1942	1943	1944	1945
Direct taxes and duties	1 202	1 586	1 639	2 497	4 398	5 542	7 467
Income tax*	–	–	–	–	–	–	(3 060)
Indirect taxes and revenues**	3 600	4 509	5 474	9 203	16 396	20 713	35 962
Revenue from public property	40	28	58	49	124	382	1 083
Revenue from public enterprises	836	720	628	1 094	1 459	1 870	2 350
Miscellaneous receipts	776	894	747	2 655	4 272	4 720	8 210
Receipts in attenuation of expenditure	37	101	103	74	118	160	160
Withdrawals from reserves	249	429	1 523	1 081	2 413	142	3 963
Receipts from Common Interests	15	400	150	–	–	1 354	–
Extraordinary receipts	736	107	–	–	–	3 000	–
Total receipts	7 491	8 774	10 322	16 653	29 180	37 883	59 195

Table A8b: *Ordinary budgets, 1946–52 (£L 000) receipts*

Receipts	1946	1947	1948	1949	1950	1951	1952
Direct taxes and duties	10 196	12 483	11 696	14 926	15 055	17 088	32 247
Income tax*	(5 260)	(11 103)	(7 392)	(10 362)	(10 107)	(11 315)	(13 546)
Indirect taxes and revenues**	50 918	63 554	57 924	62 482	58 380	75 465	74 030
Revenue from public property	259	150	746	491	888	577	599
Revenue from public enterprises	2 701	2 600	3 038	3 129	2 719	3 646	4 404
Miscellaneous receipts	9 588	6 746	5 262	6 100	6 169	8 320	13 647
Receipts in attenuation of expenditure	253	455	88	240	105	212	–
Withdrawals from reserves	5 240	16 852	14 738	21 626	18 492	17 742	22 487
Receipts from Common Interests	–	–	–	–	–	–	–
Extraordinary receipts	–	–	–	–	–	–	–
Total receipts	79 155	102 840	93 493	108 993	101 809	123 049	147 414

Notes: * The income tax category refers to the law passed in 1944. All revenues from the income tax are included in direct taxes. The amounts shown in parentheses are for information only and are not added into totals. ** Customs duties constitute over 40 per cent of indirect taxes and revenues in 1947–52.

Table A8c: *Ordinary budgets, 1939–45 (£L 000) expenditures*

Expenditures	1939	1940	1941	1942	1943	1944	1945
President of the Republic	22	24	48	98	122	179	444
Chamber of Deputies	92	–	–	–	185	448	486
Secretary of State and Prime Minister	44	43	7	94	154	310	232
Ministry of Foreign Affairs	–	–	1	24	52	155	586
Ministry of Finance*	746	545	905	1 220	2 275	2 972	2 345
Ministry of Interior**	1 490	1 683	2 265	3 771	6 737	8 198	8 875
Ministry of Justice	621	576	681	1 048	1 721	2 050	2 370
Ministry of Public Works	1 136	1 220	987	1 999	3 891	4 678	6 970
Ministry of National Education	497	527	628	975	1 783	2 615	3 096
Ministry of Supply	–	–	1	104	297	353	372
Ministry of Agriculture	129	92	99	210	384	552	910
Ministry of National Economy***	–	–	–	–	–	–	***
Ministry of PTT	383	369	425	703	1 201	1 374	1 504
Ministry of Defence	–	–	–	–	–	11	3 238
Ministry of Health	284	287	307	701	1 236	1 689	2 003
Ministry of Commerce and Industry	40	33	33	69	145	211	294
Ministry of Information	–	–	–	–	–	–	–
Ministry of Social Affairs	–	–	–	–	–	–	–
Debt due	690	636	725	1 018	1 298	1 792	1 828
Expenditures for past years	195	80	270	82	191	79	276
Reserve for emergencies	–	–	–	–	–	–	–
Amortising and interest on treasury bonds	–	–	–	–	–	–	–
Total expenditures	6 369	6 115	7 382	12 116	21 672	27 666	35 919

Table A8d: *Ordinary budgets, 1946–52 (£L 000) expenditures*

Expenditures	1946	1947	1948	1949	1950	1951	1952
President of the Republic	257	429	450	464	489	435	459
Chamber of Deputies	491	484	638	631	574	962	1 155
Secretary of State and Prime Minister	360	239	240	210	267	277	242
Ministry of Foreign Affairs	744	1 646	2 084	2 302	2 747	2 471	2 195
Ministry of Finance*	2 843	3 194	3 596	3 397	3 408	2 552	3 983
Ministry of Interior**	10 477	10 735	11 557	11 863	11 370	11 799	11 098
Ministry of Justice	2 802	2 907	2 750	2 928	3 125	3 255	3 297
Ministry of Public Works	10 251	15 330	16 781	16 328	18 013	14 711	14 771
Ministry of National Education	4 188	4 865	5 693	6 774	7 857	9 560	9 958
Ministry of Supply	292	–	–	–	–	–	–
Ministry of Agriculture	1 130	1 244	1 526	2 100	3 520	4 801	2 853
Ministry of National Economy***	***	393	548	413	508	517	447
Ministry of PTT	1 788	1 996	2 239	2 136	2 476	2 438	2 627
Ministry of Defence	11 273	9 949	13 313	17 318	14 561	17 082	17 423

Table A8d (continued): *Ordinary budgets, 1946–52 (£L 000) expenditures*

Expenditures	1946	1947	1948	1949	1950	1951	1952
Ministry of Health	2 489	3 452	3 730	4 817	4 819	4 562	4 660
Ministry of Commerce and Industry	320	–	–	–	–	–	–
Ministry of Information	–	–	–	–	572	617	593
Ministry of Social Affairs	–	–	–	–	–	–	361
Debt due	2 049	2 913	3 158	7 581	7 442	8 118	8 593
Expenditures for past years	240	947	1 765	4 141	2 775	4 896	1 713
Reserve for emergencies	–	–	–	–	–	–	–
Amortising and interest on treasury bonds	–	–	–	–	–	–	2 082
Total expenditures	51 994	60 722	70 068	83 402	84 522	90 051	88 510

Notes: * Expenditures of the Ministry of Finance are composed of: (1) financial services (2) land services. **Expenditures of the Ministry of Interior are composed of: (1) administrative services (2) gendarmerie (3) police (4) Sûreté Générale. ***The Ministry of National Economy was established in 1945 and is composed of the Ministry of Supply and Ministry of Commerce and Industry. Expenditures of this ministry for 1945 and 1946 are shown in the other two ministries.

Source: CSIC, *Recueil de statistiques*, 1942–5, 1945–7; *Bulletin statistique trimestriel*, 1950, nos 1, 2, 4; 1952, no. 4; 1953, no. 4.

Table A9: *Expenditures of the Development Works Fund, 1944–52 (£L 000)*

Year	Water	Roads	Schools	Hospitals	Other buildings	International airport	Seaports/ other airports	Army	Misc.	Total
1944	1 102.0	339.0	–	–	52.0	–	–	–	139.0	1 632.0
1945	1 674.0	3 581.0	91	–	243.0	–	–	–	502.0	6 091.0
1946	2 110.0	3 797.0	197	–	197.0	–	–	–	485.0	6 786.0
1947	2 145.0	8 296.0	100	130.0	254.0	–	64	–	483.0	11 472.0
1948	1 602.0	5 969.0	25	370.0	575.0	1 144.0	65	–	606.0	10 356.0
1949	2 517.0	3 223.0	34	814.0	753.0	7 490.0	1	–	650.0	15 482.0
1950	3 761.0	1 368.0	37	210.0	432.0	13 029.0	–	921.0	933.0	20 691.0
1951	1 330.0	538.0	18	88.0	204.0	8 821.0	–	1 875.0	648.0	13 522.0
1952	594.0	135.0	3	171.0	512.0	4 849.0	–	418.0	356.0	7 038.0
1953	816.0	54.0.	–	201.0	66.0	1 579.0	–	431.0	63.0	3 210.0
1954	2 53.04	10.0	4	119.0	518.0	1 716.0	–	382.0	463.0	5 746.0
TOTAL	20 185.0	27 310.0	509	2 103.0	3 806.0	38 628.0	130	4 027.0	5 328.0	102 026.0
% Total	19.8	26.8	0	2.1	3.7	37.9	0	3.9	5.2	99.4*

Note: *Due to rounding, total is less than 100 per cent.

Source: Raja Himadeh, *The Fiscal System of Lebanon* (Beirut, 1961).

Table A10: *Syro-Lebanese balance of payments, 1939–46 (£L 000,000)*

	1939	1940	1941	1942	1943	1944	1945	1946
Receipts								
Exports and re-exports	37.4	19.5	11	24	32	47	46	87
Exports in contraband (including gold)	–	–	–	–	–	–	–	–
Emigrants' remittances	27.2	19.4	13	10	14	31	32	35
Capital of returning emigrants			–	–	–	–	–	–
Tourist and foreign residents' expenditures	24.5		–	–	–	–	–	–
Income on investments abroad		73.3	–	–	–	–	–	–
Foreign investments in Lebanon			–	–	–	–	–	–
Commissions on trade			64	272	320	287	346	50
Allied Armies' expenditures			88	306	366	365	424	202
Sub-Total	89.1	112.2						
Payments								
Imports	75.6	57.1	40	107	110	94	131	267
Imports in contraband			–	–	–	–	–	–
Expenses of nationals abroad and representation	–	–	–	–	–		–	–
Interest on foreign investments in Lebanon			–	–	–	–	–	–
Payments for services			–	–	–	–	–	–
Investment in foreign currencies			27	41	93	205	235	–
Sub-Total	75.6	57.1	67	148	203	299	366	267
Balance	+13.5	+55.1	+21	+158	+163	+66	+58	–65

Source: Gibb, *The Economic Development of Lebanon*, Table 62; Elias Saba, *The Foreign Exchange Systems of Lebanon and Syria, 1939–57* (Beirut, 1961) Table 2.

Table A11: *Lebanon's balance of payments, 1951–2* (£L 000,000)*

	1951		1952	
	Credit	Debit	Credit	Debit
A. Goods and services				
Merchandise trade	124.9	436.4	122.1	454.2
Non-monetary gold	15.2	14.3	25.0	36.5
Foreign travel	35.0	14.7	47.6	23.1
Transportation and insurance	16.3	9.2	21.2	8.5
Investment income	15.6	11.8	16.2	9.2
Government, not included elsewhere	79.5	9.8	72.2	6.6
Miscellaneous services				
Transit	113.1	–	95.4	–
Other services	35.7	–	36.0	–
Total (A)	*435.3*	*496.2*	*435.7*	*538.1*
B. Private donations and capital movements				
Emigrant remittances and transfers	58.4	4.0	71.7	2.7
Government	0.5	–	2.5	–
Charitable and cultural institutions	10.2	–	13.5	–
Capital movements (net)	14.7	–	43.7	–
Total (B)	*83.8*	*4.0*	*131.4*	*2.7*
C. *Total* (A+B)				
Total (C)	*519.1*	*500.2*	*567.1*	*540.8*
D. *Surplus* (Credit–Debit)				
Total (D)	*18.9*	–	*26.3*	–
E. Compensatory Financing				
Monetary gold	–	23.9	–	15.3
Foreign exchange assets	0.9	–	–	10.4
Bank liabilities to non-residents	4.1	–	–	0.5
Total (E)	*5.0*	*23.9*	–	*26.3*
TOTAL	0	0	0	0

Note: *Table A11 and A12 show comparative estimates of Lebanon's balance of payments, 1951–2.

Source: Edward Fei and Paul Klat, *The Balance of Payments in Lebanon, 1951 and 1952* (Beirut, 1954).

Table A12: *Lebanon's balance of payments, 1951–2* (£L 000,000)*

	1951	1952
A. Goods and services	*–190.8*	*–205.8*
1. Merchandise: credit	831.9	809.1
Exports f.o.b	158.6	148.5
Transit and entrepôt trade	673.3	660.6
Merchandise: debit	–1 124.2	–1 120.7
Imports c.i.f.	–464.1	–473.0
Transit and entrepôt trade	–660.1	–647.7
2. Nonmonetary gold	23.9	3.2
3. Foreign travel: credit	35.0	47.6
Foreign travel: debit	–15.3	–23.7
4. Transportation: credit	16.4	21.5
Passenger fares	6.3	8.3
Shore expenditure of foreign crews	1.1	1.3
Other port expenditures	9.0	11.9
Transportation: debit	–9.2	–8.5
5. Insurance: credit	0.4	0.4
Investment income: debit	–0.6	–0.6
7. Government, n.i.e.: credit	14.7	26.8
Government, n.i.e.: debit	–2.2	–2.6
8. Miscellaneous: credit	34.6	34.7
Profit on exchange operations	10.5	11.5
Foreign companies' local expenditures	24.1	23.2
Miscellaneous: debit	–	–
B. Donations	*72.8*	*99.1*
9. Private	64.6	82.5
Personal remittances	58.4	71.7
Institutional remittances	10.2	13.5
Emigrants' transfers	–4.0	–2.7
10. Official	8.2	16.6
TOTAL (1 through 9)	–126.2	–123.3
TOTAL (1 through 10)	–118.0	–106.7

Table A12 (continued): *Lebanon's balance of payments,* 1951–2 (£L 000,000)*

	1951	1952
C. Capital and monetary flows	*–4.3*	*–7.5*
Private, excluding banks	3.1	–2.3
11. Long-term liabilities	3.5	–1.4
13. Long-term assets	–0.4	–0.9
12, 14. Short-term capital		
D. Official and banking institutions	*–7.4*	*–5.2*
15. Long-term liabilities	–4.2	–4.2
Payments to France and UK	–4.2	–4.2
IBRD loan drawings	–	–
16. Short-term liabilities	0.8	–0.5
To IMF	–3.3	–
Bank liabilities	4.1	–0.5
17. Long-term assets	–	8.9
18. Short-term assets	19.9	6.0
French francs	15.4	3.9
Other currencies	4.5	2.1
19. Monetary gold	–23.9	–15.4
Net errors and omissions	122.3	114.2
TOTAL	–7.4	–5.2

Note: *Table A11 and A12 show comparative estimates of Lebanon's balance of payments, 1951–2.

Source: IMF, *Balance of Payments Yearbook* (Washington, DC) vol. 10, April 1959.

Table A13: *Comparative estimates of agricultural land, 1945–54 (000 hectares)*

Sources	Cultivated	Cultivable but not cultivated	Total	Irrigated	Additional irrigable	Total
Gibb Report	230	160–80	390–410	44	76	120
US–Lebanon agricultural mission	270	270	540	40	162	202
Doreen Marriner	526	–	526	–	–	–
Alfred Bonné	–	–	560	–	–	–
Clapp Report III	210	298	508	44	44	88
Mazloum Report	225	–	–	30	–	–
Report on agricultural credit	273	115	388	48	34	82

Source: Gibb, *The Economic Development of Lebanon*, pp. 41–2, Diagram 4; AUB, *Report on Agricultural Credit in Lebanon*, Table 1; Alfred Bonné, 'Land and population in the Middle East: trends and prospects, *Middle East Journal*, vol. 5 (Winter 1951) Table 1, pp. 39–56.

Figure A1: *Survey of the rural Qaza of Jibb-Janine, 1952*

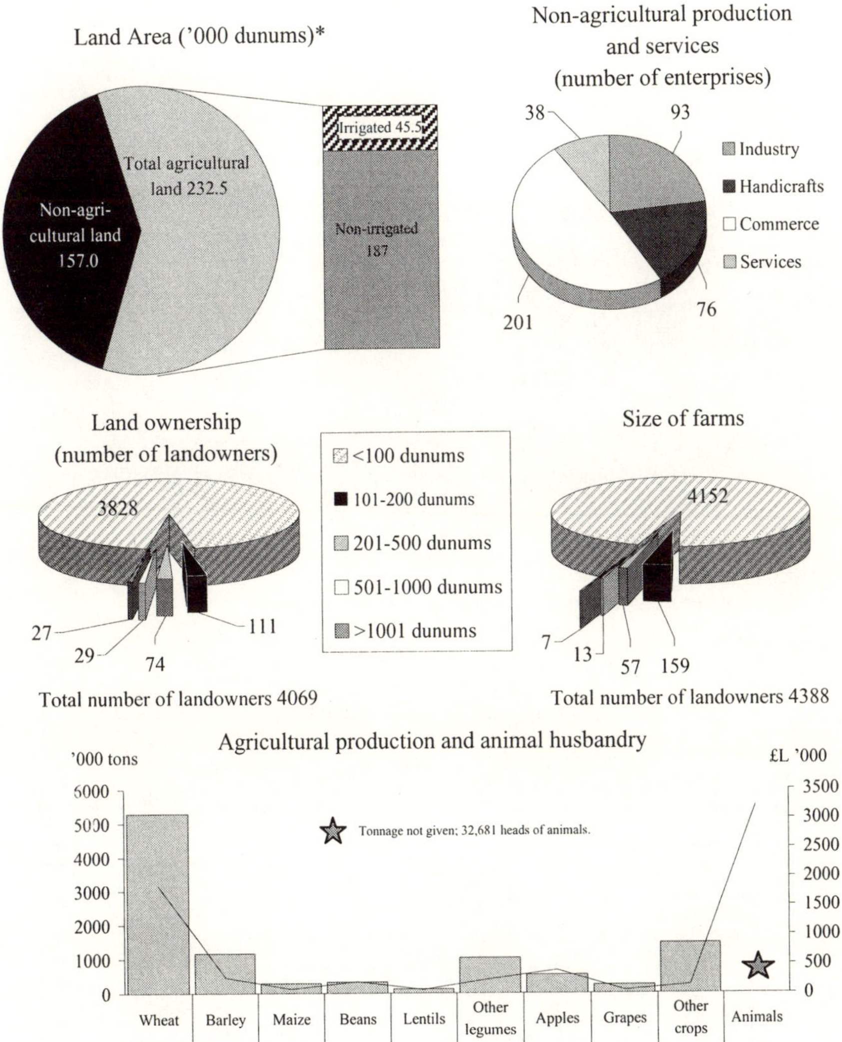

	Wheat	Barley	Maize	Beans	Lentils	Other legumes	Apples	Grapes	Other crops	Animals
Tons	5284	1168	289	329	124	1034	538	244	1465	0
£L'000	1854	271	73	197	62	239	392	49	142	3217

Notes: The Lebanese government surveyed 33 villages located in Jibb-Jannine (in the southern Beka'a plain); *Dunum ≈ 900 m^2.
Source: *Bulletin statistique trimestriel*, 1953.

Figure A2: *Tobacco production of the* Régie des tabacs, *1939–52*

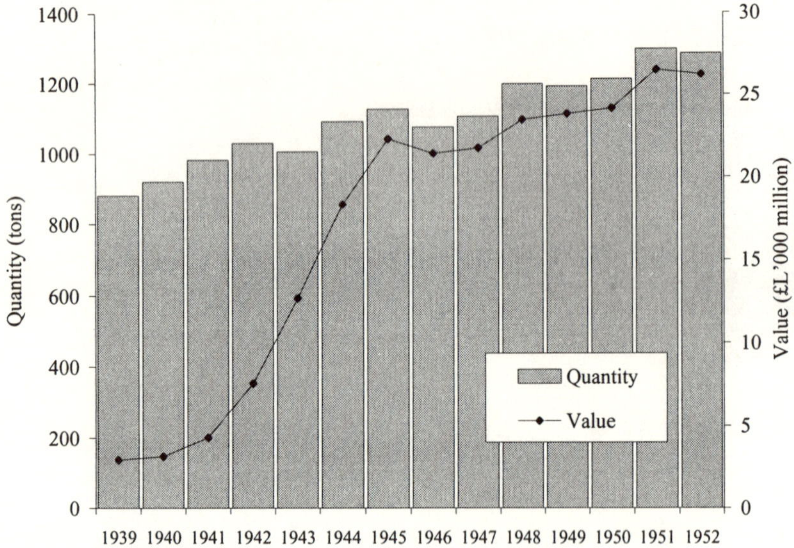

Note: *Includes processed tobacco, tombac, cigars and cigarettes.

Source: *Bulletin statistique trimestries*, 1953, vol. 4, no. 4.

Figure A3: *Establishment of industrial enterprises, 1913–55*

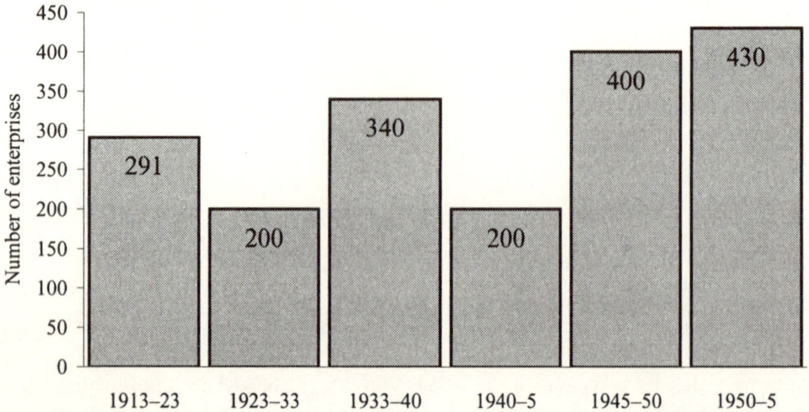

Source: IRFED, *Besoins et possibilités*, vol. 1.

Table A14: *Wheat production of Lebanon and selected countries, 1934–52*

Year	Lebanon Acreage[a]	Lebanon Bushels[b]	Lebanon Ratio[c]	Syria Acreage	Syria Bushels	Syria Ratio	Egypt Acreage	Egypt Bushels	Egypt Ratio	USA Acreage	USA Bushels	USA Ratio
1934–8[d]	168	1 286	7.7	1 169	16 865	14.4	1 453	43 505	30.0	55 429	715 620	12.9
1945	173	1 941	11.2	1 853	14 299	7.7	1 710	43 418	25.4	65 120	1 107 623	17.0
1946	161	2 576	16.0	2 002	21 243	10.6	1 646	42 727	26.0	67 105	1 152 118	17.2
1947	173	1 829	10.6	2 084	14 821	7.1	1 692	38 341	22.7	74 519	1 358 911	18.2
1948	173	1 829	10.6	1 947	24 117	12.4	1 574	39 685	25.2	72 418	1 294 911	17.9
1949	178	1 867	10.5	1 840	32 666	17.8	1 471	42 896	29.2	76 559	1 098 415	14.3
1950	178	1 984	11.1	2 451	30 497	12.4	1 423	37 405	26.3	61 609	1 019 389	16.5
1951	168	1 837	10.9	2 563	18 739	7.3	1 554	44 423	28.6	61 424	980 810	16.0
1952	168	1 837	10.9	2 224	49 270	22.2	1 455	40 011	27.5	70 925	1 298 957	18.3

Notes: [a] '000 acres, [b] '000, [c] yields, [d] average. Notes apply across all columns.

Source: International Wheat Council, *World Wheat Statistics* (London, April 1955), pp. 9–12.

Table A15: *Gross and net income arising in the agricultural sector, 1948–50 (£L 000)*

Category	1948 Gross income	1948 Production costs	1948 Net income	1949 Gross income	1949 Production costs	1949 Net income	1950 Gross income	1950 Production costs	1950 Net income
I. Agro-goods	160 412	10 213	150 199	148 304	7 350	140 954	188 086	8 231	179 855
Cereals	(39 665)			(21 904)			(23 904)		
Legumes	(20 916)			(17 668)			(19 015)		
Industrial crops	(7 142)			(5 543)			(4 945)		
Fruits	(74 635)			(87 555)			(124 770)		
Vegetables	(18 054)			(15 634)			(15 452)		
Production costs									
Seed consumption		(7 500)			(4 700)			(4 720)	
Machinery depreciation		(285)			(285)			(343)	
Fertilisers		(2 428)			(2 365)			(3 168)	
II. Animal products	28 262	14 315	13 947	25 158	11 235	13 923	35 550	13 550	22 000
III. Fishing	2 810	702	2 108	2 546	636	1 910	2 625	656	1 969
IV. Forestry	1 090*	–	1 090	1 213*	–	1 213	1 288*	–	1 288
V. Silk	1 143*	–	1 143	840*	–	840	1 375*	–	1 375
TOTAL	193 717	25 230	168 487	178 061	19 221	158 840	228 924	22 437	206 487

Note: * Net income (which is included in calculations of gross income).

Source: *Bulletin statistique trimestriel*, 1952; Albert Badre, 'The National Income of Lebanon', *Middle East Economic Papers*, 1956.

Table A16: *Economic activity of the Ubaydiyyah Cooperative, 1937–52*

Year	Membership (number)	Capital £L	Goods marketed £L 000	Goods marketed tons	Supplies purchased £L 000	Loans £L 000
1937	22	110	2.2	50	–	–
1938	41	314	7.8	186	1.8	0.2
1939	74	1 159	15.6	304	1.0	0.8
1940	98	–	37.0	500	3.3	1.0
1941	140	7 401	62.0	400	24.2	0.9
1942	203	14 304	150.0	584	26.7	1.3
1943	222	–	219.0	800	21.5	0.6
1944	226	–	176.0	–	51.3	2.6
1945	229	–	157.0	–	15.3	13.4
1946	183	–	139.0	–	25.7	14.1
1947	183	–	86.0	–	13.3	5.3
1950	183	–	88.6	–	7.6	7.0
1951	194	–	99.8	–	63.0	20.8
1952	205	–	72.1	–	73.3	14.1

Source: RG84, vol. Xi (1943), Beirut, box 31, Scott/Beirut, August 23, 1943, no. 46, 'Agricultural cooperative societies in Syria and Lebanon', p. 2; Gibb, *Economic Development*, p. 44; N. Saadeh, 'Agricultural credit in Lebanon', 1953 as cited by *Report on Agricultural Credit in Lebanon*.

Table A17: *Industrial employment in Lebanese centres 1913 and 1937 (numbers)*

City/ Category	IO	Year	Lab.	Gender and age			Wages		Employed in		Religion		Nationality			ADW (gold franc)		
				M	F	C	Day	Piece	WS	H	Ms	Ch	J	L	I	M	F	C
Beirut	Old	1913	5 765	4 620	45	1 110	3 665	2 100	5 030	735	1 438	3 610	717	5 765	0	3.24	1.13	0.37
	Old	1937	9960	7070	470	2420	4640	5320	2060	2900	3177	6458	325	5630	4330	12.60	6.30	2.95
	New	1937	16753	14682	1344	727	8478	8275	0	0	4324	12173	256	13741	3012	15.59	0	4.62
Tripoli	Old	1913	4601	3046	1130	425	3364	1237	4341	260	3574	1025	2	4601	0	2.90	1.08	0.35
	Old	1937	12532	3252	5825	1455	10846	1868	12407	125	10937	1595	0	12363	169	11.20	4.50	2.50
	New	1937	354	240	0	114	315	39	0	0	325	29	0	340	14	11.25	0	3.66
Sidon	Old	1913	993	875	0	118	339	654	993	0	709	272	12	993	0	2.33	0	0.21
	Old	1937	1427	1199	5	223	852	575	1422	5	1172	247	8	1405	22	8.88	4.00	1.92
	New	1937	60	40	0	20	60	0	0	0	55	0	5	58	2	12.00	0	3.00
Total	Old	1913	11359	8541	1175	1653	7368	3991	10364	995	5721	4907	731	11359	0			
"	Old	1937	23919	11521	6300	4098	16338	7763	15889	3030	15286	8300	333	19398	4521			
"	New	1937	17167	14962	1344	861	8853	8314	0	0	4704	12202	261	14139	3028			
Con.co.	Old	1913	3002	2699	253	50	2985	17	3002	0	1322	1595	85	3002	0	2.56	1.87	0.35
"	Old	1937	4975	3670	1189	116	4954	21	4975	0	1884	3050	41	4399	626	18.40	12.75	3.50
"	New	1937	2153	2152	0	1	2153	0	0	0	1068	1078	7	1284	869	1.84	0	5.00
Misc.	Old	1913	184491	65422	109590	9479	18194	166297	11591	172900	39570	144921	0	184491	0	1.25	0.41	0.27
"	Old	1937	70060	25549	41030	3581	5866	64194	3810	66250	19700	50360	0	70030	30	10.00	3.44	3.05
"	New	1937	914	914	0	0	914	0	0	0	247	667	0	901	13	14.20	0	0

Notes: ADW = Average daily wages; H = Home; IO = Industrial organisation; Lab. = Labour; M = Male; WS = Workshop; Ms = Muslim; L = Lebanese; F = Female; Ch = Christian; I = Immigrant; C = Child; J = Jew; Con. co. = Concessionary companies in Syria and Lebanon; Misc. = Miscellaneous companies in Syria and Lebanon.

Source: France, Ministère des affaires étrangères, *Rapport à la Société des nations sur la situation de la Syrie et du Grand Liban* (Paris, 1938), pp. 218-19.

Table A18: *Industrial employment and salaries/wages, 1950*

Sector	Entrps	Capital	Labour	Owners/managers		Technicians		Men		Women		Children	
	(No. of)	(£L000)	(No.)	No.	Salary	No.	Salary	No.	Wages	No.	Wages	No.	Wages
Food	401	24754	5334	602	400	273	500	3645	100	1064	70	352	33
Beverages	122	10650	1290	183	650	327	420	800	160	781	70	82	40*
Textiles	60	32587	5040	90	1100	120	633	2389	120	2283	50	248	42
Wearing apparel	29	3358	1068	44	1100	62	660	405	190	501	60	100	43
Wood and cork	23	1310	196	35	550	27	600*	140	140	–	–	29	20
Furniture	95	4593	1211	143	400	164	500	735	100	14	70	298	33
Paper	8	470	90	12	500	10	600*	28	80	36	33	16	40*
Printing	100	8606	855	150	600	104	600*	526	115	75	60	150	30
Leather	60	4536	731	90	600	45	685	518	130	88	160	80	40
Rubber	5	962	445	8	500	7	600*	160	100	226	45	50	30
Chemicals	55	5899	1089	83	800	61	935	636	140	306	35	86	34
Non-metallic minerals	97	35412	2697	146	875	221	595	2135	165	104	200	237	43
Metal products	30	2649	639	45	650	62	600*	408	115	90	70	79	45
Machinery	26	3233	588	39	825	36	675	452	130	6	70*	94	57
Electrical	4	1553	214	6	700*	19	600	85	141	83	70	27	40
Miscellaneous	29	6462	367	44	1016	34	1220	226	164	90	73	17	40
TOTAL	1144	147034	21854	1710	609	1572	603	13291	134	5046	54	1945	39

Notes: entrps = enterprises; no. = number; salary = average monthly salary in £L; wages = average monthly wages in £L; *Interpolated numbers.

Source: *Bulletin statistique trimestriel*, 1951.

Table A19: *Industrial production, 1950: a comparison of estimates*

Branch	Enterprises (1) (no.)	Output (£L 000)	Ents (2) (no.)	Ents (3) (no.)	Ents (4) (no.)	Output (£L 000)
Food processing	*278*	*30 335*	*227*	*401*	*455*	*30 123*
Margarine	3	1 850				
Confectionery, pastry	240	26 485				
Milk products	35	2 000				
Beverages and liquids	*775*	*20 055*	*213*	*122*	*123*	*5 603*
Olive oil	450	2 250				
Sesame oil	21	5 175				
Other vegetable oils	17	5 760				
‘Arak	140	3 600				
Alcohol	4	1 100				
Beer	3	1 050				
Other	140	1 120				
Wood:	*127*	*2 850*	*134*	*118*	*95*	*6 232*
Leather, rubber	*82*	*11 205*			*70*	*7 663*
Footwear	17	3 175	–	5		
Tanneries	65	8 030	77	60		
Textiles	*72*	*34 495*	*79*	*60*	*60*	*17 702*
Cotton yarn	8	8 000				
Cotton cloth	10	10 000				
Wool cloth	2	2 000				
Silk cloth	17	8 000				
Hosiery	5	4 375				
Other	39	2 120				
Metal industries	*81*	*9 875*	*69*	*56*	*30*	*6 496*
Foundries	50	4 000				
Ironware	2	2 000				
Other	29	3 875				

Table A19 (cont.): *Industrial production, 1950: a comparison of estimates*

Branch	Enterprises (1) (no.)	Output (£L 000)	Ents (2) (no.)	Ents (3) (no.)	Ents (4) (no.)	Output (£L 000)
Other industries	*195*	*29 275*				
Cement and products	100	18 000	115	97	156	13 461
Soap	70	9 000				
Matches	4	1 200	64	55	64	7 941
Various	21	1 075	109	170	232	24 491
TOTAL	1 610	138 090	1 087	1 144	1 285	119 712
Adjustments (5)						
Olive presses	–	–	450	350	–	–
Beverages	–		50	100	–	–
TOTAL	1 610		1 587	1 594	1 285	–

Notes: ents = enterprises.

Sources: (1) *Middle East Economic and Financial Service*, 1952; (2) Donato, 'Lebanon and its labour legislation', p. 67 and Grunwald, 'The industrialisation of the Lebanon and Syria', Table 15; (3) Industrial Survey, *Bulletin statistique trimestriel*, 1951; (4) Badre and Nasr: *NIL, Industry*, Table 6; and (5) Grunwald, Table 15.

Table A20a: *Industrial production, 1939–45*

Category	Unit	1939	1940	1941	1942	1943	1944	1945
I. Processed foods								
Jams/preserves	tons	185	215	180	600	700	1 050	1 500
Pasta		1 375	1 450	1 402	450	475	550	460
Biscuits		280	214	198	40	100	100	93
Halawé		–	–	–	200	750	750	800
Chocolate		235	145	100	–	50	60	75
Butter		n.a.	98	93	52	60	60	70
Samné		n.a.	–	–	10	–	10	10
Cheese		n.a.	89	84	53	130	180	300
II. Alcohol products								
Industrial alcohol		300	575	713	625	583	558	334
Beer	000 litres	2 347	1 821	3 434	4 794	7 033	8 325	7 027
Wine	tons	n.a.	2 297	1 535	702	1 048	864	756
'Arak		n.a.	1 122	715	754	1 090	910	1 099
III. Vegetable oils								
Olive oil		n.a.	7 500	2 700	12 000	3 500	11 000	8 000
Other oils		n.a.	1 400	500	–	–	80	700
IV. Chemicals								
Matches	000 boxes	24 500	23 930	25 695	26 560	14 960	17 420	19 900
Eau de Cologne	000 litres	n.a.	45	20	–	70	125	150
Soap	tons	n.a.	2 550	1 500	2 000	4 500	3 500	3 000
V. Leather								
Shoe leather		–	–	1 500	2 300	2 500	1 800	1 500
Box-calf	000 sq. ft	–	–	1 500	2 000	1 500	2 200	1 700
VI. Textiles								
Cotton yarn	tons	910	1 350	1 200	1 150	1 500	1 700	1 600
Cotton cloth		–	–	1 100	500	400	400	400
								(3.8)*
Stockings/socks	000 doz prs	230	320	250	300	138	100	100
VII. Minerals								
Cement	tons	156 000	89 568	67 862	171 966	118 321	136 326	148 471

Table A20b: *Industrial production, 1946–52*

Category	Unit	1946	1947	1948	1949	1950	1951	1952
I. Processed foods:								
Jams/preserves	tons	55	n.a.	n.a.	n.a.	n.a.	n.a.	n.a.
Pasta		333	n.a.	n.a.	n.a.	n.a.	n.a.	n.a.
Biscuits		152	n.a.	n.a.	n.a.	n.a.	n.a.	n.a.
Halawé		514	n.a.	n.a.	n.a.	n.a.	n.a.	n.a.
Chocolate		300	n.a.	n.a.	n.a.	n.a.	n.a.	n.a.
Butter		125	n.a.	n.a.	n.a.	n.a.	n.a.	n.a.
Samné		–	n.a.	n.a.	n.a.	n.a.	n.a.	n.a.
Cheese		600	n.a.	n.a.	n.a.	n.a.	n.a.	n.a.
II. Alcohol products								
Industrial alcohol		441	468	831	822	950	520	n.a.
Beer	000 litres	1 583	1 568	1 895	2 016	2 086	1 460	n.a.
Wine	tons	445	n.a.	n.a.	n.a.	n.a.	n.a.	n.a.
'Arak		1 233	n.a.	n.a.	n.a.	n.a.	n.a.	n.a.
III. Vegetable oils			7 000	9 000	12 000	12 000	12 000	5 600
Olive oil		2 000						
Other oils		3 000						
IV. Chemicals								
Matches	000 boxes	24 635	34 740	51 875	60 000	45 000	39 000	n.a.
Eau de Cologne	000 litres	27	n.a.	n.a.	n.a.	n.a.	n.a.	n.a.
Soap	tons	3 200	n.a.	n.a.	n.a.	n.a.	n.a.	n.a.
V. Leather								
Shoe leather		2 500	1 500	2 000	2 500	2 000	2 000	n.a.
Box-calf	000 sq. ft	2 000	2 000	2 500	2 750	2 200	2 300	n.a.
VI. Textiles								
Cotton yarn	tons	1 760	1 840	6 000	5 000	1 550	2 050	n.a.
Cotton cloth		425 (3.2)*	n.a.	(5.1)*	(5.3)*	(4.9)*	n.a.	1 100
Stockings/socks	000 doz prs	25	n.a.	n.a.	n.a.	n.a.	n.a.	n.a.
VII. Minerals								
Cement	tons	157 600	167 580	208 532	253 657	263 197	302 652	n.a.

Note: *The figures of 1945–50 cotton cloth are given in millions of square meters in parentheses; n.a. = not available.

Source: Levant States, CSIC, *Recueil de statistiques*, 1942–5, 1945–7; Ministère de l'économie national, *Bulletin statistique trimestriel*, 1950, vol. 1, nos 1–2; 1952, vol. 3, no. 1.

Table A21: *Tripoli oil refinery production, 1941–52 (tons)*

Year	Crude oil	Benzine	Kerosene	Gas oil	Fuel oil	Diesel oil
1941*	99 907	25 352	6 162	13 517	55 055	–
1942	141 505	31 682	14 320	15 455	77 216	–
1943	160 630	34 574	18 023	18 616	83 644	–
1944	190 319	38 148	24 424	22 480	105 439	–
1945	–	–	–	–	–	–
1946	226 671	51 382	27 383	29 668	120 703	–
1947	241 741	56 466	25 442	32 476	95 837	–
1948	255 788	51 248	27 584	31 924	111 228	5 147
1949	303 697	61 583	33 482	45 348	134 089	865
1950	492 095	98 049	60 456	82 389	152 205	–
1951	549 212	116 510	61 808	92 749	148 386	–
1952	546 689	114 013	66 003	92 442	188 429	–

Note: *Tripoli refinery began to produce in November 1940; the last two months of 1940 production were added to 1941 production figures.
Source: *Bulletin statistique trimestriel*, 1950, vol. 1, nos 1–2; 1952, vol. 3, no. 4.

Table A22: *Electricity production, 1939–52*

Year	Geothermal energy (kWh)	Hydroelectric energy (kWh)	Total production (kWh)
1939	n.a.	n.a.	43 000 000
1940	n.a.	n.a.	37 775 000
1941	n.a.	n.a.	35 125 000
1942	n.a.	n.a.	44 290 000
1943	n.a.	n.a.	43 210 600
1944	n.a.	n.a.	48 279 000
1945	9 261 240	47 935 000	57 196 240
1946	12 189 000	49 261 000	61 450 000
1947	22 611 556	50 772 000	72 883 556
1948	26 849 230	60 115 150	86 964 380
1949	36 145 150	67 562 740	103 707 890
1950	52 535 780	63 566 690	116 102 470
1951	54 518 520	78 025 650	132 544 170
1952	56 596 145	90 184 418	146 770 563

Note: n.a. = not available.
Source: Jewish Agency for Palestine, *Statistical Handbook of Middle Eastern Countries*; Levant States, CSIC, *Recueil de statistiques*, 1942–5, 1945–7; IRFED, vol. 1, Table 53.

Table A23a: *Evolution of foreign trade, 1938–52 (by weight)*

	Year	Weight (Tons) Imports	Exports	Re-exports	Transit
Syro-	1938	561 231	376 201	5 169	2 286 902
Lebanese	1939	542 234	325 830	5 139	2 149 997
Customs	1940	968 868	314 147	121 563	374
Union	1941	273 542	29 487	16	37 742
	1942	503 465	23 781	–	76 216
	1943	428 483	52 821	–	654 608
	1944	428 968	120 099	1 236	1 436 171
	1945	514 692	139 315	6 866	2 022 789
	1946	369 587	106 521	572	1 998 147
	1947	414 057	148 018	2 428	2 103 986
	1948	758 334	123 709	1 603	2 295 504
	1949	957 416	305 715	2 050	3 006 710
	1950a	238 871	111 783	449	1 254 898
Lebanon	1950b	606 702	150 574	5 936	5 755 985
	1951	722 775	204 311	6 334	22 476 208
	1952	811 534	203 224	16 404	23 126 710

Table A23b: *Evolution of foreign trade, 1938–52 (by value)*

	Year	Value (£SL'000)* Imports	Exports	Re-exports	Transit
Syro-	1938	70 811	39 278	760	36 659
Lebanese	1939	75 567	36 517	867	37 686
Customs	1940	57 156	19 302	173	26 679
Union	1941	40 527	11 228	44	37 336
	1942	107 085	23 753	–	67 790
	1943	110 137	32 031	–	136 033
	1944	93 643	46 195	789	157 710
	1945	130 624	43 842	1 948	128 438
	1946	266 654	85 560	1 127	101 746
	1947	362 764	83 640	3 487	182 841
	1948	483 460	78 501	1 179	232 581
	1949	516 188	111 104	1 697	342 567
	1950a	116 813	37 695	632	106 731
Lebanon	1950b	244 815	67 129	3 400	510 564
	1951	320 772	97 655	8 201	1 136 795
	1952	347 049	77 430	19 491	1 238 601

Notes: 1950a = 1 January to 13 March; 1950b = 14 March to 31 December; *Based on official exchange rates.
Source: BSL, *Rapport du Conseil d'Administration*, 1952.

Table A24a: *Composition of Syro-Lebanese imports: 1935–8, 1939–45 and 1946*

Category	1935–38* Tons	1935–38* £SL'000	1935–38* % total value	1939–45* Tons	1939–45* £SL'000	1939–45* % total value	1946 Tons	1946 £SL'000	1946 % total value
1. Live animals and animal products**	1 822	1 975	4.32	736	5 784	6.59	620	9 224	3.39
2. Vegetable products	70 987	3 559	7.78	86 114	17 290	19.69	104 863	29 653	10.90
3. Fatty substances, greases, oils and their cleavage products; prepared edible fats; waxes of animal or vegetable origin	6 174	1 127	2.46	2 160	1 333	1.52	1 488	1 947	0.72
4. Products of food industries; beverages, alcoholic liquids and vinegars; tobacco	41 977	2 728	5.96	25 611	7 515	8.56	37 836	10 961	4.03
5. Mineral products***	270 496	3 590	7.85	251 992	10 382	11.82	324 688	11 514	4.23
6. Chemical and pharmaceutical products; dyes and varnishes; perfumery, soap, candles etc.; glues and gelatines; explosives and fertilizers	12 797	2 477	5.41	9 303	5 782	6.58	16 996	17 695	6.51
7. Hides, skins, leather and fur products	4 662	1 488	3.25	2 597	2 999	3.41	3 036	6 048	2.22
8. Rubber and rubber products	1 161	591	1.29	629	1 426	1.62	8 307	4 788	1.76
9. Wood and cork products; plating materials	50 779	1 551	3.39	16 470	1 998	2.28	12 122	4 781	1.76
10. Paper products	9 032	1 113	2.43	2 560	1 396	1.59	4 444	4 186	1.54
11. Textiles and allied products	19 778	13 014	28.44	11 771	21 702	24.71	14 728	69 684	25.62
12. Footwear, hats, rainwear, umbrellas	275	280	0.61	50	156	0.18	184	455	0.17

and fashion-wear									
13. Stonework and mineral products; ceramics and glass products	10 514	805	1.76	2 211	623	0.71	6 790	3 476	1.28
14. Pearls, precious stones, metals and coins	18	2 372	5.18	9	1 077	1.23	22	52 067	19.14
15. Base metals and products	55 334	4 350	9.51	14 165	3 667	4.18	44 688	16 625	6.11
16. Machinery and tools, electrical goods	4 452	2 308	5.04	1 289	1 813	2.06	5 667	12 096	4.45
17. Transport material	2 477	1 734	3.79	1 492	2 526	2.88	9 362	13 086	4.81
18. Scientific instruments and tools; watchmaker wares and musical instruments	141	287	0.63	24	247	0.28	103	1 810	0.67
19. Arms and munitions	218	84	0.18	17	14	0.02	96	175	0.06
20. Miscellaneous goods	382	324	0.71	87	313	0.36	217	1 702	0.63
21. Objets d'art and collectors' items	3	3	0.01	–	2	–	1	11	–
TOTAL	563 479	45 760	100	429 287	88 045	100	596 258	271 984	100

Table A24b: *Composition of Syro-Lebanese imports: 1947, 1948 and 1949*

Category	1947 Tons	1947 £SL'000	1947 % total value	1948 Tons	1948 £SL'000	1948 % total value	1949 Tons	1949 £SL'000	1949 % total value
1. Live animals and animal products**	1 149	9 871	2.7	2 311	17 209	3.6	4 100	17 307	3.4
2. Vegetable products	50 270	21 077	5.8	232 870	102 940	21.3	144 391	49 619	9.6
3. Fatty substances, greases, oils and their cleavage products; prepared edible fats; waxes of animal or vegetable origin	2 053	3 000	0.8	3 377	4 105	0.9	6 158	5 955	1.2
4. Products of food industries; beverages, alcoholic liquids and vinegars; tobacco	43 480	24 587	6.8	49 336	24 350	5.0	45 971	21 057	4.1
5. Mineral products***	137 838	12 220	3.4	204 403	19 462	4.0	448 433	36 472	7.1
6. Chemical and pharmaceutical products; dyes and varnishes; perfumery, soap, candles etc.; glues and gelatines; explosives and fertilizers	19 155	17 433	4.8	30 119	21 362	4.4	30 128	21 925	4.2
7. Hides, skins, leather and fur products	2 125	4 486	1.2	2 983	4 854	1.0	4 583	6 181	1.2
8. Rubber and rubber products	4 043	6 822	1.9	3 835	6 869	1.4	3 433	6 621	1.3
9. Wood and cork products; plating materials	30 868	9 735	2.7	44 189	13 579	2.8	46 673	11 978	2.3
10. Paper products	8 161	7 659	2.1	8 448	6 743	1.4	11 197	8 400	1.6
11. Textiles and allied products	19 451	99 349	26.3	19 863	87 977	18.2	28 478	89 768	17.4
12. Footwear, hats, rainwear, umbrellas and fashionwear	155	843	0.2	86	639	0.1	275	1 195	0.2
13. Stonework and mineral products; ceramics and glass products	10 097	6 359	1.8	10 955	7 322	1.5	13 951	8 425	1.6

14. Pearls, precious stones, metals and coins	24	49 051	13.5	42	16 923	3.5	58	42 039	8.1
15. Base metals and products	60 343	29 796	8.2	110 813	58 472	12.1	128 670	62 769	12.2
16. Machinery and tools, electrical goods	12 652	32 297	8.9	19 815	50 838	10.5	26 344	78 795	15.3
17. Transport material	11 172	24 678	6.8	12 786	31 903	6.6	13 474	39 058	7.6
18. Scientific instruments and tools; watchmaker wares and musical instruments	143	2 923	0.8	280	3 700	0.8	253	4 385	0.8
19. Arms and munitions	300	924	0.3	217	957	0.2	208	903	0.2
20. Miscellaneous goods	574	3 498	1.0	603	3 197	0.7	631	3 281	0.6
21. Objets d'art and collectors' items	4	156	–	3	59	–	7	55	–
TOTAL	414 057	362 764	100	757 334	483 460	100	957 416	516 188	100

Table A24c: *Composition of Syro-Lebanese imports before separation (1 January–14 March 1950) and Lebanese imports after separation (15 March–31 December 1950)*

Category	Before separation			After separation		
	Tons	£SL'000	% total value	Tons	£SL'000	% total value
1. Live animals and animal products**	1 069	3 770	3.0	3 057	19 268	7.9
2. Vegetable products	19 475	5 901	5.1	169 559	38 403	15.7
3. Fatty substances, greases, oils and their cleavage products; prepared edible fats; waxes of animal or vegetable origin	1 718	1 171	1.0	2 741	2 269	0.9
4. Products of food industries; beverages, alcoholic liquids and vinegars; tobacco	19 457	6 593	5.6	21 479	9 576	3.9
5. Mineral products***	136 321	9 505	8.1	282 227	16 549	6.8
6. Chemical and pharmaceutical products; dyes and varnishes; perfumery, soap, candles etc.; glues and gelatines; explosives and fertilizers	5 581	4 460	3.8	20 111	9 896	4.0
7. Hides, skins, leather and fur products	1 835	1 264	1.1	2 498	3 876	1.6
8. Rubber and rubber products	1 008	1 672	1.4	1 314	2 441	1.0
9. Wood and cork products; plating materials	10 048	2 223	1.9	26 135	5 157	2.1
10. Paper products	2 973	1 461	1.2	6 553	3 323	1.3
11. Textiles and allied products	5 103	15 115	13.0	7 331	28 303	11.7
12. Footwear, hats, rainwear, umbrellas and fashion-wear	132	296	0.3	247	809	0.3
13. Stonework and mineral products; ceramics and glass products	3 018	1 658	1.4	6 976	3 175	1.3
14. Pearls, precious stones, metals and coins	8	35 247	30.4	15	61 470	25.2
15. Base metals and products	24 842	8 645	7.4	47 209	13 887	5.6
16. Machinery and tools, electrical goods	4 069	10 762	9.2	5 829	15 386	6.3
17. Transport material	1 884	5 134	4.4	2 800	6 970	2.9

18. Scientific instruments and tools; watchmaker wares and musical instruments	81	995	0.9	224	1 939	0.8
19. Arms and munitions	73	270	0.2	71	297	0.1
20. Miscellaneous goods	218	728	0.6	301	1 289	0.6
21. Objets d'art and collectors' items	2	11	–	22	540	–
TOTAL	238 915	116 881	100	606 698	244 823	100

Table A24d: *Composition of Lebanese imports, 1951 and 1952*

Category	1951 Tons	1951 £L'000	1951 % total value	1952 Tons	1952 £L'000	1952 % total value
1. Live animals and animal products**	6 337	34 266	10.7	6 968	28 457	8.2
2. Vegetable products	227 054	56 198	17.5	298 657	77 723	22.4
3. Fatty substances, greases, oils and their cleavage products; prepared edible fats; waxes of animal or vegetable origin	3 432	2 561	0.8	4 527	2 912	0.8
4. Products of food industries; beverages, alcoholic liquids and vinegars; tobacco	22 412	13 351	4.2	29 023	14 204	4.1
5. Mineral products***	282 018	20 340	6.3	323 554	25 638	7.4
6. Chemical and pharmaceutical products; dyes and varnishes; perfumery, soap, candles etc.; glues and gelatines; explosives and fertilizers	31 488	14 438	4.5	29 602	14 810	4.3
7. Hides, skins, leather and fur products	1 964	4 091	1.3	2 667	5 092	1.5
8. Rubber and rubber products	1 739	4 315	1.3	1 555	2 850	0.8
9. Wood and cork products; plating materials	32 467	7 884	2.4	27 467	7 775	2.2
10. Paper products	10 472	7 833	2.4	7 513	5 831	1.7
11. Textiles and allied products	12 814	56 958	17.9	12 397	46 094	13.3
12. Footwear, hats, rainwear, umbrellas and fashion-wear	353	1 254	0.4	216	964	0.3
13. Stonework and mineral products; ceramics and glass products	12 057	5 177	1.6	10 779	5 585	1.6
14. Pearls, precious stones, metals and coins	8	23 217	7.2	12	39 461	11.3
15. Base metals and products	64 159	22 734	7.1	41 767	21 283	6.1
16. Machinery and tools, electrical goods	8 741	21 419	6.7	9 802	26 286	7.6
17. Transport material	4 439	11 924	3.7	4 345	13 022	3.8

18. Scientific instruments and tools; watchmaker wares and musical instruments	211	2 898	0.9	191	3 570	1.0
19. Arms and munitions	204	564	0.2	103	501	0.1
20. Miscellaneous goods	338	1 591	0.5	338	1 624	0.5
21. Objets d'art and collectors' items	68	7 758	2.4	55	3 367	1.0
TOTAL	722 775	320 772	100	811 534	347 049	100

Notes: *Average; **Does not include the weight of live animals; ***Does not include oil destined for Tripoli oil refinery; tot val = total value.

Source: BSL, *Rapport du Conseil d'Administration*, 1949; CSIC, *Recueil de statistiques*, 1942–5, 1945–7; *Bulletin statistique trimestriel*, 1950–2; Lebanon, Conseil supérieur des douanes, *Statistiques du commerce extérieur, 1952* (Beirut, 1953); Syria, Ministry of National Economy, Department of Statistics, *Mudiriyat al-ihsa*, 1950 (Damascus, n.d.).

Table A25a: *Composition of Syro-Lebanese exports: 1935–8, 1942–5 and 1946*

Category	1935–38*			1942–45*			1946		
	Tons	£SL'000	% total value	Tons	£SL'000	% total value	Tons	£SL'000	% total value
1. Live animals and animal products**	7 873	2 090	10.04	675	1 130	3.10	3 782	6 098	7.13
2. Vegetable products	176 788	6 531	31.40	28 055	11 936	32.74	72 294	25 508	29.81
3. Fatty substances, greases, oils and their cleavage products; prepared edible fats; waxes of animal or vegetable origin	8 172	1 972	9.50	12	29	0.08	5 218	12 859	15.03
4. Products of food industries; beverages, alcoholic liquids and vinegars; tobacco	8 198	1 272	6.11	3 671	4 034	11.06	5 636	7 418	8.67
5. Mineral products***	63 384	442	2.12	46 162	2 134	5.85	8 091	509	0.60
6. Chemical and pharmaceutical products; dyes and varnishes; perfumery, soap, candles etc.; glues and gelatines; explosives and fertilizers	1 562	338	1.62	613	1 132	3.10	1 995	4 890	5.72
7. Hides, skins, leather and fur products	2 255	1 043	5.01	84	343	0.94	1 325	3 728	4.36
8. Rubber and rubber products	2	1	–	–	–	–	71	122	0.14
9. Wood and cork products; plating materials	2 449	247	1.19	1 522	514	1.41	564	588	0.69
10. Paper products	719	158	0.76	51	105	0.29	78	284	0.33
11. Textiles and allied products	8 428	5 184	24.92	2 619	14 067	38.58	5 140	21 111	24.67
12. Footwear, hats, rainwear, umbrellas and fashionwear	322	423	2.03	47	371	1.02	141	1 003	1.17
13. Stonework and mineral products; ceramics and glass products	3 256	62	0.30	312	304	0.83	1 000	330	0.39
14. Pearls, precious stones, metals and coins	20	264	1.27	–	45	0.12	1	128	0.15
15. Base metals and products	5 511	302	1.45	100	115	0.32	880	684	0.80

16. Machinery and tools, electrical goods	159	95	0.46	17	32	0.09	229	178	0.21
17. Transport material	643	243	1.17	10	27	0.75	2	2	–
18. Scientific instruments and tools; watchmaker wares and musical instruments	17	18	0.09	3	22	0.06	9	30	0.03
19. Arms and munitions	–	1	–	–	–	–	–	–	–
20. Miscellaneous goods	495	100	0.48	51	111	0.30	65	90	0.10
21. Objets d'art and collectors' items	36	16	0.08	–	4	0.01	–	–	–
TOTAL	290 289	20 802	100	84 004	36 455	100	106 521	85 276	100

Table A25b: *Composition of Syro-Lebanese exports: 1947, 1948 and 1949*

Category	1947 Tons	1947 £SL 000	1947 % total value	1948 Tons	1948 £SL 000	1948 % total value	1949 Tons	1949 £SL 000	1949 % total value
1. Live animals and animal products**	5 375	7 968	9.5	3 294	1 485	1.9	3 428	2 355	2.1
2. Vegetable products	106 537	28 733	34.4	79 695	15 125	32.0	244 381	52 155	46.9
3. Fatty substances, greases, oils and their cleavage products; prepared edible fats; waxes of animal or vegetable origin	1 125	2 725	3.3	851	1 626	2.1	1 906	3 390	3.1
4. Products of food industries; beverages, alcoholic liquids and vinegars; tobacco	7 826	6 591	7.9	5 258	4 485	5.7	7 703	4 985	4.5
5. Mineral products	8 984	430	0.5	8 475	723	0.9	14 367	830	0.7
6. Chemical and pharmaceutical products; dyes and varnishes; perfumery, soap, candles etc.; glues and gelatines; explosives and fertilizers	1 569	3 258	3.9	2 428	5 661	7.2	3 632	3 963	3.6
7. Hides, skins, leather and fur products	1 304	3 032	3.6	1 173	1 945	2.5	1 203	1 628	1.5
8. Rubber and rubber products	274	324	0.4	240	346	0.5	322	419	0.4
9. Wood and cork products; plating materials	610	727	0.9	1 331	891	1.1	2 068	1 249	1.1
10. Paper products	75	259	0.3	268	912	1.2	710	1 063	1.0
11. Textiles and allied products	6 506	25 867	30.9	6 492	21 823	27.8	6 407	24 462	22.0
12. Footwear, hats, rainwear, umbrellas and fashionwear	174	963	1.2	141	647	0.8	172	518	0.5
13. Stonework and mineral products; ceramics and glass products	1 079	341	0.4	875	320	0.4	2 574	544	0.5

14. Pearls, precious stones, metals and coins	–	21	–	1	23	–	–	7	–
15. Base metals and products	6 193	1 211	1.4	9 636	2 951	3.8	7 491	4 046	3.6
16. Machinery and tools, electrical goods	146	320	0.4	1 594	3 571	4.6	2 226	4 328	3.9
17. Transport material	127	355	0.4	1 872	5 589	7.1	7 041	4 835	4.3
18. Scientific instruments and tools; watchmaker wares and musical instruments	4	33	–	22	177	0.2	17	133	0.1
19. Arms and munitions	1	4	–	1	6	–	1	5	–
20. Miscellaneous goods	109	478	0.6	61	196	0.2	92	183	0.2
21. Objets d'art and collectors' items	–	–	–	–	–	–	1	6	–
TOTAL		83 640	100	123 708	78 502	100	305 715	111 104	100

Table A25c: *Composition of Syro-Lebanese exports before separation (1 January–14 March 1950) and Lebanese exports after separation (15 March–31 December 1950)*

Category	Before separation			After separation		
	Tons	£SL'000	% total value	Tons	£SL'000	% total value
1. Live animals and animal products**	582	562	1.4	1 233	544	0.8
2. Vegetable products	97 472	18 244	48.6	86 861	15 639	23.4
3. Fatty substances, greases, oils and their cleavage products; prepared edible fats; waxes of animal or vegetable origin	341	426	1.1	117	127	0.2
4. Products of food industries; beverages, alcoholic liquids and vinegars; tobacco	2 165	1 050	2.8	3 627	2 262	3.4
5. Mineral products	1 094	119	0.3	26 141	1 884	2.8
6. Chemical and pharmaceutical products; dyes and varnishes; perfumery, soap, candles etc.; glues and gelatines; explosives and fertilizers	517	796	2.1	3 048	2 322	3.4
7. Hides, skins, leather and fur products	207	286	0.8	1 335	2 667	4.0
8. Rubber and rubber products	23	23	–	693	172	0.2
9. Wood and cork products; plating materials	926	285	0.8	2 084	872	1.3
10. Paper products	451	477	1.3	1 078	1 196	1.8
11. Textiles and allied products	5 667	13 531	36.2	6 107	13 570	20.2
12. Footwear, hats, rainwear, umbrellas and fashion-wear	30	58	–	34	164	0.2
13. Stonework and mineral products; ceramics and glass products	465	113	0.1	2 366	663	1.0
14. Pearls, precious stones, metals and coins	–	532	1.4	4	15 249	22.8
15. Base metals and products	1 675	543	1.5	11 974	3 945	5.9
16. Machinery and tools, electrical goods	96	230	0.6	2 018	5 126	7.6
17. Transport material	83	316	0.9	1 810	514	0.8

18. Scientific instruments and tools; watchmaker wares and musical instruments	3	9	–	8	91	0.1
19. Arms and munitions	–	1	–	1	5	–
20. Miscellaneous goods	31	93	0.1	34	95	0.1
21. Objets d'art and collectors' items	–	1	–	–	23	–
TOTAL	111 783	37 695	100	150 574	67 129	100

Table A25d: *Composition of Lebanese exports, 1951 and 1952*

Category	1951 Tons	1951 £L'000	1951 % total value	1952 Tons	1952 £L'000	1952 % total value
1. Live animals and animal products**	1 752	1 123	1.1	1 999	1 445	1.9
2. Vegetable products	83 631	19 067	19.5	110 155	25 045	32.3
3. Fatty substances, greases, oils and their cleavage products; prepared edible fats; waxes of animal or vegetable origin	1 330	2 013	2.1	3 227	3 368	4.3
4. Products of food industries; beverages, alcoholic liquids and vinegars; tobacco	8 502	2 849	2.9	12 449	3 644	4.7
5. Mineral products	64 330	4 137	4.2	31 627	2 094	2.7
6. Chemical and pharmaceutical products; dyes and varnishes; perfumery, soap, candles etc.; glues and gelatines; explosives and fertilizers	3 549	2 263	3.3	1 286	1 793	2.3
7. Hides, skins, leather and fur products	1 661	4 348	4.5	1 029	2 680	3.4
8. Rubber and rubber products	1 217	445	0.5	1 160	233	0.9
9. Wood and cork products; plating materials	1 904	898	0.9	2 142	1 136	1.4
10. Paper products	1 597	1 905	2.0	1 006	1 373	1.9
11. Textiles and allied products	8 024	35 453	36.3	7 055	20 534	26.5
12. Footwear, hats, rainwear, umbrellas and fashion-wear	66	452	0.5	82	732	0.9
13. Stonework and mineral products; ceramics and glass products	3 441	699	0.7	3 105	1 036	1.3
14. Pearls, precious stones, metals and coins	3	8 094	8.3	–	79	0.1
15. Base metals and products	20 762	6 307	6.5	24 994	6 999	9.0
16. Machinery and tools, electrical goods	2 191	5 814	6.0	1 210	3 858	4.9
17. Transport material	300	508	0.5	616	949	1.0

18. Scientific instruments and tools; watchmaker wares and musical instruments	11	126	0.1	21	195	0.2
19. Arms and munitions	2	10	–	2	19	–
20. Miscellaneous goods	38	138	0.1	54	201	0.3
21. Objets d'art and collectors' items	–	6	–	1	17	–
TOTAL	204 311	97 655	100	203 224	77 430	100

Notes: *Average; **Does not include the weight of live animals.

Sources: BSL, *Rapport du Conseil d'Administration*, 1949; CSIC, *Recueil de statistiques*, 1942–5, 1945–7; *Bulletin statistique trimestriel*, 1950–2; Lebanon, *Statistiques du commerce extérieur, 1952*; Syria, *Mudiriyat al-ihsa*, 1950.

Table A26: *Syro-Lebanese and Lebanese imports, order of country of origin, 1938–51*

Country	1938	1939	1940	1941	1942	1943	1944	1945	1946	1947	1948	1949	1950*	1951**
Saudi Arabia	–	–	–	–	–	–	–	–	–	–	–	7		–
Egypt	–	10	10	5	6	6	8	5	8	9	8	–		–
USA	4	4	4	6	3	7	5	1	1	1	2	1		2
France	2	1	1	10	–	–	–	–	3	3	3	3		3
Great Britain	1	2	3	8	5	5	2	3	2	2	1	2		4
India	–	–	–	2	1	1	6	8	4	10	–	9		–
Iraq	10	–	9	1	2	2	1	2	5	8	6	5		5
Japan	3	3	2	3	8	10	–	–	–	–	–	–		–
Palestine	7	9	7	4	4	3	4	4	6	7	–	–		–
Transjordan	–	–	–	9	–	–	–	9	9	–	–	–		–
Turkey	–	–	–	7	7	4	3	7	7	6	7	8		10
Iran	–	–	–	–	9	8	7	6	10	–	10	–		–
Italy	8	5	8	–	–	–	–	–	–	4	4	4		6
Romania	5	6	5	–	–	–	–	–	–	–	–	–		–
Germany	6	7	–	–	–	–	–	–	–	–	–	–		8
Belgium	9	8	6	–	–	–	–	–	–	9	5	6		7
USSR	–	–	–	–	–	–	10	10	–	–	–	–		–
Netherlands	–	–	–	–	–	–	–	–	–	–	9	–		9
Switzerland	–	–	–	–	10	9	–	–	–	–	–	10		–
Syria	–	–	–	–	–	–	–	–	–	–	–	–		1

Notes: *Data for 1950 are not given because of the dissolution of the Syro-Lebanese Customs Union in 1950; **Lebanese imports only.
Source: CSIC, *Recueil de statistiques*, 1942–5, 1945–7; *Bulletin statistique trimestriel*, 1952, vol. 4, no. 4.

Table A27: *Syro-Lebanese and Lebanese exports, order of country of destination, 1938–52*

Country	1938	1939	1940	1941	1942	1943	1944	1945	1946	1947	1948	1949	1950*	1951**	1952**
Egypt	6	8	6	8	7	6	6	2	5	7	5	4		3	5
USA	5	8	2	2	4	8	5	6	3	4	4	9		2	4
France	2	2	1	–	–	–	2	5	2	5	3	7		7	3
Great Britain	4	4	7	3	3	2	1	3	7	–	9	5		8	6
Iraq	9	9	4	4	6	3	4	1	1	2	1	1		–	–
Palestine	1	1	3	1	2	1	3	1	1	1	7	6		–	–
Transjordan	8	6	5	7	5	4	7	7	6	6	2	2		6	8
Turkey	10	–	8	6	8	10	–	–	9	–	–	–		–	–
Saudi Arabia	–	–	–	9	9	–	–	9	10	8	6	8		4	2
Cyprus	–	–	–	–	–	7	8	8	–	–	–	–		–	10
Switzerland	–	–	–	5	–	–	–	–	8	–	–	–		–	10
Greece	–	–	9	–	–	–	–	–	–	–	–	–		–	–
Italy	3	5	–	–	–	–	–	10	–	3	8	3		5	9
Germany	7	7	–	–	–	–	–	–	–	–	–	–		–	–
Belgium	–	10	–	–	–	–	–	–	–	9	–	10		–	–
Romania	–	–	10	–	–	–	–	–	–	–	–	–		–	–
Czechoslovakia	–	–	–	–	–	–	–	–	–	10	10	–		–	–
Syria	–	–	–	–	–	–	–	–	–	–	–	–		1	1
Netherlands	–	–	–	–	–	–	–	–	–	–	–	–		9	–

Notes: * Data for 1950 are not given because of the dissolution of the Syro-Lebanese Customs Union in 1950; ** Lebanese exports only.

Source: CSIC, *Recueil de statistiques*, 1942–5, 1945–7; *Bulletin statistique trimestriel*, 1952, vol. 4, no. 4.

Table A28: *Port of Beirut shipping activities, 1939–52*

Year	Ships entered	Goods entered* (tons)	Goods exported* (tons)
1939	2 128	522 300	110 445
1940	1 259	263 888	50 270
1941	847	183 531	21 102
1942	876	279 925	15 600
1943	1 003	155 355	10 830
1944	769	–	–
1945	765	127 528	36 590
1946	1 160	300 079	86 771
1947	1 470	456 809	62 818
1948	1 744	772 514	119 234
1949	1 801	806 075	143 094
1950	2 109	832 475	219 006
1951	2 038	911 196	225 086
1952	2 044	878 905	241 649

Note: *Does not include weight of live animals.

Source: *Compagnie du Port de Beyrouth* as cited by Ministère de l'économie national, *Bulletin statistique trimestriel*, 1952, vol. 3, no. 4.

Bibliography

1. Publications

Abdel-Fadil, Mahmoud, *The Political Economy of Nasserism: a Study in Employment and Income Distribution Policies in Urban Egypt, 1952–1972* (Cambridge, UK, 1980)

Aboussouan, B., *Le problème politique syrien* (Paris, 1924)

Abu-Iziddin, F. and George Hakim, 'A contribution to the study of labour conditions in the Lebanon', *International Labour Review* (November 1933) pp. 673–82

Adelman, Irma, *Theories of Economic Growth and Development* (Stanford, 1961)

Adelman, Irma and Cynthia T. Morris, *Economic Growth and Social Equity in Developing Countries* (Stanford, 1973)

Ali, Ifzal, 'Strategies and policies for structural transformation in Asia', *Asian Development Review*, vol. 8, no. 2 (1990) pp. 1–27

Amin, Samir, *Unequal Development: an Essay on the Social Formations of Peripheral Capitalism* (New York and London, 1976)

Amsden, Alice, *Asia's Next Giant: South Korea and Late Industrialization* (New York, 1989)

Ariff, Mohamed and Hal Hill, *Export-oriented Industrialization: the ASEAN Experience* (Sydney, 1985)

Asfour, Edmond, 'Industrial development in Lebanon', *Middle East Economic Papers* (1955) pp. 1–16

— *Syria: Development and Monetary Policy* (Cambridge, MA, 1959)

Association of Lebanese Industrialists, *Guide to Lebanon's Industries, 1949–1950* (Beirut, 1950)

Azhari, Naaman, *L'évolution du système économique libanais; ou la fin du laissez-faire* (Paris, 1970)

Badre, Albert, 'Al-siyasa al-iqtisadiyya al-lubnaniyya' [Lebanese economic policy], *Les conférences du Cénacle libanais*, vol. 10 (1 June 1956) pp. 351–70

— 'The national income of Lebanon', *Middle East Economic Papers* (1956) pp. 1–37

— 'Economic development of Lebanon', in Charles Cooper and Sidney Alexander (eds) *Economic Development and Population Growth in the Middle East* (New York, 1972) pp. 161–207

Badre, Albert and Apogig Altounian, 'Income arising in the construction sector', *National Income of Lebanon*, monograph 2 (Beirut, 1951)

Badre, Albert and As'ad Nasr, 'Income arising in the industrial sector', *National Income of Lebanon*, monograph 3 (Beirut, 1953)

— 'Income arising in the services sector', *National Income of Lebanon*, monograph 4 (Beirut, 1953)

Bain, J. S., *Industrial Organization* (New York, 1968)

Banque de Syrie et du Liban, *Bulletin annuel de la Banque de Syrie et du Liban, 1932–1952* (Paris)

— *Rapport du Conseil d'administration*, 1947–1952 (Paris)

Basile, A., 'La vocation régionale de la place financière de Beyrouth', *Proche-Orient études économiques* (January–December, 1973)

Baumol, William, 'The transactions demand for cash: an inventory theoretic approach', *Quarterly Journal of Economics*, vol. 66 (November 1952)

Beyhoum, Mohammed, *Al-naza'at al-siyasat bi lubnan, 1918–1945* [Political Attitudes in Lebanon, 1918–1945] (Beirut, 1977)

Bhagwati, Jagdish N., 'Directly-unproductive, profit-seeking (DUP) activities', *Journal of Political Economy*, vol. 90 (1982) pp. 988–1002

— 'Export-promoting trade strategy: issues and evidence', in Chris Milner (ed.) *Export Promotion Strategies: Theory and Evidence from Developing Countries* (New York, 1991

Bonné, Alfred, *State and Economics in the Middle East: a Society in Transition* (London, 1955)

— 'Land and population in the Middle East: trends and prospects', *Middle East Journal*, vol. 5 (Winter 1951) pp. 39–56

— *Economic Development of the Middle East* (London, 1943)

Bornschier, Volker, 'Multinational corporations and economic growth: a cross-national test of the decapitalization thesis', *Journal of Development Economics*, vol. 7 (1980) pp 191–210

Bornschier, Volker and Christopher Chase-Dunn, *Transnational Corporations and Underdevelopment* (New York, 1985)

Buheiry, Marwan, *Beirut's Role in the Political Economy of the French Mandate, 1919–1939*, Centre for Lebanese Studies, *Papers on Lebanon*, no. 4 (Oxford, 1987)

Bureau d'étude et de documentation (ed.) *L'annuaire financier du Liban, 1965* (Beirut, n.d.)

Burns, Norman, *The Tariff of Syria, 1919–1932* (Beirut, 1933)

Burns, Norman and Allen Edwards, 'Foreign trade', in Sa'id Himadeh (ed.) *Economic Organization of Syria* (Beirut, 1936) pp. 229–59

Centre d'études et de recherches sur le Moyen-Orient, *Etat et perspectives de l'industrie au Liban* (Beirut, 1978)

Chamoun, Camille, *Mudhakkirati* [My Memoirs] (Beirut, 1969)

— *Crise au Moyen-Orient* (Paris, 1963)

Chandler, Alfred D. Jr, *Scale and Scope, the Dynamics of Industrial Capitalism* (Cambridge, MA, 1990)

Chenery, Hollis B., S. Shishido and T. Watanabe, 'The pattern of Japanese growth, 1914–1954', *Econometrica*, vol. 30 (1962)

Chenery, Hollis B. and Moshe Syrquin, *Patterns of Development 1950–1970* (Oxford, 1975)

— *Patterns of Development 1950–1983* (Washington, DC, 1986)

Chevallier, Dominique, 'Lyon et la Syrie en 1919; les bases d'une intervention', *Revue historique*, vol. 224 (October–December 1960) pp. 275–320

— 'Western development and eastern crisis in the mid-nineteenth century: Syria confronted with the European economy', in William Polk and Richard Chambers (eds) *Beginning of Modernization in the Middle East* (Chicago, 1968)

— 'Les cadres sociaux de l'économie agraire dans le Proche-Orient au début du XIXe siècle: le cas du Mont-Liban', in M. A. Cook (ed.) *Studies in the Economic History of the Middle East: From the Rise of Islam to the Present Day* (London, 1970) pp. 333–45

— *La société du Mont Liban à l'époque de la révolution industrielle en Europe* (Paris, 1971)

— 'Signes de Beyrouth en 1834', *Bulletin d'études orientales*, vol. 25 (Damascus, 1972)

Chiha, Michel, *Le Liban d'aujourd'hui* (Beirut, 1949)

— 'Le Liban dans le monde: perspectives d'avenir', *Les conférences du Cénacle libanais*, vol. 5 (December 1951) pp. 256–82

— *Politique intérieure* (Beirut, 1964)

Cline, William, 'Can the East Asian model of development be generalized?', *World Development* (February 1982)

Coase, R. H., 'The nature of the firm', *Economica*, November 1937, pp. 386–405

Corm, Georges, 'Bilan des finances publiques libanaises, 1945–1965', *Le Commerce du Levant* (3 March 1965) pp. 10–13

Couland, Jacques, *Le mouvement syndical au Liban: 1919–1946* (Paris, 1970)

Cuinet, V., *Syrie, Liban et Palestine*, vol. 5 (Paris, 1896)

Dahir, Mas'ud, *Tarikh lubnan al-ijtima'i: 1914–1926* [The Social History of Lebanon: 1914–1926] (Beirut, 1974)

— *Lubnan, al-istiqlal, al-mithaq wa-al-sigha* [Lebanon, Independence, the National Pact and the Confessional System] (Beirut, 1977)

David, Philipe (compiler), *Recueil des actes administratifs du haut-commissariat de la République française en Syrie et au Liban*, 1919–1932 (Beirut)

de Monicault, Jacques, *Le port de Beyrouth et l'économie des pays du Levant sous le mandat français* (Paris, 1936)

Debbané, François, 'Finances publiques et redistribution des revenus, l'économie libanaise et le progrès social', *Semaine sociale au Liban* (Beirut, 1955) pp. 105–44

Delvolvé, Pierre, *L'administration libanaise* (Paris, 1971)

Diab, Mohammed, 'Foreign trade of Lebanon (1951–1960)', *Middle East Economic Papers* (1962) pp. 16–37

Dollar, David, 'Outward-oriented developing economies really do grow more rapidly: evidence from 95 LDCs, 1976–1985', *Economic Development and Cultural Change*, vol. 40, no. 3 (1992) pp. 523–44

Donato, Joseph, 'Lebanon and its labour legislation', *International Labour Review*, vol. 55 (January 1952) pp. 64–92

Dubar, Claude and Salim Nasr, *Les classes sociales au Liban* (Paris, 1976)

Ducousso, Gaston, *L'industrie de la soie en Syrie et au Liban* (Beirut and Paris, 1913)

Duchâtel, 'Une grande voie internationale: l'avenir d'Alexandrette', *Bulletin de l'union économique de Syrie*, vol. 7, 1982

Ducruet, Jean, *Les capitaux européens au Proche-Orient* (Paris, 1964)

Evans, H. David, 'Outward orientation: an assessment', in Chris Milner (ed.) *Export Promotion Strategies: Theory and Evidence from Developing Countries* (New York, 1991)

Farley, J. L., *Two Years in Syria* (London, 1858)

Fawaz, Leila, *Merchants and Migrants in Nineteenth Century Beirut* (Cambridge, MA, 1983)

Fei, Edward and Paul Klat, *The Balance of Payments in Lebanon, 1951 and 1952* (Beirut, 1954)

France, Haut-commissariat de la République française en Syrie et au Liban, *Bulletin économique trimestriel des états du levant sous mandat français*, 1926–38 (Beirut, n.d.)

— *Bulletin officiel des actes administratifs du haut-commissariat*, 1919–44 (Beirut, n.d.)

— *La Syrie et le Liban en 1921* (Paris, 1922)

— *La Syrie et le Liban en 1922* (Paris, 1923)

— *Recueil des actes administratifs du haut-commissariat*, 1921–32 (Beirut, n.d.)

— Ministère des affaires étrangères, *Rapport à la Société des nations sur la situation de la Syrie et du Grand Liban*, 1923–1938 (Paris)

Gates, Carolyn L., *The Historical Role of Political Economy in the Development of Modern Lebanon*, Centre for Lebanese Studies, *Papers on Lebanon*, no. 10 (Oxford, 1989)

— 'Laissez-faire, outward-orientation, and regional economic disintegration: a case study of the dissolution of the Syro-Lebanese Customs Union', in Youssef Choueiri (ed.) *State and Society in Syria and Lebanon* (Exeter, UK, 1993)

Gemayel, Maurice, *La planification intégrale des eaux libanaise* (Beirut, 1951)

Gibb, Sir Alexander and Partners, *The Economic Development of Lebanon* (London, 1948)

Gouraud, Henri, *La France en Syrie* (Paris, 1922)

Great Britain, Department of Overseas Trade, *Iraq, Syria, the Lebanon, Cyprus: British Goodwill Trade Mission* [Davidson Mission], *Report*, 31 August (London, 1946)

Greenaway, David and David Sapsford, 'What does liberalization do for exports and growth?', *Weltwirtschaftliches Archiv*, vol. 130, no. 1 (1994) pp. 152–74

Griffin, Keith, *Alternative Strategies for Economic Development* (London, 1989)

Grindle, Merilee S., 'The new political economy positive economics and negative politics', *Working Papers*, World Bank, Macroeconomic Adjustment and Growth, WPS 304, December 1989

Grunwald, Kurt, *The Government Finances of the Mandated Territories in the Near East* (Tel Aviv, 1932)

— 'The industrialization of the Lebanon and Syria', *Weltwirtschaftliches Archiv*, vol. 76, no. 1 (1956)

Grunwald, Kurt, and Joachim Ronall, *Industrialization in the Middle East* (New York, 1960)

Hafez, Mohamed Amine El-, *La structure et la politique économique en Syrie et au Liban* (Beirut, 1953)

Hakim, George, 'Fiscal system', in Sa'id Himadeh (ed.) *Economic Organization of Syria* (Beirut, 1936)

— 'Industry', in Sa'id Himadeh (ed.) *Economic Organization of Syria* (Beirut, 1936) pp. 119–73

— 'Land tenure reform', *Middle East Economic Papers* (1954) pp. 76–90

Hanna, 'Abd Allah, *Al-haraka al-'ummaliyya fi suriyya wa lubnan, 1900–1945* [The Labour Movement in Syria and Lebanon] (Damascus, 1973)

— *Al-qadiyya al-zira'iyya wa-al-haraka al-falahiyya fi suriyya wa lubnan* [The Agrarian Question and the Peasant Movement in Syria and Lebanon], 2 vols, 1820–1920 and 1920–45 (Beirut, 1975)

Hannush, Basim, 'The present socio-economic conditions in Lebanon and the prospects for economic development', *Middle East Economic Papers* (1962) pp. 40–52

Harbison, Frederick and Charles Myers, *Management in the Industrial World: An International Analysis* (New York, 1959)

Harfouche, Jamal Karam, *Social Structure of Low-Income Families in Lebanon* (Beirut, 1965)

Havard, G. T. and F. C. Ogden, *Report on Economic and Commercial Conditions in Syria and the Lebanon* 1932, 1936, 1936–1938 (London)

Heckscher, Eli, 'The effect of foreign trade on the distribution of income', reprinted in H. Ellis and L. Metzler (eds) *Readings in the Theory of International Trade* (1949)

Hershlag, Zvi, *Introduction to the Modern Economic History of the Middle East* (Leiden, 1972)

Himadeh, Raja, *The Fiscal System of Lebanon* (Beirut, 1961)

Himadeh, Sa'id, *Monetary and Banking System of Syria and Lebanon* (Beirut, 1935)

— (ed.) *Economic Organization of Syria* (Beirut, 1936)

— 'Monetary and banking system', in Sa'id Himadeh (ed.) *Economic Organization of Syria* (Beirut, 1936)

— 'Mashakil al-iqtisadiyya wa-kayf nu'alijuha' [Economic problems and how we should deal with them], *Les conférences du Cénacle libanais* (Beirut, 1947)

Holmstrom, Bengt R. and Jean Tirole, 'The theory of the firm', in R. Schmalensee and R. D. Willig (eds), *Handbook of Industrial Organization*, vol. 1 (Amsterdam, 1989) pp. 61–133

Hoss, Salim, 'Economic concentration in Lebanon', *Middle East Economic Papers*, (1963) pp. 55–74

Hudson, Michael, *The Precarious Republic: Political Modernization in Lebanon* (New York, 1968)

International Labour Review, 'Working conditions in handicrafts and modern industry in Syria', vol. 29, no. 3 (March 1934) pp. 407–11

— 'Conditions of work in Syria and the Lebanon under French mandate', vol. 39, no. 4 (April 1939) pp. 513–26

International Monetary Fund, *Financial Statistics*, 1948–1952 (Washington, DC)

— *International Financial News Survey*, 1948–1952 (Washington, DC)

— *Balance of Payments Yearbook*, 1950–1951 (Washington, DC, 1952)

International Wheat Council, *World Wheat Statistics* (London, April 1955)

Issawi, Charles (ed.) *The Economic History of the Middle East, 1800–1914* (Chicago and London, 1966)

— *An Economic History of the Middle East and North Africa* (New York, 1982)

— *The Fertile Crescent 1800–1914: A Documentary History* (New York and Oxford, 1988)

Jewish Agency for Palestine, Economic Research Institute, *Statistical Handbook of Middle Eastern Countries* (Jerusalem, 1945)

Joarder, Safiuddin, *Syria under the French Mandate: the Early Phase, 1920–1927* (Dacca, 1977)

Jumblatt, Kamal, *Démocratie nouvelle*, Lectures 1950–5 (Beirut, n.d.)

— *Al-haqiqa 'an al-thawra al-lubnaniyya* [The Truth about the Lebanese Revolution] (Beirut, 1959)

— *Fi majra al-siyassa al-lubnaniyya* [In the Course of Lebanese Politics] (Beirut, 1960)

Jung, W. S. and G. Lee, 'The effectiveness of export promotion policies: the case of Korea', *Weltwirtschaftliches Archiv*, vol. 122 (1986)

Keen, Bernard A., *Agricultural Development of the Middle East* (London, 1946)

Khalaf, Nadim, 'Concentration in the Lebanese economy', *Middle East Economic Papers* (1964) pp. 34–51

Khalaf, Samir, 'Lebanese labour unions: some comparative features', *Middle East Economic Papers* (1968) pp. 111–38

— 'Adaptive modernization: the case for Lebanon', in Charles Cooper and Sidney Alexander (eds) *Economic Development and Population Growth in the Middle East* (New York, 1972) pp. 568–98

Khalaf, Samir and Emilie Shwayri, 'Family firms and industrial development: the Lebanese case', *Economic Development and Cultural Change*, vol. 15, no. 1 (October, 1966)

Khoury, Bishara al-, *Haqa'iq lubnaniyya* [Lebanese Truths], 3 vols (Beirut, 1961)

Khuri, Albert, 'Agriculture', in Sa'id Himadeh (ed.) *Economic Organization of Syria* (Beirut, 1936) pp. 73–115

Kirkpatrick, C. H., *Export-led Development, Labour-market Regulation and the Distribution of Income in Asian NICs: the Case of Singapore* (Paris, 1987)

Klat, Paul, 'Labour movement in Syria and Lebanon', *Political Affairs* (New York, 3 June 1948) pp. 75–6

— 'Labour legislation in Lebanon', *Middle East Economic Papers* (1959) pp. 69–81

Kravis, Irving, 'Trade as a handmaiden of growth: similarities between the nineteenth and twentieth centuries', *Economic Journal* (December 1970) pp. 850–72

Krueger, Anne O., 'The political economy of the rent-seeking society', *American Economic Review*, vol. 64 (1974) pp. 291–303

— *Trade and Employment in Developing Countries: Synthesis and Conclusions* (Chicago, 1982)

Krugman, Paul R., 'Is free trade passé?', *Journal of Economic Perspectives*, vol. 1 (1987) pp. 131–44

Kuwait Fund for Arab Economic Development, *Report on the Lebanese Economy and its Development Projects* (Kuwait, 1976)

Kuznets, Simon, *Economic Growth of Nations: Total Output and Production Structure* (Cambridge, MA, 1971)

— *Economic Growth and Structure: Selected Essays* (New York, 1965)

La Syrie et le Liban sous l'occupation et le mandat français, 1919–1927 (Paris)

Labaki, Boutros, *Introduction à l'histoire économique du Liban: soie et commerce extérieur en fin de période ottomane (1840–1914)* (Beirut, 1984)

League of Nations, Permanent Mandates Commission, *Minutes of the Permanent Mandates Commission* (Geneva) 1st– 37th sessions, 1921–1940 (Lausanne)
Lebanon, Conseil supérieur des douanes, Direction générale des douanes, *Statistiques du commerce extérieur, 1952* (Beirut, 1953)
— *Industrial Census of Lebanon, 1955* (Beirut, 1957)
— *Al-jarida al-rasmiyya*, 1949–1957 [Official Gazette] (Beirut)
— *Journal officiel de la république libanaise*, 1922–1947 (Beirut)
— *Débats parlementaires*, Chambre des députés, 1936–1938 (Beirut)
Lebanon, Ministère de l'économie national, Service de statistique générale, *Bulletin statistique trimestriel* (Beirut, 1950–3)
Lebanon, Ministère du plan et mission IRFED, *Besoins et possibilités de développement du Liban*, étude préliminaire, 2 vols (Beirut, n.d.)
Leudde-Neurath, R., *Import Controls and Export Oriented Development: a Re-assessment of the South Korean Case* (Boulder and London, 1986)
Levant States, Conseil supérieur des intérêts communs (CSIC), Douanes de la Syrie et du Liban, *Eléments statistiques des états de Syrie et du Liban*, no. 20, 1947 (Beirut, 1948)
— Service d'études économiques et de statistiques, *Recueil de statistiques de la Syrie et du Liban*, 1942–5 (Beirut, 1946); 1945–7 (Beirut, 1948)
— *Statistiques du commerce extérieur*, 1944 (Beirut, 1946)
Lewis, W. A., 'The slowing down of the engine of growth', *American Economic Review*, vol. 70 (1982) pp. 555–64
Libesny, Herbert. 'A digest of the labor code of Lebanon', *Middle East Journal*, vol. 1, no. 1 (Winter 1947) pp. 89–91
Little, I. M. D., 'The experience and causes of rapid labour-intensive development in Korea, Taiwan Province, Hong Kong and Singapore; and the possibilities of emulation', in E. L. H. Lee (ed.) *Export-led Industrialisation and Development* (Bangkok, 1981)
Longrigg, Stephen, *Syria and Lebanon under French Mandate* (London, 1958)
Mallat, Raymond, *70 Years of Money Muddling in Lebanon, 1900–1970* (Beirut, 1970)
Menassa, Gabriel, *Plan de reconstruction de l'économie libanaise et de réforme de l'état* (Beirut, 1948)
— 'Reconstruction de l'économie libanaise', *Les conférences du Cénacle libanais*, vol. 2 (21 June 1948) pp. 55–76
Mill, J. S., *Principles of Political Economy* (London, 1902)
Mills, Arthur E., *Private Enterprise in Lebanon* (Beirut, 1959)
— 'Economic change in Lebanon', *Middle East Economic Papers* (1956) pp. 75–97
Milner, Chris (ed.) *Export Promotion Strategies: Theory and Evidence from Developing Countries* (New York, 1991)
Mirrlees, James A. and N. H. Stern, *Models of Economic Growth* (New York, 1973)
Mitchell, Tony, 'South Korea: vision of the future for labour surplus economies', in Manfred Bienefeld and Martin Godfrey (eds) *The Struggle for Development: National Strategies in an International Context* (Chichester, 1982)
Moussali, Negib, *Etudes économiques sur la Syrie et le Liban* (Beirut, 1957)
Mushahwar, Amin, *Précis de législation fiscale libanaise* (Beirut, 1945)

Near East Economic Research Company, *A Memorandum on the Near East Economic Research Company and a Report on the Project of an American, Syro-Lebanese Corporation* (Beirut, n.d.)

Nelson, Richard R. and Sidney G. Winter, *An Evolutionary Theory of Economic Change* (Cambridge, MA, 1982)

Nickoley, Edward, 'Transportation and communications', in Sa'id Himadeh (ed.) *Economic Organization of Syria* (Beirut, 1936) pp. 177–95

Nolan, Peter, 'Assessing economic growth in the Asian NICs', *Journal of Contemporary Asia*, vol. 20, no. l (1990)

North, Douglass C., *Institutions, Institutional Change and Economic Performance* (Cambridge, UK, 1990)

— 'A transaction cost approach to the historical development of polities and economies', *Journal of Institutional and Theoretical Economics,* 145 (1989) pp. 661–8

Nurkse, Ragnor, 'Some international aspects of the problem of economic development', *American Economic Review* (May 1952)

— 'Patterns of trade and development', *Wicksell Lectures* (Stockholm, 1959)

Nusuli, Mustafa al–, 'Le régime de la zone franche et son importance par rapport à l'économie libanaise', *L'économie libanaise et arabe*, no. 10 (October 1952) section II, pp. 7–14

— 'Min al-hirfa ila al-sina'a' [From craft to industry], *Muhadarat al-nudwa* [*Les conférences du Cénacle libanais*] (Beirut, 1953)

— *Nahwa ghadan afdal li-as-sina'a al-lubnaniyya* [Towards a better tomorrow for Lebanese industry] (Beirut, 1968)

O'Hearn, Denis, 'TNCs, intervening mechanisms and economic growth in Ireland: a longitudinal test and extension of the Bornschier model', *World Development*, vol. 18, no. 3 (1990) pp. 417–29

Odeh, B. J., *Lebanon Dynamics of Conflict* (London, 1985)

Ohlin, Bertil, *Interregional and International Trade* (Cambridge, MA, 1933)

Organisation for Economic Cooperation and Development, *The Newly Industrialising Countries* (Paris, 1988)

Owen, Roger, *The Middle East in the World Economy, 1800–1914* (London and New York, 1981)

Page, Sheila, 'The role of trade in the new NICs', *Journal of Development Studies,* vol. 27, no.3. pp. 39–60

Pharaon, Henri, *Au service du Liban et son unité* (Beirut, 1959)

Picard, Elizabeth, *Etat de discorde, des fondations aux guerres fratricides* (Paris, 1988)

Polk, William and Richard Chambers (eds), *Beginning of Modernization in the Middle East* (Chicago, 1968)

Prebisch, Raoul, 'The economic development of Latin America and its principal problems', *Economic Bulletin for Latin America*, vol. 7, no. 1 (February 1962)

— *Towards a New Trade Strategy for Development: Report by the Secretary-General of the UN Conference on Trade and Development* (New York, 1964)

Prest, A. R., *War Economics of Primary Producing Countries* (Cambridge, UK, 1948)

Puaux, Gabriel, *Deux années au Levant* (Paris, 1952)

Review Group on Private Sector Development, *Developing the Private Sector: A Challenge for the World Bank Group* (Washington DC, 1989)
Riashi, Iskandar, *Qabl wa ba'd* [Before and After] (Beirut, 1953)
— *Al-ayyam al-lubnaniyya* [Lebanese Days] (Beirut, 1957)
— *Ru'asa' lubnan kama 'araftuhum* [Presidents of Lebanon as I Knew Them] (Beirut, 1961)
Ricardo, David, *Principles of Political Economy and Taxation* (1817, reprinted London, 1957)
Riedel, James, 'Trade as the engine of growth in developing countries, revisited', *Economic Journal*, vol. 84 (1984) pp. 56–73
Rizk, Charles, *Le régime politique libanais* (Paris, 1966)
Roberts, Stephen, *History of French Colonial Policy (1870–1925)* vol. 2 (London, 1929)
Rondot, Pierre, *Les institutions politiques du Liban* (Paris, 1947)
— 'L'expérience du mandat français en Syrie', *Revue générale de droit internationale publique* (1948) pp. 387–409
Rosenfeld, Félix, 'Les échanges commerciaux entre la Syrie et le Liban et les autres pays du Proche-Orient', *L'économiste européen*, vol. 98, no. 2 (25 November 1945) pp. 332–5
— 'Les statistiques officielles et semi-officielles en Syrie, au Liban et en Palestine', *Journal de la société statistique de Paris*, vol. 9, no. 1 (September–October 1945) pp. 233–6
— 'Variations des prix et de la circulation monétaire en Syrie et au Liban au cours de la deuxième guerre mondiale', *Journal de la société de statistique de Paris*, Berger-Levrault edition (Paris, 1946)
Saba, Elias, 'The Syro-Lebanese Customs Union: causes of failure and attempts at re-organisation', *Middle East Economic Papers* (1960) pp. 91–108
— 'Lebanon's liberal foreign exchange system', *Middle East Economic Papers* (1961) pp. 98–112
— *The Foreign Exchange Systems of Lebanon and Syria 1939–1957* (Beirut, 1961)
— 'The implications of the foreign sector in the Lebanese economy', *Middle East Economic Papers* (1962) pp. 140–54
Salam, Saeb, *Lubnan wahid la lubnanain* [One Lebanon, Not Two] (Beirut, 1961)
Salibi, Kamal, *The Modern History of Lebanon* (London, 1965 and New York, 1977)
Samuelson, Paul, 'International trade and equalization of factor prices', *Economic Journal* (June 1948) pp.163–84
Sarc, Omar Celal, 'Ottoman industrial policy, 1840–1914', in Charles Issawi (ed.), *Economic History of the Middle East, 1800–1914* (Chicago and London, 1966)
Sayegh, Yusif, 'Lebanon: special economic problems arising from a special structure', *Middle East Economic Papers* (1957) pp. 60–88
— *Entrepreneurs of Lebanon: the Role of the Business Leader in a Developing Country* (Cambridge, MA, 1962)
Sayegh, Yusif and Muhammad Atallah, *Nazra thaniya li al-iqtisad al-lubnaniyya* [A second look at the Lebanese economy] (Beirut, 1966)
Scitovsky, Tibor, 'Economic development of Taiwan and South Korea, 1965–1981', in L. J. Lau (ed.), *Models of Development: A Comparative Study of Economic Growth in South Korea and Taiwan* (San Francisco, 1986)

Semaine sociale, *L'agriculture, richesse nationale* (Beirut, 1942)

Shehadi, Nadim, *The Idea of Lebanon: Economy and State in the Cénacle Libanais, 1946–1954*, Centre for Lebanese Studies, *Papers on Lebanon*, no. 5 (Oxford, 1987)

Shorrock, William, *French Imperialism in the Middle East: the Failure of Policy in Syria and Lebanon, 1900–191* (Madison, 1976)

Siba'i, Badr al-Din al-, *Adwa' 'ala al-rasmal al-anjabi fi surriyya 1850–1958* [Foreign Capital in Syria 1850–1958] (Damascus, 1968)

Siksek, S., A. Baaklini and A. Daouk, *Preliminary Assessment of Manpower Resources and Requirements in Lebanon* (Beirut, 1959)

Smilianskaya, Irina M., 'From subsistence to market economy: the disintegration of feudal relations in Syria and Lebanon in the middle of the nineteenth century', in Charles Issawi (ed.), *The Economic History of the Middle East, 1800–1914* (Chicago, 1966) pp. 226–47

— *Al-haraka al-fallahiyya fi lubnan, al-nisf al-awwal min al-qarn al-tasi' 'ashar* [The Peasant Movements of Lebanon during the First Half of the Nineteenth Century], translated from the Russian (Beirut, 1972)

Smith, Adam, *The Wealth of Nations*, edited by Edwin Cannan (New York, 1937)

Spears, General Sir Edward, *Fulfilment of a Mission: the Spears Mission to Syria and Lebanon, 1941–1944* (Hamden, CN, 1977)

Staffs of the World Bank and the International Monetary Fund, 'The contribution of the private sector to development, and the roles of the Bank Group and the Fund', *Development Issues: Presentations to the Development Committee, May 8, 1990* (Washington, DC, 1990)

Streeten, Paul, 'Trade strategies for development: some themes for the seventies', in Paul Streeten (ed.) *Trade Strategies for Development, Papers of the Ninth Cambridge Conference on Development Problems, September 1972* (London, 1973)

Streeten, Paul, 'A cool look at "outward-looking" strategies for development', *World Development*, 1982

Syria, Ministry of National Economy, Department of Statistics, *Mudiriyya al-ihsa'* [Statistical Abstract], 1950 (Damascus, n.d.)

Syrquin, Moshe and Hollis B. Chenery, 'Patterns of development, 1950 to 1983', *World Bank Discussion Papers*, no. 41

Tannous, Raja, 'Food and technology: a developing industry in Lebanon', in T. S. Stickley, J. A. Asmar, A-R. Sagher, N. Atallah and P. L. Pellet (eds), *Man, Food and Agriculture in the Middle East* (Beirut, 1969) pp. 675–92

Theil, Henri, *Optimal Decision Rules for Government and Industry* (Amsterdam, 1964)

Thobie, Jacques, *Intérêts et impérialisme français dans l'empire ottoman: 1895–1914* (Paris, 1977)

Thompson, Arthur A. Jr, *Economics of the Firm, Theory and Practice* (New York, 1985)

Thompson, Virginia and Richard Adloff, 'French economic policy in tropical Africa', in Peter Duignan and Lewis Gann (eds), *Colonialism in Africa, 1870–1960*, vol. 4 (Cambridge, 1975) pp. 127–64

Tinbergen, Jan, *Economic Policy: Principles and Design* (Amsterdam, 1956)

Tobin, James, 'The interest elasticity of the transactions demand for cash', *Review of Economics and Statistics*, vol. 38 (August 1956)

— 'Liquidity preference as behavior toward risk', *Review of Economic Studies*, vol. 25 (February 1958)

Tuéni André, 'Al-muwazana wa nizam al-dara'ib fi lubnan' [The Budget and Tax System in Lebanon], lecture by the Director-General of Finance, delivered on 8 May 1950, *Les conférences du Cénacle libanais*, vol. 4, nos 5–6 (25 May 1950) pp. 75–99

Union des ingénieurs et techniciens de la France combattante (Section du Levant) *Vingt-cinq ans d'effort français au Levant (1920–1944)* (Beirut, 1944)

United Nations, Département des questions économiques, *L'évolution économique au Moyen-Orient, 1945 à 1954* (Supplément au rapport sur l'économie mondiale, 1953/4) (New York, 1955)

— Department of Economic and Social Affairs, *Review of Economic Conditions in the Middle East, 1945* to *1954* (Supplements to World Economic Report, 1949/50–1954/5) (New York)

— Food and Agriculture Organization, *Mediterranean Development Project, Country Report: Lebanon* (Rome, 1959)

— Statistical Office, *Monthly Bulletin of Statistics*, 1947–1958 (New York)

United States, Department of Agriculture, *Report of the United States–Lebanon Agricultural Mission*, IAG Series, no. 7 (Washington DC, 1948)

— Department of Commerce, *Foreign Commerce Weekly* (Washington DC, 1950)

— Department of Commerce, *World Trade Information Service* (June 1956)

— Department of State, *Foreign Relations of the United States* (Washington DC, 1919–57)

US Embassy, Lebanon, Directory of Lebanese Government Officials and Religious Leaders (as of January 1981) (Beirut, n.d.)

Verney, Noel and George Dambmann, *Les puissances étrangères dans le Levant* (Paris, 1900)

Wade, Robert, *Governing the Market: Economic Theory and Role of Government in East Asian Industrialization* (Princeton, 1989)

Weulersse, Jacques, *Paysans de Syrie et du Proche-Orient* (Paris, 1946)

White, Gordon (ed.), *Developmental States in East Asia* (London, 1988)

Williamson, Oliver E., *The Economic Institutions of Capitalism: Firms, Markets and Relational Contracting* (New York and London, 1985)

Wilmington, Martin, *The Middle East Supply Centre* (Albany and London, 1971)

World Bank, *The East Asian Miracle, Economic Growth and Public Policy* (New York and Oxford, 1993)

Yaffi, Talha, 'La réforme bancaire au Liban', *Le Commerce du Levant* (24 October 1949)

— 'A case for banking reforms in Lebanon', *Middle East Economic Papers* (1958) pp. 93–114

Younes, Sadr, 'Liban: le mouvement syndical', *Cahiers internationaux* (Paris, July–August 1961) pp. 60–8

2. Unpublished sources

Private collected papers

General Sir Edward Spears Papers, St Antony's Private Papers, Oxford

Government papers

France: Les archives du Ministère des affaires étrangères, Paris (MAE)

Guerre 1939–1945: Londres: Comité national français (CNF) vols 39–65; Alger (CFLN–GPRF) June 1943–September 1944; Levant: vols 999–1025; Vichy-Levant: vols 25–70

Papiers d'agents: Gabriel Puaux; Henry de Jouvenal

Série E-Levant 1918–40: Syrie-Liban 1918–29, vols 1–437; *Syrie-Liban 1930–40*, vols 456–637

Série EU–Europe, URSS, 1949–55, vols 72–7

Great Britain: Public Record Office

Foreign Office (Embassy and Consular) and War Office Archives, London

Series: FO226 files 27, 31, 60, 278, 332, 462, S8/177

FO371 Lebanese, Syrian and Middle East files, 1920–52

FO684 France: (Damascus) files, 9, 37A

FO921 (Minister of State/Cairo) files 8, 8 (2) 22, 50 (1), 54 (9), 79, 79 (1–18), 82, 82 (1–13), 117 (21), 143 (8)

FO922 (MESC, 1939–45) files 461, 860/07, 979/07, 1766, 1781, 1892, 1950, 1982, 3102, AP, FS, GO, IN, IP, MS, S83, S86, SS

WOl69 (British Security Mission in Syria) file 15961, box 172/2, vols 31–41

WOl78 (War Office Diaries: Military Missions) files 10–13, vols 1–30

United States: National Archives and Record Administration, Washington DC

Record Groups:

59 (General Records of the Department of State, central files, 1920–1954)

84 (Records of the Foreign Service Posts, regional files, 1920–1954)

165 (Office of Strategic Services, Military Attaché Reports, G–2 regional files)

169 (MESC operations)

319 (Military intelligence reports and G–2 alphabetical file, Lebanon and Syria, 1938–52; Egypt, 1942–7)

ID file, 1950–8

Theses, papers and reports

American University of Beirut, Economic Research Institute, *Report on Agricultural Credit in Lebanon*, Conference on Agricultural Credit sponsored by the Ford Foundation and organised by the AUB (Beirut, 12–14 October 1953)

— *Agenda, Working Materials and Proceedings*, Conference on Agricultural Credit sponsored by the Ford Foundation and organised by the AUB (Beirut, 12–14 October 1953)

Badre, Albert, *The Economic Development of Lebanon with Special Emphasis on Finance*, Ph.D. dissertation (State University of Iowa, 1950)

Bohsali, Kamal, *Contribution à l'étude de la situation de la classe ouvrière au Liban*, thèse de droit (Paris, 1951)

Da'uq, Bashir, *Growth in Agricultural Output of Syria and Lebanon, 1925–1954*, Ph.D. dissertation (University of Wisconsin, 1957)

Durand, H., *L'expérience d'union économique entre la Syrie et le Liban*, thèse de droit (Université de Grenoble, 1953)

Gates, Carolyn L., *The Development of the Modern Political Economy of Lebanon: the State and the Economy from Colonialism to Independence, 1939–1952*, D.Phil. thesis (Oxford University, 1985)

— 'Development strategy, the state and institutional change: the case of Lebanon', paper presented at a conference organised by the Centre for Lebanese Studies, *Current Research on Lebanon* (Oxford, 1986)

— 'Governance and economic restructuring in Lebanon, 1948–1970', unpublished paper presented at the University of Amsterdam, Faculty of Economics and Econometrics and Department of International Relations, October 1991

— 'Choice, content and performance of a "service-oriented open economy" strategy: the case of Lebanon, 1948–1958', paper presented at conference organised by Texas University, Austin and the Centre for Lebanese Studies, Oxford, *A Look Back at Lebanon, 1958* (Austin, September 1992)

Kalla, M. S., *Role of Foreign Trade in the Economic Development of Syria, 1831–1914*, Ph.D. dissertation (American University, Washington, DC, 1969)

Klat, Paul, *Land Tenure in Syria and Lebanon and its Economic and Social Effects with Some Suggestions for Reform*, B.Litt. thesis (Oxford University, 1948)

Medawar, George, *Monetary Problems in Lebanon*, Ph.D. dissertation (Cornell University, 1963)

Mitri, Bassam, *The Dependence Features of the Lebanese Economy*, Ph.D. dissertation (University of Arizona, 1970)

Saba, Paul, *The Development and Decline of the Silk Industry*, B.Litt. thesis (Oxford University, 1977)

Sehnaoui, Nada, *L'occidentalisation de la vie quotidienne à Beyrouth, 1860–1914: Mémoire de maîtrise* (Paris, X-Nanterre, 1981)

Index